# PIETY AND FANATICISM

# PIETY AND FANATICISM

## RABBINIC CRITICISM OF RELIGIOUS STRINGENCY

SARA EPSTEIN WEINSTEIN

JASON ARONSON INC.
Northvale, New Jersey
London

This book was set in 11 pt. Stempel Schneidler by Alabama Book Composition, Inc., Deatsville, AL.

**Library of Congress Cataloging-in-Publication Data**

Weinstein, Sara.
    Piety and fanaticism : rabbinic criticism of religious stringency / Sara Weinstein.
        p.        cm.
    Includes bibliographical references and index.
    ISBN 1-56821-976-8 (alk. paper)
    1. Supererogation in rabbinical literature.    2. Rabbinical
literature—History and criticism.    3. Asceticism—Judaism.
4. Fanaticism.    5. Jewish law—Interpretation and construction.
I. Title.
BM496.9.S95W45      1997
296.7'1—dc20                                                96–41188

Manufactured in the United States of America. Jason Aronson Inc. offers books and cassettes. For information and catalog write to Jason Aronson Inc., 230 Livingston Street, Northvale, New Jersey 07647.

To my husband, Bernie,
for always believing in me.

To my children,
Tehila, Aryeh, Netanel, and Elisheva,
may HaShem grant you the opportunity to pursue your dreams.

To my parents,
Max and Rhoda Epstein,
who taught me that learning Torah and
being a woman are harmonious.

# Contents

# Acknowledgments

My deepest thanks go to Professor Lawrence H. Schiffman, my adviser at New York University. His consistent encouragement, wisdom, and excellent guidance throughout this long process were invaluable. I also wish to thank Professor Jeffrey Rubinstein, for his careful reading of this study and his helpful comments and suggestions. Some of the most important issues dealt with in this study were formulated during discussions with Professors Robert Chazan and Baruch Levine. Professor Levine's consistent enthusiasm about my topic was very encouraging. Helpful advice was also given to me by Professors Frank Peters, Steven Fraade, Vincent Wimbush, Elliot Wolfson, and Michael Swartz. I would also like to thank the Memorial Foundation for Jewish Culture and the National Foundation for Jewish Culture for granting me Doctoral Dissertation Fellowships that helped finance my years of research. Henry Resnick of the Klau Library at Hebrew Union College graciously provided much needed assistance in locating many books.

To Ruth Weinstein, my mother-in-law, I wish to express my deep appreciation, for being there for me whenever the need arose. To my parents, Rhoda and Max Epstein, I feel especially grateful, for all of their help over the years. They tried their very best to ensure that I receive the best education possible. By sending me to the Yeshivah of Flatbush, they enabled me to begin studying Talmud at age 11. This was truly a rare opportunity for a young Orthodox Jewish girl; it was an opportunity that opened the doors of Talmud Torah (in all of its forms) to me and, I believe, was the first step along the path leading me to the writing of this book. While I was writing this book, they spent many days caring for my children and attending to the many mundane matters of everyday life for me, so that I could be free to pursue my more "ethereal" pursuits. My brothers, Daniel and Asher Epstein, also deserve a deeply felt thanks, for their help and encouragement; Asher read this entire manuscript and made most insightful comments.

To my four wonderful children, Tehila, Aryeh, Netanel, and Elisheva, I would like to say thank you for your patience, for your tolerance of my need to work so many hours, and, most of all, for sharing in my joy. May HaShem, who has granted me the opportunity to fulfill so many of my dreams, reward you in the same manner.

Finally, *aharon aharon haviv,* I would like to thank my husband, Bernie, for his loving encouragement, interest, patience, help, and pride in my accomplishments. His editing talents remain unsurpassed and have added a tremendous amount to the clarity of this book. His unwavering emotional support, throughout the many years of my work, helped me complete this study, and for that I will always be grateful.

# Abbreviation Key

B. = Babylonian
M. = Mishnah
P. = Palestinian
T. = Tosefta
BT = Babylonian Talmud
PT = Palestinian Talmud

# Introduction

## STATEMENT OF PURPOSE

Religious zeal represents the passionate desire to serve God. Within traditional Judaism, religious zeal or piety express themselves in both the strictest observance of Jewish law as well as in practices above and beyond the demands of the law. The passionate desire to serve God should, ideally, inspire individuals who are deeply committed to the values of the halakhic system to become especially kind, spiritually sensitive, and compassionate people.

While religious zeal or piety often do yield these positive results, they can at times result in religious excess, fanaticism, or elitism. What, then, are the limits of individualized strictness? When is zealously self-imposed religious stringency—above and beyond the requirements of the law—actually criticized in Talmudic literature?

The extreme diversity of opinion within Talmudic literature regarding the issue of religious stringency has given rise to a great deal of secondary literature about rabbinic praise of supererogatory behavior. The word *supererogatory*, which literally means "going

1

beyond what is commanded or required,"[1] is a key term in this study and will be used synonymously with "self-imposed religious stringency" and with the Hebrew *humra*. Many articles and books have been written discussing terms such as "above and beyond the letter of the law" (*lifenim mishurat hadin*), "extremely pious behavior" (*midat hasidut*), and "whoever is especially stringent shall be blessed" (*hamahamir tavo alav berakhah*).[2]

On the other hand, rabbinic criticism of self-imposed religious stringency has received much less attention in the secondary literature. True, many articles and books discussing Jewish asceticism and piety mention sources with anti-ascetic motifs. There is, however, no systematic study of Talmudic criticism of supererogatory behavior that includes both ascetic and non-ascetic practices. The purpose of this study is to begin to bridge this gap.

This study will start by examining when supererogation for the individual was generally permitted and when it was criticized. It will then focus on specific types of people who were criticized for their supererogatory behavior, such as the "foolish pietist" and "the ascetic woman." When stringent behavior was considered "common" or "arrogant" will be examined as well. The different contexts within which these terms appear will be examined in order to reach the broadest possible understanding of their meaning.

The issue of being stringent (*mahamir*) within the context of a Halakhic debate, however, in which one rabbi rules leniently and the other stringently, will not be discussed here. This analysis will be limited to stringency that is self-imposed, above and beyond the recommendations of any specific Halakhic ruling, rather than stringency that had legal-rabbinic prescription. Understanding when either the more stringent (*mahamir*) or the more lenient (*meikel*) path within Halakhic debate itself was chosen or criticized by a particular Rabbi[3]—although clearly conceptually related to the concern of this book—belongs to another study.

---

1. *The Compact Edition of the Oxford English Dictionary* (Oxford: Oxford University Press, 1971), Vol. II, p. 3159.

2. For a discussion of these terms, as well as an extensive bibliography, see Aaron Kirschenbaum, *Equity in Jewish Law, Beyond Equity* (Hoboken, NJ: Ktav, 1991; New York: Yeshiva University Press, 1991), pp. xv–xix, 59–136.

3. See, for example, *B. Bezah.* 2b: "the power of leniency is stronger" (*koah deheteira adif*). See also Haym Soloveitchik's analysis of the relatively recent proliferation of *humra* within the Halakhic community: "Rupture and

As this study will focus on the Talmudic sources, the chrono-logical time period covered will include the tannaitic and amoraic periods (1 c.e. to approximately 500 c.e.). Jewish sectarian, Greco-Roman, and early Christian practices and attitudes will also be explored when parallel (or opposing) traditions exist. Ultimately, the conclusions derived may serve as paradigms for evaluating the dynamics of an individual's quest for personal spiritual expression within the confines of any organized religion.

This study is extremely timely, given the recent proliferation of religious extremism in various countries throughout the world. The atmosphere of extreme stringency that prevails within today's Orthodox Jewish community seems, to some extent, to be part of this global trend. This "stringent" atmosphere, however, manifests itself primarily within the context of Halakhic debate, in which the more stringent rabbinic rulings are promoted and viewed as spiritu-ally superior to more lenient viewpoints.

While it does not, in the main, express itself via the forms of supererogatory behaviors examined in this study (i.e., stringencies that are clearly above and beyond the legal requirements of *any* Halakhic authority), the motivations behind both types of stringency may be similar. The purpose of embracing either the self-imposed or the rabbinically prescribed stringency is, presumably, to better serve one's Creator by adopting a more difficult way of life. Rabbinic criticism of self-imposed *humra* may, then, apply at times to rabbini-cally prescribed *humra* as well. This study can then aid in the evaluation of whether the Talmudic ideal of Judaism, if such a term can indeed be used, would encourage or discourage the current state of affairs.

## RELIGIOUS ISSUES

### Fanaticism, Elitism, and Subjectivity

As mentioned, one of the dangers of extreme religious passion is that it can lead to religious excess or fanaticism. A fanatic is "character-ized, influenced or prompted by excessive and mistaken enthusiasm,

---

Reconstruction: The Transformation of Contemporary Orthodoxy," *Tradi-tion* 28:4 (1994): 64–130.

especially in religious matters."[4] The excessiveness of fanatical behavior is that "the fanatic attaches too much importance to his cause, or to certain of his values. . . . [H]is obsession [with his particular cause] prevents him from paying sufficient attention to other things that he values or professes to value [such as other aspects of his religion]." Furthermore, his "overvaluing" of his particular cause "leads him to adopt a callous attitude toward certain innocent human beings or their interests."[5]

Religious fanaticism, according to this definition, is problematic for two interrelated reasons. First, it results in a distortion of what is of ultimate import in "the fanatic's" own religion, for he "overvalues" his particular cause at the expense of other, more fundamental religious values. Second, his particular cause can become so important in his mind that the feelings and even lives of other people take on a mere secondary level of significance.[6] This study will examine the criteria used by the Talmud to limit individualized strictness, out of concern lest religious zeal lead to fanaticism.

The second problem to which unrestrained religious passion could lead is the growth of an elitist class of pietists who could become a separatist branch of Judaism, thus destroying Jewish unity. Steven Fraade raises this issue, asking just how much abstinence was permitted to the rabbinic elite in particular. He writes:

> The Rabbis differed regarding the extent to which a rabbinic elite should adopt an abstinent course of conduct more demanding than what could be expected of the people under its authority. Did the halakhah determine both the norms and *limits* of

---

4. *The Compact Edition of the Oxford English Dictionary* (Oxford: Oxford University Press, 1971), Vol. I, p. 959.

5. Jay Newman, *Fanatics and Hypocrites* (Buffalo: Prometheus Books, 1986), pp. 52, 57. Newman discusses the phenomenon of fanaticism from a philosophical, psychological, and historical point of view and provides references for further investigation of this phenomenon. See also Josef Rudin, *Fanaticism, A Psychological Analysis,* trans. Elisabeth Reinecke and Paul C. Bailey (Notre Dame, IN: University of Notre Dame Press, 1969).

6. For a discussion of the philosophical literature concerning the relationship between supererogation and morality, see Joshua Halberstam, "Supererogation in Jewish Halakhah and Islamic Shari'a", *Studies in Islamic and Judaic Traditions,* ed. William M. Brinner and Stephen D. Ricks, Brown Judaic Studies 110 (Atlanta: Scholars Press, 1986), pp. 85–89.

abstinence, or were individuals free to abstain from what was otherwise permitted . . . ?[7]

While Fraade limits his question to the rabbinic elite and abstinence, this study addresses this issue as a general phenomenon, affecting both common people and scholars and involving both ascetic and nonascetic behavior. The purpose of this study is to investigate how this question was answered in the rabbinic sources.

The rabbinic critique of individualized strictness appears to revolve around the limitations that objective Jewish law placed on subjective[8] religious expression. Two different types of subjective religious expression will be addressed here. One involves observing a religious commandment from which one is exempt only temporarily, such as a bridegroom reciting the Shema. (Although generally obligated to recite the Shema, he is exempt on his wedding night.) The second involves accepting a new religious obligation that one was never obligated to observe under any other circumstance, such as praying extra daily prayers or fasting extra fasts. For a woman who, according to Talmudic law, is generally exempt from time-dependent positive commandments, accepting any of these commandments upon herself as an obligation would be another example of this latter type of subjective religious expression (i.e., supererogatory behavior). Thus, although Talmudic Judaism certainly allowed for the expression of personal, subjective needs for spiritual fulfillment through extensions of (or additions to) Jewish law, conformity to legal-communal norms often precluded the individualized subjective prerogative to extend (or add to) those norms. At times, therefore, the rabbis condemned the supererogatory practices described earlier. This study will attempt to define the parameters of these limitations.

---

7. Fraade continues, by stating, "This question, never answered within Rabbinic Judaism, was inherited by medieval Jewish philosophers, mystics, and legal authorities." While the question was never answered in any systematic, explicit, or authoritative way in rabbinic Judaism, this study will investigate the various answers that were, in fact, provided by the Talmudic literature ("Ascetical Aspects of Ancient Judaism", *Jewish Spirituality I,* ed. Arthur Green [New York: Crossroad, 1987], p. 272).

8. The word *subjective* is used here to mean personal or individualistic; it does not refer to the term *subjective* as used in the philosophical literature.

*Asceticism*

The broader topic of asceticism in Talmudic Judaism is extremely relevant to this study. The term *asceticism* has been defined in many different ways;[9] the following definition will be used in this study. It is "the exercise of disciplined effort toward the goal of spiritual perfection . . . which requires abstention . . . from the satisfaction of otherwise permitted earthly, creaturely desires."[10] Although primarily antiascetic sources will be presented here, this approach is by no means intended to portray the Talmudic literature as exclusively antiascetic. For just as many sources criticize ascetic types of behavior, many express praise for it.

This conflict, reflected in the sources, has led to a debate among scholars as to whether Talmudic Judaism was primarily ascetic or antiascetic. Most late nineteenth- and early twentieth-century scholars, both Jewish and Christian, held that Talmudic Judaism was basically antiascetic.[11] Although many accepted the notion that there were some ascetic tendencies within Judaism, they nevertheless agreed that ascetic behavior in that time period was a deviation from the norm.[12]

Yitzchak Baer, on the other hand (the first to analyze the

---

9. See Fraade, "Asectical Aspects," pp. 253–257.

10. Fraade, "Ascetical Aspects," p. 257. For further discussion of the origins of asceticism and the various forms of asceticism found in different religions, see Walter O. Kaelber, "Asceticism," *The Encyclopedia of Religion,* ed. Mircea Eliade (New York: Macmillan, 1987), vol. I, pp. 441–445.

11. Ephraim E. Urbach, "Iskizm VeYisurim beTorat Hazal," *Sefer HaYovel LeYitzchak Baer* (Jerusalem: Historical Society of Israel, 1960), pp. 48–49; David Halivni (Weiss), "On the Supposed Anti-Asceticism or Anti-Naziritism of Simon the Just," *Jewish Quarterly Review* 58 (1968), p. 243.

12. George Foot Moore, *Judaism in the First Centuries of the Christian Era* (Cambridge, MA: Harvard University Press, 1966), vol. II, pp. 263–266; Urbach, "Iskizm," p. 48. Joseph Bonsirven, however, in his search for "an anticipation of Christian asceticism" within Jewish sources, writes that there was a strong ascetic strain in first-century Palestinian Judaism; he basically classifies all of Jewish law as a form of asceticism. See *Palestinian Judaism in the Time of Jesus Christ,* trans. William Wolf [New York: Holt, Rinehart and Winston, 1964], pp. 158–161.

sources historically), argued against this general attitude. He claimed that the hasidim-scholars[13] in Second Temple times and the early tannaim were, in fact, ascetics who served as prototypes for later Christian monks and whose ideals influenced Pharisaic/rabbinic Judaism.[14] He holds that although more extreme ascetic practices were eliminated with the passage of time, this ascetic way of life left a distinctive mark on Judaism, since echoes of the "Torah" of these early ascetics can be found within much of tannaitic literature.[15]

Ephraim Urbach cogently argues against Baer's thesis and denies that there is evidence from the sources that the early tannaim or even the hasidim of the Second Temple period were ascetics.[16] He claims, instead, that all of the ascetic practices found in the Talmud were reactions to two specific tragic events, namely, the destruction of the Temple and the later Hadrianic persecutions.[17] Urbach thus accepts the general scholarly consensus that Talmudic Judaism was, otherwise, antiascetic.

Steven Fraade, in his excellent critical evaluation of the Baer-Urbach controversy,[18] explains that one of the underlying issues in the Baer-Urbach debate is the fact that these two scholars are actually using different definitions of asceticism. Baer uses the word in a very broad sense, as a "positive sense of moral and spiritual self-discipline and exercise," whereas Urbach uses a very narrow, specific definition of asceticism as a "negative sense of dualistic abnegation of the body."[19] These different definitions resulted in different conclusions regarding whether the hasidim and early tannaim were actually ascetics. Fraade's suggested definition of asceticism, which was quoted earlier and will be used in this study, is neither as broad as Baer's nor as narrow as Urbach's.

---

13. See John Kampen's exhaustive survey of the literature on the term *hasidim* in his *The Hasideans and the Origin of Pharisaism* (Atlanta: Scholars Press, 1988), especially pp. 1–45, 187–222.

14. Yitzchak Baer, *Yisrael Ba-Ammim* (Jerusalem: Mossad Bialik, 1955), pp. 27, 39.

15. Ibid., pp. 40, 48.

16. Kampen, though, holds that "Clearly the Talmudic tradition saw the 'pious' to be related to the ascetic movement, probably to the Nazirites" (*The Hasideans*, p. 203).

17. Urbach, "Iskizm," p. 56.

18. Fraade, "Ascetical Aspects," pp. 258–260.

19. Ibid., p. 259.

Fraade himself argues that although a catastrophic event such as the Temple's destruction certainly did engender ascetic responses, Urbach's claim that the many ascetic practices found in the Talmud were limited, isolated responses to two particular tragic events is untenable. He correctly observes that "Urbach's *own* evidence" suggests that the ascetic responses to the destruction were "sharpened expressions of tension and tendencies already present," and not solely new developments responding to specific tragedies. The attitude of the rabbis toward asceticism was simply far more complex and diverse than Urbach acknowledged. For there is such diversity of opinion regarding asceticism to be found in the Talmud (including multiple authors, time periods, and geographic locations), that the evidence does not fit into neat, highly specific categories. Fraade's own conclusion regarding the basis of ancient Jewish asceticism is that the many conflicting opinions in the Talmud reflect "ascetic tension," caused by the rabbis' struggle with "the tension between the realization of transcendent ideals and the confronting of this-worldly obstacles to that realization."[20]

The goal of this study is, however, not to generate any new conclusions as to whether the rabbis of the Talmud were, on the whole, inclined toward or against asceticism.[21] Instead, chapters 2, 3, and 4 will simply be limited to the rationales behind the antiascetic opinions expressed within Talmudic literature.

Recently published studies of asceticism in ancient religions illustrate that "ascetic behavior represent[ed] a range of responses to social, political, and physical worlds often perceived as oppressive or unfriendly, or as stumbling blocks to the pursuit of heroic personal or communal goals, life styles, and commitments."[22] This study (specifically Chapters 2 through 4) focuses on when Jews, who responded to these "worlds" by adopting ascetic behavior, were

---

20. Fraade, "Ascetical Aspects," pp. 260, 269–277.

21. Other important works dealing with the history of Jewish asceticism are Adolf Buchler, *Types of Jewish Palestinian Piety* (London: Jew's College, 1922); S. Lowy, "The Motivation of Fasting in Talmudic Literature," *Journal of Jewish Studies* 9 (1958), pp. 19–38; and A. J. Heschel, *Torah min haShamayim beAspaklarya shel haDorot* (London: Soncino, 1962), vol. I, pp. 127–133.

22. Vincent Wimbush, *Ascetic Behavior in Greco-Roman Antiquity*, p. 2. See also *Semeia* (1992), vol. I and II.

criticized by the rabbis. This study of rabbinic assumptions regarding the motivating factors behind Jewish asceticism in Talmudic times and when they criticized the ascetic behavior, thus, advances the modern study of asceticism.[23]

A relatively new focus of modern research, one that has emerged predominantly in the last decade as women's studies have become more prevalent, is on the ascetic behavior of women in Greco-Roman antiquity. Many books and articles have been written on this subject, focusing especially on early Christian women.[24] Chapter 3 of this study, which deals with the ascetic woman of *M. Sotah* 3:4, will add the perspective of the Talmud to the rapidly growing literature on this topic.

The difference, though, between this study and the modern study of asceticism lies in two crucial factors. One is the different nature of the asceticism being studied. For even though Chapters 2, 3, and 4 deal with rabbinic criticism of ascetic behaviors, the behaviors addressed never reached the extremes of Christian asceticism. Early Christian monks would, for example, withdraw from society and live in isolation in caves or on mountain tops, eating only plants and berries, never bathing or cutting their hair or nails. As Arthur Voobus points out:

---

23. Within modern scholarship, some see asceticism in a very broad sense, "as a kind of MS-DOS of cultures, a fundamental operating ground on which the particular culture, the word processing program itself, is overlaid." Since all cultures are ethical, they therefore impose on their members the essential ascetic discipline of "self-denial," meaning the resistance to "nature and nature's appetites." This imposition of self-discipline, termed the "ascetic imperative" is then a primary, transcultural structuring force. It is, then, applied to a study of capitalism, literature, and art. (Geoffrey Galt Harpham, *The Ascetic Imperative in Culture and Criticism* [Chicago: University of Chicago Press, 1987], pp. xi–xii, xvi, and subsequent chapters.) This study, however, will focus on asceticism in a more traditional, limited sense, as it relates to self denial within the spheres of religion and spirituality.

24. See, for example, the works of Elizabeth A. Clark, such as *Ascetic Piety and Women's Faith* (Lewiston, N.Y.: Mellen, 1986), Susan Ashbrook Harvey, *Asceticism and Society in Crisis* (Berkeley: University of California Press, 1990), and the many articles in *Semeia* (1992). A classic work on this topic is Caroline Walker Bynum, *Holy Feasts and Holy Fasts* (Berkeley: University of California Press, 1987). Bynum's work, however, focuses primarily on medieval Christian women.

While many facets of ancient Syrian Christianity can be traced
back to Jewish Christian origin, yet in the factor of asceticism,
however, we encounter a phenomenon so astonishing that it
seems to be entirely outside of the Jewish mold which stands at
the beginning of the development.[25]

The "astonishing" severity of the asceticism that characterized
the Christian monastic movement was, essentially, a phenomenon
unique to Christianity[26] and not found within Judaism. Even when
the rabbis did criticize ascetic behavior, they were not generally
addressing people living lives of hardship in monastic settings but
"regular" people living within families and communities.

The second distinguishing feature between the asceticism of
this study versus the asceticism in the modern literature lies in the
fact that this study addresses the issue of asceticism as part of a
broader study of rabbinic criticism of supererogation in general.
Thus, Chapters 5, 6, and 7 (the foolish pietist, the commoner, and
the issue of arrogance), although dealing with self-imposed stringencies, do not necessarily involve ascetic self-denial. Consequently,
many of the supererogatory practices discussed here are not, in fact,
ascetic practices at all.

*Intention*

The issue of intention in religious behavior is of crucial importance
in this study. The idea that one's thoughts can imbue one's actions
with meaning is very basic to the Halakhic system. This concept,
known as *kavvana,* is of critical importance in various areas of Jewish
law. Among these are the laws of sacrifices, tithing, prayer, the
Sabbath, homicide, personal injury, civil offenses, and transfer and
ownership of property.[27]

---

25. Arthur Voobus, *History of Asceticism in the Syrian Orient* (Louvain:
Secretariat du CorpusSCO, 1958), vol. I, p. 14.

26. For more information regarding these extreme practices, see
Arthur Voobus, *History of Asceticism: The Sayings of the Desert Fathers
(Apophthegmata patrum),* trans. Benedicta Ward (London: Mowbray, 1980),
and *The Desert Fathers,* trans. and ed. Helen Waddell (NewYork: Holt, 1936).

27. For further discussion of this topic, see Y. D. Gilath, "Kavana
U'Ma'aseh BaMishnah," *Annual of Bar-Ilan University* IV–V (1967), pp.

In the laws of the Sabbath, for example, one is not liable for having violated one of the thirty-nine forbidden work categories unless one intended to do the forbidden category (*melekhet mahshevet*). If one did something by accident or with no intention, then that person is generally not liable.[28] Similarly, if one recites the Shema without intending to fulfill one's obligation, then that obligation in fact remains unfulfilled (*M. Berakhot* 2:1).

An important question to be addressed in this study of supererogatory behavior is, thus, to what extent the rabbis' criticism of such behavior considered why the individual imposed on himself the specific stringency. Were sincere intentions alone a sufficient reason for granting legitimacy to the supererogatory behavior? Alternatively, did insincere intentions, in and of themselves, invalidate the supererogatory behavior? If the latter were true, then self-imposed stringency would follow the model of the sacrificial laws, in which improper intentions alone can render the sacrifice invalid (Leviticus 19:7).

## HISTORICAL CONTEXT

Jewish pietists are referred to in the literature from as early as the times of the Macabbees. The Hasmoneans joined forces with the hasidim, who originally would not fight Antiochus's forces on the Sabbath day. The Talmud is full of references to the early pietists (*hahasidim harishonim*), and pietists and men of good deeds (*hasidim veanshei ma'aseh*). Samuel Safrai holds that there was a distinct group of hasidim, with their own set of alternate halakhot (known as *mishnat hasidim*), in tannaitic times.[29] The pietists discussed in the

---

104–116; Michael Higger, "Intention in Talmudic Law," *Studies in Jewish Jurisprudence*, vol. I (New York: Hermon, 1971), pp. 235–293; Bernard S. Jackson, "Liability for Mere Intention in Jewish Law," *Essays in Jewish and Comparative Legal History* (Leiden: Brill, 1975), pp. 202–234; Jacob Neusner, *Judaism: The Evidence of the Mishnah* (Chicago: University of Chicago Press, 1981), pp. 270–283; and Howard Eilberg Schwartz, *The Human Will in Judaism* (Atlanta: Scholars Press, 1986). For further references, see Eilberg Schwartz, ibid., p. 201, note 3.

28. B. Shabbat 29b, 73a, Maimonides *Yad,* Laws of Shabbat 1:1–14.

29. Safrai, "Teaching of Pietists," *Journal of Jewish Studies* XVI (1965), pp. 15–33. Cf. Kampens's study, *The Hasideans,* pp. 1–42, 187–222.

Talmud are generally spoken of with great respect. As already noted, however, this study will examine only those cases in which their practices are criticized.

This study begins with the start of the tannaitic period (first century)—a time of tremendous upheaval in Palestine. Three main groups of Jews were described by Josephus: the Pharisees, Saducees, and Essenes (as well as other sectarians, such as the Dead Sea Sect). The Essenes and Dead Sea Sect were groups of people dedicated to a separatist lifestyle. The influence of these sects, however, on the Talmudic era was short-lived. After the destruction, the different sects basically disappeared, and Pharisaic Judaism became mainstream.

In Palestine, the revolt against the Romans and the destruction of the Temple, followed by the Hadrianic persecutions of the second century, led to depression, despair, and economic hardship. The destruction of the Temple was a traumatic event for the nation.[30] Talmudic sources describe how segments of the community adopted severely ascetic mourning rituals after the destruction. Rabbinic attempts to curb the more extreme among them will be examined in Chapter 2.

At this same time, Christianity was slowly developing, first within Palestine and then spreading throughout the Roman Empire. Communities of Jewish Christians began to grow during the middle of the first century, consisting of Jews who believed in Jesus yet wanted to remain Jewish and continue observing the commandments. Eventually these Jewish Christians split from Judaism as Christianity became a separate religion. Soon after the destruction of the Temple, they were rejected by the sages. Nonetheless, there were continuing contacts between the Jewish Christians and individual Jews, both common and scholarly, throughout the second and third centuries.[31]

The interrelationship between early Christianity and Judaism is relevant to this study, since ascetic practices such as fasting, virginity,

---

30. Baruch M. Bokser, "Rabbinic Responses to Catastrophe: From Continuity to Discontinuity," *Proceedings of the American Academy for Jewish Research* 50 (1983), p. 61.

31. Gedaliah Alon, *The Jews in Their Land in the Talmudic Age,* ed. and trans. G. Levi (Jerusalem: Magnes, 1980), p. 26; Lawrence H. Schiffman, *Who Was A Jew* (Hoboken, NJ: Ktav, 1985), pp. 52–54, 61, 64–67.

celibacy, and poverty were glorified in early Christianity. Hermits who practiced extreme forms of asceticism were regarded as holy men. This issue will be discussed primarily in Chapter 3, which deals with the ascetic woman.

There was, certainly, contact between Jews and early Christians in Palestine; the influence of the early Christians on the Jews in Palestine, however, probably declined as the years went by, since the attitude of Judaism to Christianity was that of a majority to a minority. Once Paul began preaching Christianity to the Gentiles, then Christianity's importance for the Jews of Palestine diminished. Only a relatively small Jewish Christian community was left in Palestine, which declined steadily throughout the second, third, and fourth centuries.[32]

Christian influence on the Jewish community in Babylonia was probably minimal, since the Christians in the Babylonian empire represented a persecuted minority, whereas the Jews of Babylonia were relatively free of anti-Semitic attacks and religious persecution.[33] As such, it is unlikely that this persecuted minority could have presented a serious challenge to the larger and more stable Jewish community.

There is even evidence that the Christians felt the need to defend themselves against Jewish proselytizing.[34] Aphrahat, the fourth-century Christian bishop at Mar Mattai (near Ninveh, in northern Mesopotamia), defends Christian practices against the critique of the Jews of his time.[35] Aphrahat's "Demonstrations" show that there was Jewish-Christian dialogue in fourth-century Babylonia and that the Jews in the Babylonian empire spoke out against Christian practices and beliefs.

Whereas Louis Ginzberg and other scholars held that Aphrahat was strongly influenced by rabbinical Judaism,[36] Neusner strongly

---

32. Michael Avi-Yonah, *The Jews of Palestine* (New York: Schocken, 1976), pp. 138–140.

33. Gafni, *Yehudei Bavel*, pp. 151–152.

34. Ibid., p. 146. Cf. *B. Pesahim* 87b, "God exiled the Jews amongst the nations only in order to attract proselytes."

35. Frank E. Talmage, *Disputation and Dialogue: Readings in the Jewish-Christian Encounter* (New York: Ktav and the Anti-Defamation League of B'nai Brith, 1975), p. 17.

36. Louis Ginzberg, "Aphraates, The Persian Sage," *The Jewish Encyclo-*

disagrees with this contention[37] and questions whether Aphrahat, who lived in northern Mesapotamia, had any connection with the rabbis of the Babylonian communities of Sura, Pumbedita, and Mahoza, which lay to the south. Neusner, however, represents a minority opinion, and most scholars agree that Aphrahat was in contact with rabbinic scholars.[38] Gafni goes so far as to suggest that there might be a correlation among Aphrahat's defense of Christianity, the Persian authorities' persecution of Christians in the early fourth century, and the Talmudic evidence of converts to Judaism during the same period. The persecuted Christians in Babylonia, then, who may even have felt religiously threatened by Judaism, did not, in all likelihood, present a serious threat to the Jewish religion.

Evidence from the Talmud demonstrates that the Jews of Babylonia lived in close proximity to their gentile neighbors. They worked and traded together peacefully. It is, thus, not surprising that the influence of various Babylonian folk beliefs, such as astrology, demonology, and medical practices, can be found in Talmudic literature.[39] Nonetheless, even if Babylonian folk beliefs did infiltrate the Jewish community, the Babylonian religion did not seem to be of major concern to the rabbis. According to Neusner, the Babylonian rabbis had "no interest in, and slight knowledge of, other religions besides Christianity. Mazdaeism, the religion of the state, elicited only a limited polemic."[40]

The economic situation of the Jews in amoraic times is also an important factor to consider. In Palestine, from the second half of the second century through the third and fourth centuries, the political situation basically stabilized. Palestinian Jewry did not, at that time, undergo religious persecution and still enjoyed some degree of political autonomy.

Life in Palestine became terribly difficult, however, in approxi-

---

*pedia,* vol. I (New York: Funk & Wagnall, 1912), pp. 663; Jacob Neusner, *Aphrahat and Judaism* (Leiden: Brill, 1971), pp. 150–158.

37. He devotes a long chapter of his book *Aphrahat and Judaism* (pp. 158–195) to disproving Ginzberg's claim.

38. Gafni, *Yehudei Bavel,* p. 144, note 118.

39. Gafni, *Yehudei Bavel,* pp. 149–166, and Maimonides, "Commentary to the Mishnah," *Abodah Zara* 4:7.

40. Neusner, *Aphrahat,* p. 125.

mately 235 C.E.[41] This development resulted from the great crisis that shook the Roman empire throughout the remainder of the third century. During this time, a loss of central control over the empire and tremendous political instability occurred.[42] Rulers changed frequently—twenty-two different emperors ruled for a total of fifty-eight years; all but two of them rose to power after their predecessor had met a violent death.[43]

As a result of this crisis, civil war between different Roman factions was a common sight, and people would easily lose their property or their life.[44] Famine and epidemics were commonplace, and the tax burden became unbearable. The Jewish community was thus reduced to grinding poverty,[45] and, as a result, the Jewish population of the country declined steeply during this period.[46]

Although not enough data are available to describe the economic status of the average Babylonian Jew, what seems clear is that they were far better off than were their brothers in Palestine. Wages were higher in Babylon; land was less expensive, and livestock, wheat, dates, and possibly clothing were all cheaper than they were in Palestine.[47] Babylonian Jewry underwent difficult time periods, but they were never subjected to the devastating wars, oppressive taxes, and steep inflation of the Roman empire.[48]

Significant differences thus existed between the economic and political conditions in Palestine and Babylonia. Whether there is a correlation between these differences and rabbinic criticism of self-imposed stringency in the Palestinian versus Babylonian Talmud will, consequently, be investigated.

---

41. Gedaliah Allon, *The Jews in Their Land in the Talmudic Age,* vol. II, ed. and trans. G. Levi (Jerusalem: Magnes, Hebrew University, 1984), p. 746.
42. Yonah, *The Jews of Palestine,* p. 90.
43. Ibid., p. 91.
44. Ibid., pp. 90–91.
45. Ibid., p. 104.
46. Ibid., p. 89.
47. Louis Jacobs, "The Economic Conditions of the Jews in Babylon in Talmudic Times Compared with Palestine," *Journal of Semitic Studies* 2 (1957), pp. 352–353.
48. Ibid., p. 352.

# RELATED ISSUES

*Oaths and Vows*

The topic of taking oaths and vows in general (*shevu'ot* and *nedarim*) is also related to the issue of supererogatory behavior. One of the religious means used by people to impose stringencies on themselves was by taking an oath not to do (or to do) certain things or by vowing to avoid deriving benefit from certain objects or people. Although people made many types of vows for a multitude of reasons,[49] some vows were made for ascetic purposes. For example, people would vow that certain foods were forbidden to them. Likewise, they might vow not to benefit in any way from their spouse; sexual pleasure would be included in that vow.

Nonetheless, the topic of rabbinic criticism of vows in general does not belong in this study. This is because when vows are criticized, the tanna or amora is usually criticizing the very act itself of taking a vow (because of the difficulty involved in keeping it). They are not, generally, criticizing the behavior chosen as the content of the vow. When, though, rabbinic criticism of vows does provide information regarding rabbinic criticism of specific supererogatory behaviors, those sources will be examined.

*Baraita deNiddah*

*Baraita deNiddah* is a source that contains numerous religious stringencies. Many extreme practices forbidding contact with a menstruating woman are found in this work, including considering the ground on which she walks and any food or utensil that she touches to be impure and hence forbidden to use.[50] These stringencies, however, will not be discussed in this study, as *Baraita deNiddah* is post-Talmudic.[51] Additionally, the practices described in this work

---

49. See Saul Lieberman, "Oaths and Vows," *Greek in Jewish Palestine*, (New York: Jewish Theological Seminary, 1942), pp. 115–143.

50. *Baraita deNiddah*, ed. Chaim Horovitz, *Tosefta Atikata* V, pp. 3, 12–13, 1970.

51. It is dated in the Geonic period, though the author is unknown (Mordechai Margaliot, *HaHilukim sheBein Anshei Mizrah uBenei Eretz Yisrael* [Jerusalem: Eretz Yisrael 1938], p. 115).

were not necessarily supererogatory. For *Baraita deNiddah,* like the *mishnat hasidim* of tannaitic times, may have reflected a different Halakhic tradition as to what is actually required by halakhah (and not self-imposed).[52]

It should be noted that some of the practices described in this work have their origins in tannaitic times[53] or even Second Temple times.[54] Some of the very basic laws of *niddah* as formulated in the Talmud may thus have aimed specifically at opposing the extreme practices that already existed at the time and were preserved in *Baraita deNiddah.*[55] For example, R. Huna's statement in *B. Ketubot* 61a that a woman who is *niddah* may perform virtually all everyday household chores may have been formulated to counter those who claimed that anything that a *niddah* touched became impure. If this is correct, then normative laws of *niddah* would in and of themselves constitute an unspoken yet extremely powerful critique of excessive purity rituals. This study, however, will be limited to explicit, verbalized criticisms of self-imposed religious stringencies. It will not deal with possible unspoken censure of stringencies that can be read into formulated Talmudic laws, as may be the case here.[56]

---

52. Safrai, "Teaching of Pietists," pp. 15–33.

53. Yedidiah Dinari, "Minhagei Tumat HaNiddah-Mekoram VeHish-talshelutam," *Tarbiz* 49:3–4 (1980), pp. 305–310; and *M. Niddah* 7:4.

54. The Temple Scroll refers to special places that were designated for menstruant women. See Yigal Yadin, *Megilat HaMikdash* (Jerusalem: Ha-Hevra LeHakirat Eretz Yisrael veAtikotehah, 1977), vol. III, column 48:14–17, plate 63, and comments in vol. I, pp. 305–307.

55. Dinari, pp. 311–315.

56. Another example of this type of silent but potent criticism can be read into the discussion in *B. Niddah* 38a–b of how the early pietiests used to have sexual intercourse with their wives only on Wednesdays. This practice is described without censure—no negative comments are recorded regarding this custom, even though it most flagrantly violates the precepts of *onah* as we know them. (*Onah* is the marital obligation of a husband to fulfill his wife's sexual needs.) The Babylonian Talmud, however, voices a silent criticism, as it corrects the baraita to say "from Wednesday onward" rather than only on Wednesdays. As Safrai notes, this is not the simplest meaning of the baraita, and the Talmud's correction in and of itself can be seen as an objection to the practice of the early pietists (Safrai, "Teaching of Pietists," p. 25). In this case, through, as well as in the case of *Baraita deNiddah,* the behavior described may not have been supererogatory.

## SUMMARY OF CHAPTERS

Chapter 1 focuses on the issue of when supererogatory behavior is permitted and when it is forbidden. This issue is discussed in the context of *M. Ta'anit* 1:4, which states that "the individuals" begin fasting for rain two weeks before the rest of the community is instructed to do so. *T. Ta'anit* 1:7 (with its parallels in *B. Ta'anit* 10b and *P. Berakhot* 2:9) discusses just who qualifies as "an individual" and in what other situations people may or may not impose religious obligations on themselves.

The Tosefta divides supererogatory behavior into two types: matters of praise and matters of anguish. Matters of praise are observances that will elicit the praise of other people. The individual who accepts these observances will be viewed as a particularly pious or learned person and will gain more respect within the community. Examples of matters of praise are reciting extra prayers and dressing and behaving as a scholar. Matters of anguish are ascetic types of practices, such as restricting the types of foods one eats, fasting, and practicing sexual abstinence.

The Tosefta thus provides general policy statements regarding when self-imposed stringency is permitted or forbidden. Since it is one of the few sources that provides such a general approach, it is discussed in the first chapter of this study. Furthermore, the two categories of behavior that it describes—matters of anguish and matters of praise—will be referred to repeatedly in later chapters to see how the other Talmudic sources compare and contrast to the Tosefta's position.

Chapter 2 considers matters of anguish and discusses when and why the rabbis criticized self-imposed ascetic behaviors. It is divided into two sections. The first deals with rabbinic criticisms of self-

---

Instead, it may have represented an alternative Halakhic tradition. Another possible example of "silent criticism" can be found in *M. Keritut* 6:3, where R. Eliezer permits the offering of a suspensive guilt offering on any day and at any time one pleases (*asham hasidim*), whereas the rabbis forbid such behavior and permit this offering only as atonement for very specific sins. One could claim that the rabbis wanted to place limits on voluntary sacrificing (cf. the discussion in Chapter 1 regarding voluntary prayer). The Talmudic sugya, though, gives a different explanation for the Rabbis' position (*B. Keritut* 25a).

imposed anguish because of the negative results to which it would lead. For example, frequent fasting is viewed, in principle, as positive and is criticized only in situations in which it leads to physical weakness or illness. The second section deals with rabbinic evaluations of self-imposed anguish as being inherently negative. Frequent fasting, according to these sources, would be negative in and of itself, even if it did not lead to physical weakness or illness.

The third, fourth, and fifth chapters discuss three of the categories of people singled out in *M. Sotah* 3:4 as people who bring destruction upon the world. Chapter 3 deals with one of these categories—"the ascetic woman" (*ishah perushah*), establishing what type of behavior was being condemned in the Mishnah and why it was criticized so vehemently. This chapter is a continuation of the theme of rabbinic criticism of matters of anguish, since the woman was condemned for her ascetic behavior. The fourth chapter discusses another category of people criticized in the Mishnah, namely, "the wounds of the separatists" (*makot perushim*). *B. Sotah* 22b lists seven types of "separatists" who bring destruction upon the world; the relevant categories are defined and analyzed. The majority of these categories also involve ascetic behaviors.

Chapter 5 focuses on a third category singled out for criticism in *M. Sotah* 3:4—the foolish pietist. This category, though found in the same Mishnah as the separatist woman and the wounds of the separatists, does not fit into the category of matters of anguish. Consequently, it is dealt with in a new unit in this study. This unit (comprising Chapters 5 through 7) focuses primarily on nonascetic supererogatory behavior, some of which falls into the category of "matters of praise."

After discussing *M. Sotah* 3:4 in Chapters 3 through 5, I return in Chapter 6 to *P. Berakhot* 2:9. The central organizing motif of this chapter revolves around the phrase "Whoever does something from which he is exempt is called a commoner (*hedyot*)." The meaning of the term *commoner,* the type of supererogatory behavior that "merited" this label, and the reasons for this negative attitude are all discussed. The possible connection between the label "commoner" and "the foolish pietist" will also be examined.

In the final chapter, the concept of arrogance (*yohara*) is addressed. This concept seems to be a paramount concern underlying much of the rabbinic criticism of the supererogatory behavior discussed in all of the other chapters. The issue of arrogance is discussed in *B. Berakhot* 17b and in two other sources in the Babylonian Talmud. The term does not appear at all in the Palestinian Talmud, but the idea certainly does surface, though possibly with a different focus from that found in the Babylonian Talmud.

## METHODOLOGY

The relevant sources have been gathered through the use of Talmudic cross references, concordances, encyclopedias, the Judaic Classics Library, Bar-Ilan Responsa project computer data banks, and other reference materials. These sources are examined with all available tools of research. Tannaitic material, including the Mishnah, Tosefta, and relevant Midrashic material, has been analyzed, using manuscripts and critical editions. All amoraic material has likewise been studied with available manuscripts and *Dikdukei Soferim*. Relevant passages in both the Babylonian and Palestinian Talmud are researched and compared. The historical development of each passage has been analyzed, to discover the various layers of text and place them in proper historical context.

Whenever appropriate, tannaitic and amoraic statements have first been analyzed as independent units, and then examined as parts of the context within which they appear. The differences and similarities between the Babylonian and Palestinian sources have also been addressed. The Talmudic sources will be discussed in the body of the text; many of the formulations of medieval and modern commentators will be cited in the notes. While examining these sources, geographic, historical, and teacher-student patterns of thought that can be detected within the various rabbinic statements are investigated.

Geographic patterns involve detecting philosophical differences between the Palestinian and Babylonian amoraim. Historical patterns involve determining whether there were changing attitudes from tannaitic to amoraic times, or even between different centuries or generations. Attitudes toward self-imposed stringency may have become more positive, or more negative, with the passage of time. Finally, schools of thought may be detected that are influenced by teacher-student or father-son relationships, independent of other geographic or historical considerations. To investigate these possible thought patterns, the dates, locations, teachers, students, families, and colleagues of the tannaim and amoraim quoted are determined.

Related statements made by these scholars are compared and contrasted.

This study will also compare the self-imposed stringencies criticized in the Talmud to related practices of the various Jewish sects, Greco-Roman religions, and the early Christians. To this end, the Dead Sea Scrolls, Josephus, Philo, the New Testament, and other relevant primary and secondary sources were consulted. Whether these other groups influenced or were influenced by the Pharisees (i.e., "Pre-Rabbinic" Judaism) or the later rabbinic Judaism of the Talmud will be discussed. The possibility of parallel practices arising independently will, obviously, also be considered.

# 1

# The Permissibility of Self-Imposed Religious Stringency

The individual's desire for personal, subjective religious expression above and beyond the requirements of the law (i.e., supererogatory behavior) was sometimes permitted or even praised in the Talmud. At other times, this type of behavior was criticized or even forbidden. The Talmudic discussion of "Who may declare themselves individuals?" is critical to the study of when supererogatory behavior was permitted or even praised versus when conformity to legal-communal norms precluded the individual's subjective prerogative to extend (or add to) those norms.

The discussion begins with *M. Ta'anit* 1:4, which outlines the community's response to an impending drought:

> I.   If the seventeenth of the month of Mar Heshvan has arrived and rains have not yet fallen, *the individuals* begin fasting three fasts. . . .[1]

---

1. The same terminology is used in *B. Ta'anit* 6a (and *B. Nedarim 63a*). The Talmudic sugya quotes R. Yosi, who disagreed with this Mishnah:

23

II. If the first day of the month of Kislev arrives and rain still has not fallen, the court decrees three fasts on the entire community."

Although the Mishnah declares that "the individuals" begin fasting three fasts, it does not define just who qualified to be "an individual." Another factor that remains unclear is whether the Mishnah was describing a practice that was permitted (or even encouraged) versus an actual obligation. The second part of the Mishnah, which states that the court decrees three fasts on the entire community, may provide the answer to this question. The Mishnah states that the community's fasts were based on a court decree, but, regarding the individual's fasts, it just says "the individuals begin fasting." This seems to indicate that the fasts of the individuals, not having been decreed by the court, were voluntary. The Mishnah, then, would be encouraging supererogatory fasting in this situation, to help bring rain for the community. One can argue, though, that the individuals' fasts were, in fact, obligatory but that no actual court decree was needed, since "the individuals" may have referred to a specific group of especially pious people who were aware of their obligations.

## DEFINITIONS OF THE TERM *THE INDIVIDUALS*

There are two possible definitions of the term *the individuals* (*hayehidim*) in the Mishnah. The first, a very inclusive definition of the term, is that it refers to any individual who felt motivated to fast. The term *an individual* (*yahid*) is used countless times throughout Talmudic literature as a reference to any individual (as opposed to the community).[2] Any person who felt that he or she wanted to do something special to help bring about the rain was encouraged to

"And thus did R. Yosi say, 'The individuals do not begin fasting until the first day of Kislev.'" (The Mishnah rules that they begin fasting after the seventeenth of Mar Heshvan, the month before Kislev.)

2. See H. Y. Kassowski, *Otzar Leshon HaMishnah* (Jerusalem: Massadah, 1957), *Otzar Leshon HaTosefta* (Jerusalem: Jewish Theological Seminary, 1961) and *Otzar Leshon HaTalmud* (Jerusalem: Ministry of Education and Culture, Government of Israel and Jewish Theological Seminary, 1982), s.v. *yahid*.

fast after the seventeenth of Tamuz.[3] The second definition, based on the plural term *the individuals,* specifically defines them as "the special people,"[4] a distinctive group of people, thus curbing the prerogative of just any individual to fast. The linguistic basis for favoring this "exclusive" definition of *the individuals* is the fact that the Mishnah does not merely state "individuals" (*yehidim*) but instead uses the definite article *the* (*ha*)—"the individuals" (*hayehidim*)—which seems to indicate that the Mishnah was referring to a specific group of individuals.

This latter, "exclusive" definition is found in both the Babylonian and Palestinian Talmudic sugyot following this Mishnah. Both ask, "Who are the individuals?" and then proceed to answer the question. While this same question is also asked in *T. Ta'anit* 1:7, it is not answered in that source. Instead, the Tosefta discusses who is allowed to declare him- or herself an individual and exactly what types of supererogatory behaviors are encouraged or discouraged. This Tosefta passage will, consequently, be examined after the definitions of *the individuals*—found in four other sources—are first clarified. The four sources defining "who are the individuals" presented are: *B. Ta'anit* 10a–b, *P. Ta'anit* 1:4(64b), *Tosefta Yoma* 1:10, and *Leviticus Rabbah* 30:7.

## B. Ta'anit 10a–b

I.  Who are "the individuals"?

II.  R. Huna says: "the Rabbis (*rabanan*)" . . .

III.  The Rabbis taught:

IV.  "A person must never say: I am a student (*talmid*), and I am not worthy of being "an individual"; rather, all students of sages (*talmidei hakhamim*) are individuals."

V.  Who is an individual and who is a student (*talmid*)?

VI.  An individual is one who is worthy of being appointed a community leader.

VII.  A student (*talmid*) is one who is asked any question of

---

3. R. Eleazar Azkiri in the *Perush MiBa'al Sefer Haredim* defines *the individuals* here as "people who have fear of sin even though they are *not* scholars, and not ignoramuses" (*P. Berakhot* 2:9).

4. R. Natan b. Yehiel, *Sefer Arukh HaShalem,* ed. A. Kohut (Vienna: Menorah, 1926), vol. III, s.v. *yahid,* p. 121.

Halakhah connected with his studies and can answer it—even if it is on a subject dealt with in the Tractate *Kallah.*

According to R. Huna, the individuals are the Rabbis. According to the baraita (sections III–IV), all students of sages (*talmidei hakhamim*) may consider themselves individuals in this situation. The Talmudic sugya (sections V, VI, and VII) continues to refine the distinction between an individual and a student. We see from the baraita in section IV and from the Talmudic sugya in section VII that the term *a student* (*talmid*) here is used synonymously with the term *student of the sages* (*talmid hakham*–scholar) and will be translated hereafter as "student of the sages" or simply "scholar."

While R. Huna and the baraita are contextually merely defining the term *the individuals,* their definitions lead to certain necessary conclusions. These conclusions are quite germane to this study. According to their definition of *the individuals*—referring to a limited, very specifically defined group and not to "anyone who wishes to may fast"—there are two possible interpretations of the Mishnah.

The first is that, according to R. Huna, the Mishnah permitted fasting only to the rabbis (i.e., sages and teachers), perhaps excluding even "students of the sages" (general *talmidei hakhamim*). The BT sugya, though, broadens his definition by quoting the baraita (sections III and IV), declaring that all students of sages (*talmidei hakhamim*) are "individuals" and are, therefore, permitted to fast. The anonymous sugya (sections V, VI, and VII) further expands on the baraita, explaining that an individual is worthy of being appointed a leader of the community, whereas a student is defined as someone who has an excellent command of his studies, since he can answer questions on anything he has learned, including the Tractate *Kallah.*[5]

---

5. The medieval commentaries discuss these definitions at length (see, e.g., Tosafot here, s.v. *eizehu yahid*). They also clarify the reference to "Tractate Kallah." One opinion is that it was the short Tractate called Kallah, which was not very well known and therefore would indicate a particularly high level of scholarship (R. Yom Tov Alashvili, *Hiddushei HaRitva, Ta'anit* 10b [Jerusalem: Mossad HaRav Kook, 1980]). Another opinion is that it was the Tractate that was studied during the month of the Kallah, when the community would assemble to study. If it is the latter, then that tractate would be well known and the title "student" would be

The common person, then, according to all accounts, would not be allowed to fast.

The second interpretation is that the Mishnah was not limiting the permission to fast but rather the obligation to fast. According to R. Huna, the Mishnah obligated only the rabbis (the sages-teachers), while, according to the baraita, all students of sages (*talmidei hakhamim*) are included in the category of rabbis.[6] The Mishnah, then, would be delineating who was obligated to fast. The common person, according to this interpretation, would still retain the right to fast but would not have the obligation. When the new moon of the month of Kislev, however, arrived, and rain still did not fall, then that right (according to this second interpretation), or perhaps that prohibition (according to the first interpretation), became an obligation.

What is clear from this passage, according to both of these explanations, is that R. Huna and the *B. Ta'anit* Talmudic sugya are clearly defining *the individual* as a member of a specific group. They can, thus, be labeled as proponents of the exclusivist position— limiting the right or obligation to fast to an exclusive group.

*P. Ta'anit* 1:4 (64b)

I.   Who are the individuals?
II.  Those who are appointed community leaders.
III. Just because he is appointed a community leader, will his prayers necessarily be answered?

---

easier to attain. See H. Albeck, *Mavo LaTalmudim* [Tel Aviv: Dvir, 1969], pp. 601–604, for further discussion of this issue. The exact difference in proficiency between a student and an individual, however, is not crucial here, since what primarily concerns us is that an individual is not just any common person but instead a student of the sages, whether he be on a high or a low level.

6. The Ritva holds that only the actual sages were obligated to fast, while the students were permitted to fast but not obligated (*Hiddushei HaRitva*, ibid.). Likewise, R. Yeshaya of Trani (*Piskei HaRid*) writes that an individual (*yahid*—i.e., an actual sage) was obligated to fast, even against his will, while a student was permitted to fast and would not be perceived as arrogant if he did so (*Piskei haRid, Ta'anit* ad loc. [Jerusalem: Makhon HaTalmud HaYisraeli HaShalem, 1971], p.174).

IV. Rather, since he was appointed a community leader, he has proven himself trustworthy to pray and be answered.

The *P. Ta'anit* Talmudic sugya limits "the individuals" to the community leaders (*parnas al hatzibur*).[7] Whether a community leader also had to be a scholar is not clear.[8] The *P. Ta'anit* sugya's view, then, is also "exclusivist"; *the individuals* refers to a very specific group of community leaders. While the *P. Ta'anit* and *B. Ta'anit* may differ in their criteria for membership in this exclusive group, they both agree that only an exclusive group of people were either obligated or allowed to fast.

The *P. Ta'anit* sugya here, like R. Huna and the baraita in the parallel *B. Ta'anit* sugya discussed earlier, is simply defining a term in the Mishnah and does not discuss whether these individuals were the only ones permitted to fast or the only ones obligated to fast. When, however, these definitions of *the individuals* are applied to the Mishnah, then the necessary conclusion is that if, in fact, community leaders, rabbis, and scholars were the only people allowed to fast, then there would be an actual rabbinic prohibition of supererogatory behavior for certain population groups. For if only the individuals were permitted to fast, then everyone else was forbidden to do so.[9] The population groups forbidden to fast would be men who were not scholars (unless, perhaps they were community leaders according to the *P. Ta'anit*) and (virtually) all women.

Women would not be allowed to fast since women in Talmudic times were not students (i.e., scholars, except for the few well-known exceptions such as Beruriah). Women, then, by virtue of their not being scholars, would be forbidden to take on a supererogatory

---

7. These community leaders are understood as being specially appointed by the community to represent them before their enemies in times of danger; R. Eliezer b. Joel Halevi, *Sefer Ra'avyah*, ed. A. Optowitzer (New York: Mekitzei Nirdamim, 1983), vol. III, no. 850, pp. 599–600. See also Saul Lieberman, *Tosefta Kifeshuta, Ta'anit* (New York: Jewish Theological Seminary, 1972), p. 1070, regarding the Ra'avyah's reading of the Tosefta.

8. Whether *parnasim* were also scholars is discussed by S. Fraade, *From Tradition to Commentary* (Albany: State University of New York Press, 1991), pp. 98–99, and note 115 on p. 245.

9. This is how many medieval commentators understand these sources. These include Maimonides, *Yad, Ta'anit* 3:1, *Kitzur Piskei HaRosh* Ta'anit, par. 5, the *Ritva*, the *Rid*, and the *Meiri* on *B. Ta'anit* 10a.

fast of this nature. Possible exceptions to this, however, would be the wives of the rabbinic class, according to the principle that "the wife of a scholar is like a scholar (*eshet haver harei hee kehaver*).[10] Men and women[11] who were very pious but who were not scholars (or wives of scholars) would not have been allowed to fast, according to this interpretation. If, though the sources were mandating fasting for the scholarly population, rather than simply permitting it, then the option of imposing supererogatory fasts would be left open to the rest of the population. The nonscholarly but especially pious members of the community would still be allowed to fast and so express their piety.

Perhaps the idea of only scholars fasting and not the common people was to avoid placing an undue burden on the community and/or actually to create a separation between the scholars and the common people. This separation would accomplish at least two valuable goals. It would give the common people a sense of respect for the scholars of the community, who were fasting to help them, and it would give the scholars themselves an increased sense of responsibility for the rest of the nation, since they were the ones expected to fast the extra fasts. ("The individuals" were expected to fast three times a week throughout the winter, until the end of Nissan, if no rain fell;[12] they were, thus, assigned an extremely difficult task.)

## *The individuals* in Two Other Contexts

Before continuing with the discussion of the sources in *Ta'anit*, a slight digression is in order. The term *the individuals* is used in two other unrelated sources; one of them is a Tosefta passage, and the other is in *Leviticus Rabbah*. The usage of this term in these other

---

10. *B. Shebuot* 30b, *B. Abodah Zarah* 39a, cf. the "important woman" (*isha hashuvah*)—*B. Shabbat* 59b, *B. Pesahim* 108a. Rabbinic attitudes toward women who fasted when they were not obligated to do so will be discussed in Chapter 3.

11. The commentary attributed to Rashi in *Ta'anit* 6a, s.v. *yehidim,* in fact says that the individuals were very pious people (*hasidim*). Rashi on *Ta'anit* was not written by Rashi himself—see Jonah Fraenkel, *Darko shel Rashi bePerusho leTalmud Bavli* (Jerusalem: Magnes, 1975), p. 305, note 9. Rashi on *Ta'anit* will therefore be cited as Pseudo-Rashi in future references.

12. *M. Ta'anit* 1:7.

contexts will be examined to further enhance our understanding of its meaning.

## Tosefta Yoma 1:10

The term *the individuals* (*hayehidim*) is found in *Tosefta Yoma* 1:10 and *Tosefta Sukkah* 4:16. The Mishnah (in *Yoma* 2:1) to which this passage refers describes the count that would take place among the priests in the Temple to determine who would win the privilege of sweeping the ashes from the altar (*terumat hadeshen*):

I.    . . . the officer would say to them [to all the priests]:

II.   "Raise the finger!" And how many did they put forth?

III.  One or two, but one did not put forth the thumb in the Temple . . .

Each priest would raise one or two fingers. The officer would pick a number and then count the raised fingers until he reached that number. The priest with whom the number was reached won the privilege of sweeping the altar.

The Tosefta passage explains the count a bit more clearly:

I.    How is the count done? . . .

II.   They would stand in a circle, and the officer would take the headdress off one of them, and they would know that the count would begin from him.

III.  They would not put forth two fingers each, but rather one finger each.

IV.  The individuals (*hayehidim*) among them would put forth two fingers each,

V.   but the extra one would not be counted.

The Tosefta does not explain who these "individuals" were or why they were allowed to put forth two fingers each. The Talmudic sugya in *B. Yoma* 23a quotes a variant of this passage as part of its discussion of the Mishnah, and contains more information:

I.    "And how many did they put forth? One or two."

II.   If they may put forth two, why is it necessary to mention that they may put forth one?

III. R. Hisda said: "This is no difficulty. The one speaks of healthy persons, the other of sick ones.
IV. Thus has it been taught:
V. "One finger is put forth, but not two."
VI. [To whom does this rule apply?
VII. To a healthy person, but an ill one may put forth even two.][13]
VIII. But *the individuals* put forward two and only one of them is counted."

Although many of the words in this Tosefta parallel are different from the Tosefta passage quoted earlier, the basic content is the same. Information is added regarding the difference between a healthy and an ill person. The identity of these individuals is not explained in the Talmudic sugya. The Geonim, though, define the term by using R. Huna's definition in *B. Ta'anit* 10b and say that the individuals were priests who were also rabbis.[14] They also explain that "the individuals—i.e. Rabbis" were referred to as ill people (who were allowed to raise two fingers due to their weakness) because "they always fasted and made themselves ill because of the community (*al hatzibur*)."[15]

A second definition of *the individuals* is that they were the ill people referred to in the immediately preceding phrase in *B. Yoma* 23a (section VII) and have no connection to scholars. These ill

---

13. Lines VI and VII are not found in the Munich manuscript or other manuscripts and are not in the Tosefta (R. N. Rabinowitz, *Dikdukei Soferim,* ad loc. note 5).

14. *Otzar HaGeonim Yoma, "HaTeshuvot,"* p. 10; and *Teshuvot HaGeonim mitokh haGenizah,* ed. Simcha Assaf (Jerusalem: Darom, 1929), p. 98.

15. Ibid., p. 10; R. Hananel, ad loc.; and R. Natan b. Yehiel, the *Arukh* entry *yahid,* and the *Bah B. Yom.* 23a, note a. A passage in *B. Nedarim* 49a is cited as evidence that the rabbis were called ill people (*holim*). Maimonides (*Yad,* Laws of Temidin 4:3) leaves out the whole discussion regarding the healthy versus the ill and the individuals, though he does mention "the weak" and "the strong" in his Commentary to the Mishnah on *Yoma* 2:1. R. Abraham diBoton (the *Lehem Mishneh*) suggests that he must have had a different reading of the text, but we have no specific manuscripts that would solve the difficulties that he raises.

individuals do not sit together with other people but instead lie or sit by themselves.[16]

A third explanation, similar to the second in the idea that the individuals were people who stayed by themselves, is that instead of "the individuals" (*hayehidim*), the text should be emended to "the arrogant ones" (*hayehirim*)—"arrogant people who are not satisfied doing what others are doing and feel that it is beneath their dignity."[17] According to this emendation, "the arrogant ones" would raise two fingers to distinguish themselves from other priests.

*The individuals* in this *Yoma* source, thus clearly refers to an exclusive, specific group of some sort. (According to the Geonic interpretation, they were priests who were also rabbis. According to Pseudo-Rashi, they were ill people and, according to the third explanation, they were "the arrogant ones.") This usage of the term would support the notion that in our Mishnah, *the individuals* also refers to an exclusive group, even if it is not the same as the group in the *Yoma* source.

*Leviticus Rabbah* 30:7

This source[18] (explaining Leviticus 23:40), uses the term *the individuals* and also discusses fasting, just like *M. Ta'anit* 1:4. It divides the Jewish nation into three different groups and shows how each group plays a role in obtaining God's forgiveness on the Day of Atonement.

---

16. Pseudo-Rashi, ad loc. s.v. *viyehidim*. Pseudo-Rashi's s.v. here and in the Venice edition of the Talmud (1522–1523) is "and individuals (*viyehidim*)" as opposed to "and the individuals" (*vehayehidim*) found in our text. This is insignificant, however, since there are Talmudic manuscripts that also have "*veyehidim*" here in the text instead of *vehayehidim* (*Dikdukei Soferim, Ta'anit* 10a note 5).

17. *Otzar HaGeonim*, "HaPeirushim," p. 51, and the *Arukh*, entry *yahid*, suggest this emendation "and there are those who learn. . . ."

18. *Leviticus Rabbah*, ed. M. Margaliot (New York: Jewish Theological Seminary, 1993), vol. II. There are many parallels to this passage, such as *Ecclesiastes Rabbah* 9:7, *Yalkut Shimoni* Leviticus 641, and *Pesikta deRAv Kahana*, ed. S. Buber, 28:60, or ed. D. Mandelbaum (New York: Jewish Theological Seminary, 1987), vol. II, 27:7, p. 412. For a discussion of the many textual variants, see Buber's *Pesikta*, p. 183, note 91.

I.    . . . On the eve of the New Year, the greatest leaders of the generation [*gedolei hador*] fast, and God forgives a third of [the nation's] sins.

II.   From New Year's until the Day of Atonement, *the individuals[19]* fast, and God forgives a third of [the nation's] sins.

III.  And on the Day of Atonement everyone fasts—men, women and children, and God says to Israel: "What has passed, is already passed; from now on, the [new] reckoning begins."

In this source, the term *the individuals* indicates some group of people whose status lies somewhere in between the greatest leaders of the generation, and the general population. It is not clear, though, whether "the individuals" consisted of a specific, clearly defined group (such as scholars) or included any person who wished to fast. While *the individuals* in the *Yoma* source discussed earlier clearly refers to an exclusive group of some sort and not just to any individual, this passage can support both the exclusive as well as the inclusive definitions of the term which were suggested as explanations of *M. Ta'anit* 1:4.[20]

## WHO MAY DECLARE HIMSELF "AN INDIVIDUAL"?

Having presented the definitions of the term "the individuals," *T. Ta'anit* 1:7 can now be addressed. As noted above, this passage, which also asks, "Who are the individuals?" never actually answers this question directly. Nonetheless, it does deal with the pivotal question of this study: who may declare him- or herself an individual and exactly what types of supererogatory behaviors are encouraged or discouraged. There are parallels to this Tosefta passage in both the Babylonian and Palestinian Talmuds.

---

19. Some of the texts have "the pious ones" *(hakesheirim)* instead of "the individuals" (Margaliot, *Leviticus Rabbah,* ibid., Mandelbaum, *Pesikta* ibid., and Buber's note, ibid.).

20. For further discussion of this passage and of the historical evolution of the customs that it describes, see Jacob Gartner, "Fasting and Penitential Prayers before Rosh HaShanah," *HaDarom* 38 (1974), pp. 69–77.

*T. Ta'anit* 1:7

This Tosefta passage has several variant readings. The text of the Tosefta quoted below is based on the London and Erfurt[21] manuscripts of the Tosefta as well as the *B. Ta'anit* 10b parallel to this Tosefta passage:

I.    Who is an individual?

II.   R. Simeon b. Eleazar said, "Not every person who wishes to declare himself an individual may do so (*oseh*),[22]

III.  A scholar may do so (*oseh*),

IV.   unless the court has appointed him as a community leader."

V.    R. Simeon b. Gamaliel said, "For a matter of anguish, he who wishes to declare himself an individual may do so,

VI.   And a scholar does so, and is deserving of a blessing.

VII.  For a matter of praise, [however], not every person who wishes to-declare himself an individual may do so,

VIII. [but] a scholar may do so,

IX.   unless the court has appointed him as a community leader."

---

21. The first printing of the Tosefta (Lieberman's *daled* text) makes no sense; Lieberman (ibid.) dismisses it as corrupt.

22. Lieberman's Tosefta, based on the Vienna manuscript, does not have the words *may do so* (*oseh*) in section II. This text would be read as "Not every person who wishes to declare himself an individual—i.e., a scholar, may do so." *An individual, a scholar* would be synonyms, and the text would then be providing an internal definition of the term *an individual*. A second way of reading this text is to add the word *or* between the words *an individual* and *a scholar*: "Not every person who wishes to declare himself an individual *or* a scholar may do so," meaning that not just anybody is permitted to behave as an individual (and to fast), and not just anybody is permitted to adopt the practices of a scholar, such as wearing scholar's clothing. (R. David Pardo, *Hasdei David* [Livorno, 1776] ad loc., and Lieberman, *Toseftah Kifeshutah Ta'anit* p. 1070, lines 29–31. This explanation is taken from Pseudo-Rashi on the *B. Ta'anit* 10b parallel to this Toseftah passage, which will be discussed later.) In this study, however, the text of the London and Efurt manuscripts was quoted since this text is consistent with the rest of the passage that presents R. Simon b. Gamaliel's point of view. Additionally, the term *an individual-scholar* (*yahid-talmid hakham*) is redundant, and the word *or* is not found in any Tosefta text or parallel.

## R. SIMEON B. ELEAZAR

As just quoted, this Tosefta passage delineates the positions of R. Simeon b. Eleazar and R. Simeon b. Gamaliel. R. Simeon b. Eleazar's position will be explained first. The phrase "a scholar may do so" (section III) should be read as a parenthetical statement, while sections II and IV constitute one complete sentence:

I.   Who is an individual?

II.  R. Simeon b. Eleazar said, "Not every person who wishes to declare himself an individual may do so,

III. ([though] a scholar may do so),

IV.  unless the court has appointed him as a community leader.

A simplified paraphrasing of R. Simeon b. Eleazar would read as follows: Any person appointed by the court as a community leader—be he scholar or commoner—may declare himself an individual. If not appointed as a community leader, only a scholar (and not a commoner) may declare himself an individual. This concurs with the *P. Ta'anit's* definition of *the individuals* as the community leaders and also assumes that one does not have to be a scholar to be appointed as a community leader.[23] R. Simeon b. Eleazar thus severely limits supererogatory behavior, for if a common person (not appointed as a communal leader) wishes to fast for rain, for example, then he is not permitted to do so.

This position may have been based on the assumption that only scholars and/or community leaders—and not mere commoners— have the capacity to determine what type of behavior was religiously valuable and what was not. Alternately, if the masses were allowed to freely engage in supererogatory behavior, R. Simeon b. Eleazar might have argued that confusion could have resulted

---

23. If section III (a scholar may do so) is not read parenthetically, then R. Simeon b. Eleazar's position would be that only scholars who have *not* been appointed as community leaders (*parnas al hatzibur*) are permitted to declare themselves individuals. This reading is problematic, since it results in the unlikely scenario in which the students in an academy would be permitted (or encouraged) to fast, whereas the head of the academy or perhaps the community leader would be forbidden to do so. Fasting would be permitted for the disciples but forbidden for their spiritual leader.

between what is really required by the law versus what was casually chosen. The negative consequences would then be laxity in the observance of the objective requirements of the law. In a similar vein, since every stringency demands money, time, or physical or psychic energy, perhaps he was concerned that people would expend those important resources in observing stringencies. They, in turn, would not have enough money, time, or energy left to perform true Halakhic obligations.[24]

## R. SIMEON B. GAMALIEL

Rabban Simeon b. Gamaliel (sections V–X cited earlier) disagrees with R. Simeon b. Eleazar, taking a very different approach to the issue of supererogatory behavior. He uses a more inclusive definition of *yahid* and states that any individual who wishes to fast may do so. The basis of his position revolves around his division of supererogatory behavior into two categories: matters of anguish (*davar shel tza'ar*) and matters of praise (*davar shel shevah*). Common people are allowed to impose religious stringencies on themselves, as long as they are matters of anguish. Supererogatory matters of praise, however, are permissible only to an elite group of people (examples will be given later). Matters of anguish are ascetic practices, of which fasting is the primary example since that is the direct focus of the Mishnah. Other ascetic practices that also fit into this category will be discussed in Chapter 2.

Rabban Simeon b. Gamaliel's position thus contradicts the baraita brought by the *B. Ta'anit* sugya and R. Huna's position, which limited *the individuals* to the Rabbis and the students of the sages. The *P. Ta'anit* sugya that defined *the individuals* as community leaders also conflicts with Rabban Simeon b. Gamaliel, who stated that in matters of anguish, anyone who wishes to declare himself an individual may do so.

When we generalize from this case to other possible scenarios, we can assume that according to Rabban Simeon b. Gamaliel, the common person is permitted supererogatory matters of anguish, and, for a scholar, this behavior is even considered especially

---

24. Leo Levi, in the name of R. Y. Z. Gustman, *Sha'arei Talmud Torah* (Jerusalem: Feldheim, 1981), p. 123.

praiseworthy. In addition to the fasting discussed in *M. Ta'anit* 1:4, another example of the type of matter of anguish to which Rabban Simeon b. Gamaliel was referring might be the case of working on the Ninth of Ab, found in *M. Pesahim* 4:5:

I.    Where it is the custom to do work on the ninth of Ab, one may do it; where it is the custom not to do work, one may not do it.

II.   And in all places scholars cease [from work on that day].

III.  Rabban Simeon b. Gamaliel said:

IV.   "All men should declare themselves scholars."

In this case, Rabban Simeon b. Gamaliel encourages all men to behave as scholars. His reason here could be that he viewed not working on the ninth of Ab as a matter of anguish. Refraining from working would create hardship for the average person, since a day's salary would be lost.[25] Yet Rabban Simeon b. Gamaliel encouraged the average person to refrain from work, since he held that in matters involving anguish, the common person was permitted (in this case, encouraged) to engage in supererogatory behavior.

As noted, although Rabban Simeon b. Gamaliel permitted supererogatory matters of anguish, he limited self-imposed religious stringencies if they involved praise. Matters of praise involve adding to or extending one's religious observances in a manner that would elicit the praise of other people. While such obligations might make life more difficult, they are not ascetic practices involving self-denial.

One example of a matter of praise is (as was discussed earlier) dressing and behaving as a scholar does, practices that would distinguish the individual by increasing the respect or honor that he is accorded. These practices include wearing the shirt of a scholar (which was very modest),[26] keeping one's bed the way a scholar does, or making oneself look special by donning the robe of a scholar.[27] Another example of matters of praise involves reciting the Shema even when not obligated to do so (*P. Berakhot* 2:9 [5d]). This type of supererogatory prayer allows the individual to stand out

---

25. *Perush miBa'al Sefer Haredim* ad loc.

26. Cf. Mark 12:38, who describes the scribes as those who like to wear long robes.

27. *B. Baba Batra* 57b.

from those around him; his reputation as being particularly pious is then affirmed and strengthened.

These matters of praise were permitted only to scholars and community leaders, who already stood out among the general population—this type of behavior was expected of them. The permission to stand out as being particularly pious was not granted to common people, presumably because it would be perceived as presumptuous and arrogant.[28] This idea will be developed further in Chapter 7, which deals with the issue of arrogance as limiting the extent to which people may be involved in supererogatory behavior.

Private self-imposed stringencies, such as private supererogatory prayer,[29] though, would still be permissible to all individuals, since it would not constitute a matter of praise. This is precisely because it occurs in private; no one would see the behavior and then praise the individual. Rabban Simeon b. Gamaliel's differentiation between common people and scholars thus applies only to public self-imposed stringency.

A modern-day example of a matter of praise could be that when a rabbi of a congregation prays for a longer period of time than the rest of the congregation or prays in a particularly demonstrative manner, he is respected even more for the quality of his prayers. When, however, a congregant who is not otherwise known as being particularly pious prays for a particularly long time or in an especially demonstrative manner, the same behavior might be viewed with suspicion.

According to *P. Berakhot* 2:9 (5d), the recital of the Shema by a bridegroom on his wedding night is considered a matter of praise by Rabban Simeon b. Gamaliel. This issue is discussed in *M.*

---

28. R. Joseph David Epstein, *Mitzvat HaShalom* (New York: Torat Ha'Adam, 1969), p. 104.

29. The topic of individualized voluntary prayer (*tefilat nedavah*), though conceptually related to this study, will not be included here, since it is an issue developed by the medieval commentators. The limitations placed by these commentators on voluntary prayer are based on *B. Berakhot* 21a, where R. Eleazar states that if one is not sure if one prayed, then one must not pray again. His position is understood as a concern lest one transgress the prohibition of "Do not add" (*bal tosif*) (Deuteronomy 13:1), which is discussed in Chapter 2 (see Alfasi, ad loc., Maimonides, *Yad*, "Laws of Tefilah," 10:6, *Tur Orah Hayim* 107).

*Berakhot* 2:5–6. The first Mishnah states that a bridegroom is exempt from reciting the Shema, but that R. Gamaliel (Rabban Simeon b. Gamaliel's father) nevertheless recited it on his wedding night, explaining that he did not want to remove himself from "the kingship of heaven even for a moment":

I. A bridegroom is exempt from the recital of the Shema from the first night until the end of the Sabbath, if he has not consummated the marriage.

II. It happened with R. Gamaliel that when he married he recited the Shema on the first night.

III. So his disciples said to him:

IV. "Our Master, you have taught us that a bridegroom is exempt from the recital of the Shema."

V. He replied to them:

VI. "I will not listen to you to remove from myself the kingship of heaven even for a moment." ([*M. Berakhot* 2:5])

The second Mishnah rules that even though a bridegroom is exempt from reciting the Shema, he may still do so. Rabban Simeon b. Gamaliel dissents and rules that only certain very special people who are truly deserving of being called scholars are permitted to waive their exemption (as did his father, R. Gamaliel):

I. If a bridegroom desires to recite the Shema on the first night, he may do so.

II. Rabban Simeon b. Gamaliel says: "Not everyone who desires to take the name [of a scholar][30] may do so."[31] [*M. Berakhot* 2:6]

In the case of the Shema, he stated that not just anyone may take the name of a scholar and recite the Shema. This is because he views reciting the Shema as a bridegroom as a matter of praise[32] and holds

---

30. Rashi, s.v. *lo kol harotzeh* (*B. Berakhot* 17b).

31. This Mishnah, as well as Mishnah *Pesahim* 4:5 discussed earlier, will be analyzed more completely in Chapter 7.

32. The *P. Ta'anit* Talmudic sugya on this Mishnah, which will be discussed later, quotes R. Simon b. Gamaliel's opinion stating that not just anyone may impose matters of praise on themselves. This is a parallel to R.

that supererogatory matters of praise are prohibited for common people. Only someone who is already well respected by the masses as a scholar and a pious person may say the Shema; otherwise, he is considered arrogant, since he is acting as if he can concentrate when he really is not able to do so.[33] In other words, a common person who prays (in public) when he is exempt from doing so is assumed to be insincere; his motivation is to enhance his reputation, not to feel closer to God.

This Mishnah, as well as the Mishnah regarding the ninth of Ab, provide actual applications of Rabban Simeon b. Gamaliel's policy delineated in *T. Ta'anit* 1:7. As the case of the bridegroom reciting the Shema demonstrated, not just anyone can "declare himself an individual." In this case, the wording used is "take the name [of a scholar]" (and impose "matters of praise" on himself); only a true scholar may do so. Rabban Simeon b. Gamaliel, thus, seems to have defined the individuals as "the scholars" or "the rabbis," which is the same definition quoted later in the *B. Ta'anit* sugya in the name of R. Huna. Rabban Simeon b. Gamaliel's position was that in matters of praise, not just any person who wished to was allowed to consider himself an individual (i.e., a scholar).[34] In other words, supererogatory behavior, in matters of praise, is limited by Rabban Simeon b. Gamaliel.

## SUMMARY OF *T. TA'ANIT* 1:7

Tosefta *Ta'anit* 1:7 thus delineates the following policies regarding supererogatory behavior:

I.   R. Simon b. Eleazar:

Only actual scholars and community leaders may declare themselves individuals. In other words, supererogatory behavior, even if it involves matters of anguish, is forbidden to everyone

---

Simeon b. Gamaliel in the Mishnah, where he states that not just anyone may recite the Shema as a bridegroom.

33. Rashi, ad loc.

34. The Geonim who define *the individuals* in *B. Yoma* 23a as "the rabbis" (according to R. Huna in *B. Ta'anit* 10b) also state that the raising of two fingers instead of one by "the individual" (rabbinic) priests was a matter of praise (of one's reputation, presumably) and hence limited to these rabbinic priests (*Otzar HaGeonim*, *Yoma*, "HaTeshuvot," p. 10).

except scholars or community leaders. R. Simeon b. Eleazar thus represents the "exclusive" school of thought regarding supererogatory behavior.[35]

II.    Rabban Simeon b. Gamaliel:

A.    Supererogatory matters of anguish are permissible for any individual and considered praiseworthy behavior for scholars. He thus represents the "inclusive" school of thought with regard to supererogatory matters of anguish; any individual who wanted to fast for rain, for example, was permitted to do so. He does not limit this option only to scholars and community leaders.

B.    Supererogatory matters of praise, which involve public, nonascetic acts of stringency, however, are permissible only to scholars and community leaders. In this respect, his position is the same as R. Simeon b. Eleazar's; with regard to matters of praise, Rabban Simeon b. Gamaliel is a member of the "exclusive" school of thought.

## B. *Ta'anit* 10b

B. *Ta'anit* 10b records a parallel to the Tosefta passage just explored. This parallel text, itself, contains two versions of the same disagreement: R. Meir versus R. Yosi, and R. Simeon b. Eleazar versus R. Simeon b. Gamaliel.

I.    The Rabbis taught:

II.    "Not every person who wishes to declare himself an individual may do so,

---

35. It is possible, though, that he referred either only to matters of anguish or only to matters of praise. If he referred only to matters of praise, then he would be in complete agreement with R. Simeon b. Gamaliel. (Even though R. Simeon b. Eleazar's statement precedes R. Simeon b. Gamaliel's in the text, R. Simeon b. Gamaliel lived at least fifty years before R. Simeon b. Eleazar.) The Tosefta may have quoted only his remarks regarding matters of praise, while quoting R. Simeon b. Gamaliel to give the rest of the information. This last possibility is difficult, since it goes against the general context of the Tosefta, which is discussing fasting. Nonetheless, this is how the baraita in *B. Ta'anit* 10b that contains a parallel to this Tosefta explains his position.

III. [but] a student (*talmid*)[36] may do so,"[37] said R. Meir.
IV. R. Yosi said: "He does so, and is deserving of a blessing, since it brings him no praise, but, instead, brings him anguish."
V. We have learned in a different version:
VI. Not every person[38] who wishes to declare himself an individual may do so,
VII. [but] a student may do so," said R. Simeon b. Eleazar.
VIII. Rabban Simeon b. Gamaliel said:
IX. "To what do these remarks pertain?[39]
X. To matters of praise, but in matters of anguish, one does so—and receives a blessing on this account, since it brings him no praise but instead brings him anguish."

---

36. The word *student* (*talmid*) in section III is used instead of *scholar* (*talmid hakham*), which is found in the Tosefta parallel. The Munich manuscript here, and several medieval commentators, have *the students* (*vehatalmidim*) instead of *a student*. (Among these are the Rif, Rashi, and the Rosh. Malter here substitutes the word *vehatalmidim* for *talmid* [Henry Malter, *The Treatise Ta'anit* [New York: American Academy for Jewish Research, 1930], ad loc.]). These differences, however, are insignificant, since the words are being used synonymously. See R. N. Rabinowitz, *Dikdukei Soferim*, ad loc., note 40. Another difference between the Tosefta and this *B. Ta'anit* parallel is that the community leader (*parnas al hatzibbur*) found in the Tosefta text is not even mentioned in this source.

37. The Rosh and certain versions of the Rif have "The students *do not* declare themselves individuals." There are, however, other manuscripts of the Rif that are the same as the printed Talmud. See Malter, *Ta'anit*, ad loc. note 20; and S. Lieberman, *Hilkhot HaYerushalmid LeHaRambam* (New York: Jewish Theological Seminary, 1948), *Berakhot* 2:9, note 45.

38. The Rif here has "A common person (*am ha'aretz*) may not declare himself an individual," whereas a manuscript version has "not every person" (*Hilkhot Rav Alfas*, ed. R. Nissan Zaks (Jerusalem: Mossad HaRav Kook, 1969). The Bah emends the Rif to read "not every person." The reading of "a common person," like the *P. Ta'anit*'s reading of "anyone" (*kol*), strengthens R. Simeon b. Gamaliel's point—that anyone, even a common *am ha'aretz*, can take matters of anguish on himself. The Bah may simply be inserting the Talmudic text into the Rif; there are, though, manuscripts to support his emendation.

39. The phrase "To what do these matters pertain (*bame devarim amurim*) is not found in the Munich manuscript, and Malter leaves it out of his *Ta'anit* text. The Rif (ed. Zaks) also does not have this line.

Assuming that the attributions are correct, then the first version of this source (sections I–IV) would indicate that the debate between R. Simeon b. Eleazar and Rabban Simeon b. Gamaliel began during the times of R. Meir and R. Yosi. R. Meir's position (sections II–III) parallels R. Simeon b. Eleazar in the Tosefta (version II); in fact, R. Simeon b. Eleazar, who lived during the time of R. Judah the Prince, during the last generation of tannaim (second half of the second century), often quotes R. Meir.[40] R. Yosi's statement (section IV) is parallel to Rabban Simeon b. Gamaliel's position. Rabban Simeon b. Gamaliel is Rabban Simeon b. Gamaliel II, who lived during the first half of the second century. He lived at the same time as R. Yosi and R. Meir. He was probably younger than they were and both argues with them and teaches in their names.[41] In *B. Pesahim* 100a, Rabban Simeon b. Gamaliel defers to R. Yosi's authority, calling him *"berabi,"* meaning "the most revered scholar of the generation."[42] Rabban Simeon b. Gamaliel and later R. Simeon b. Eleazar were, thus, continuing a controversy that had preceded them.

When R. Meir's view (sections II–III) is seen as an independent entity, it is a general statement that would restrict both matters of anguish and matters of praise. If, however, we understand his statement in conjunction with R. Yosi's ensuing statement (section V), then R. Meir, like R. Yosi who states explicitly that "it is anguish for him," would also be referring only to matters of anguish. R. Meir's position, then, would restrict the general population from taking matters of anguish on themselves, while permitting students to do so.

R. Yosi's statement "He can do so, and is deserving of a blessing" is the opposite of R. Meir's position with regard to matters of anguish. He holds that any person can declare himself an individual in matters of anguish, since "it is of no praise to him, it brings only anguish to him."[43]

---

40. A. Hyman, *Toledot HaTannaim VeHaAmoraim* (Jerusalem: Kiryah Ne'emanah, 1964), vol. III, p. 1157.

41. A. Hyman, ibid., vol. III, p. 1166.

42. Rashbam ad loc. s.v. *berabi.*

43. Pseudo-Rashi, s.v. *R. Yose omer;* R. Nissim on the Rif, s.v. *vehatalmidim;* and R. Yeshaya Aharon (*Piskei Ri'Az,* in *Piskei haRid, Piskei Ri'Az* [Jerusalem: Makhon HaTalmud HaYisraeli HaShalem, 1971], *Ta'anit* 1:11. One can claim that R. Yose actually agreed with R. Meir regarding a

In the second version of this source (sections V–X), we first have R. Simeon b. Eleazar's position (sections VI–VII), which parallels R. Meir's statement. Rabban Simeon b. Gamaliel's position (sections IX–X) is the same as R. Yosi's statement.[44] Rabban Simeon b. Gamaliel's (and R. Yosi's) position is the same as that attributed to him in the Tosefta: supererogatory matters of praise are prohibited to common people but permitted to scholars, and supererogatory matters of anguish are permitted to common people and regarded as praiseworthy for scholars.

The addition of the clause "To what do these words apply" (*bameh devarim amurim,* section VII) before Rabban Simeon b. Gamaliel's position, however, ties R. Simeon b. Eleazar's statement to Rabban Simeon b. Gamaliel's statement, by explaining that even R. Simeon b. Eleazar excluded the commoner only from matters of praise but agreed that a common person could impose "supererogatory anguish" on himself. With the addition of that clause, then, there is no difference of opinion between the two tannaim.[45] In the first version of this baraita, however, conflict most definitely does exist between the views of R. Yosi and R. Meir.[46]

---

common person and differed with him only with regard to students — whereas R. Meir permitted only students to fast, R. Yose held that a student is even deserving of praise if he does so. *He,* then, would refer only to students. This is unlikely, however, since the phrase "since it is of no praise to him, it brings only anguish to him" (section IV) would apply equally to the commoner as well as the scholar. According, however, to the Rosh's text, which states that R. Meir's position is that "the students may *not* make themselves individuals," this interpretation of R. Yose's view would be correct. R. Netanel Weil states this explicitly (*Korban Netanel,* note 8).

44. R. Hananel (ad loc.) states explicitly that R. Simon b. Gamaliel and R. Yosi are making the same statement.

45. As was already mentioned, this is how Rashi explains the second version of the passage (s.v. *R. Yosi omer*). He explains that R. Simon b. Eleazar's statement should be read as follows: "Not just everyone who wishes to declare himself an individual *[or]* a student may do so." Declaring oneself a student involves dressing and behaving like a student and is considered a matter of praise. The sugya then continues by stating that R. Simeon b. Eleazar's remarks were, in fact, limited to matters of praise.

46. R. Joseph Karo in the *Beit Yosef (Tur Orah Hayim* 575) and the *Lehem Mishneh* (Laws of Ta'anit 3:1) discuss this conflict between R. Meir and R. Yosi in their comments on Maimonides, ruling that only scholars fast

This clause "to what do these words apply?" (*bameh devarim amurim*), though, in all likelihood was not part of Rabban Simeon b. Gamaliel's original statement and must have been inserted by later generations to clarify the ambiguity left by the original sources. Neither the Tosefta passage nor the *P. Ta'anit* passage contains this phrase, and it does not appear in the Munich manuscript. Furthermore, since R. Simeon b. Eleazar lived after Rabban Simeon b. Gamaliel, their disagreement could not have taken place face to face, and the clause "to what do these words refer?" could not have referred to the words of R. Simeon b. Eleazar, whose position was not yet formulated.

Thus, the possibility remains that R. Simeon b. Eleazar, following in R. Meir's footsteps, really did disagree with Rabban Simeon b. Gamaliel regarding matters of anguish. The tradition of Rabban Simeon b. Gamaliel was recorded in the Tosefta and in *B. Ta'anit* after R. Simeon b. Eleazar's position, presumably to show the contrast between them. In our case, then, we see that this disagreement was first recorded in the name of R. Meir and R. Yosi. Rabban

---

(declare themselves individuals) in the case of impending drought (*Yad Laws of Ta'anit* 3:1). Maimonides thus ruled according to R. Meir and R. Simeon b. Eleazar and against R. Yosi and R. Simeon b. Gamaliel. The problem raised by R. Joseph Karo is that in a conflict between R. Yosi and R. Meir, the law is supposed to follow R. Yosi; Maimonides then should have legislated according to R. Yosi that even common people were allowed to fast. Leiberman discusses Maimonides's ruling in his *Hilkhot HaYerushalmi, Berakhot* 2:9, note 30.

This same issue surfaces with regard to the Rosh's ruling, according to the *Kitzur Piskei HaRosh Ta'anit*, par. 5, which states that the Rosh ruled that only rabbis and students should fast, "and not the rest of the nation." This ruling, though, is supported by his Talmudic text (which differs from the printed Talmud), for the Rosh records R. Meir's statement as "Not anyone who wishes to declare himself an individual may do so, and the students *may not* do so." R. Yosi's statement "They do so, and receive a blessing on this account" refers, then, only to the students. R. Yosi and R. Meir's conflict, according to the Rosh's textual reading, dealt only with scholars, and the law was, in fact, determined according to R. Yosi who permitted them to fast. Leiberman suggests that Maimonides too had this textual reading and, therefore, ruled (like the Rosh) that only students could fast (*Hilkhot HaYerushalmi*, ibid.). See also R. N. Rabinowitz, *Dikdukei Soferim*, ad loc., note 40, for further discussion of the various textual readings.

Simeon b. Gamaliel then stated his position (which agreed with that of R. Yosi), and years later, R. Simeon b. Eleazar stated his position, which concurred with R. Meir's. The compiler of the baraita, faced with ambiguity, connected the two positions together with the phrase "to what do these words refer?" (*bameh devarim amurim*), perhaps to minimize the conflict between them.[47]

Summary

The following policies regarding supererogatory behavior are, thus, found in *B. Ta'anit* 10b:

Version I:

R. Meir: Supererogation in general (both praise and anguish) is permitted only to students.

R. Yosi: Supererogatory anguish is considered praiseworthy for every individual.

Version II:

1. The texts without "to what do these words apply" (*bameh devarim amurim*) are exactly parallel to Tosefta *Ta'anit* 1:7—R. Simeon b. Eleazar and Rabban Simeon b. Gamaliel disagree regarding matters of anguish.

2. According to the texts with "to what do these matters apply" (*bameh devarim amurim*), both R. Simeon b. Eleazar and Rabban Simeon b. Gamaliel agree that supererogatory matters of praise are forbidden to common people and permitted only to students, but supererogatory matters of anguish are permitted to everyone.

---

47. As Abraham Goldberg writes, "The phenomenon of minimization of conflicts (*tzimtzum hamahloket*) was not started by the amoraim, but is a general phenomenon which is widespread in all of Talmudic literature. In all of the generations of the tannaim and amoraim we find the tendency amongst later generations to minimize . . . the controversies of the preceding generations." Goldberg discusses various phrases and mechanisms used by the Amoraim to narrow or limit conflicts. While he does not mention "to what do these words refer" in his article, the use of this phrase in our baraita certainly fits into the general phenomenon which he documents. Abraham Goldberg, "Derakhim shel tzimtzum mahloket etzel amoraei Bavel," *Mehkerei Talmud* I, ed. Jacob Sussman and David Rosenthal (Jerusalem: Magnes, Hebrew University, 1990), p. 135.

*P. Berakhot* 2:9 (5d)

The Palestinian Talmud's version of the *T. Ta'anit* 1:7 is not found after the Mishnah in *Ta'anit*. We do, however, find Rabban Simeon b. Gamaliel's position quoted as an anonymous baraita in *P. Berakhot* 2:9 (5d).

   I.    They taught [*tanei*]: "For any matter that involves anguish, anyone who wishes to declare himself an individual may do so.

   II.    A student may do so, and is deserving of a blessing.

   III.    But in any matter involving gain, not everyone who wishes to declare himself an individual may do so;

   IV.    (a student may do so), unless the court has appointed him as a community leader."

This passage is quoted by the *P. Berakhot* sugya to explain *M. Berakhot* 2:6 regarding the bridegroom reciting the Shema on his wedding night. In other words, the *P. Berakhot* sugya connects Rabban Simeon b. Gamaliel's statement in the *M. Berakhot* 2:6 to his position in the *T. Ta'anit* 1:7.[48] As already noted, there is an obvious parallel between the Tosefta and the Mishnah. In the Mishnah (*Berakhot* 2:6), Rabban Simeon b. Gamaliel states that not everyone who wishes to call himself a scholar (and recite the Shema when he is not obligated to) may do so. In the Tosefta (*Ta'anit* 1:7), we are taught that not just anyone may call himself an individual and voluntarily observe matters of praise. The words *an individual* and *taking the name (of a scholar)* are being used synonymously here by the *P. Berakhot* sugya,[49] and the Shema is thus understood as an example of a matter of praise.[50]

Since *P. Berakhot* quotes only the position of R. Simeon b. Gamaliel

---

48. In the Paris and London manuscripts, in fact, R. Simeon b. Gamaliel's name is actually mentioned explicitly in the baraita—see *Synopse zum Talmud Yerushalmi*, ed. Peter Schafer and Hans-Jurgen Becker (Tubingen: Mohr, 1991), ad loc.

49. The Meiri also uses these terms synonymously in *Ta'anit* 10b, *Beit haBehirah* (Jerusalem: Kedem, 1976), p. 37.

50. R. Eleazar Azkiri, *Perush Miba'al Sefer Haredim,* and R. Moses Margaliot, *Mar-eh HaPanim,* ad loc.

(leaving out R. Simeon b. Eleazar's position), we can infer that *P. Berakhot* accepted R. Simeon b. Gamaliel's position, differentiating between matters of anguish and matters of praise. Supererogatory behavior involving anguish was permitted to the general population and praised for the scholar. Supererogatory behavior involving praise was forbidden to the general population and permitted only to scholars and community leaders.

In the *P. Berakhot* version of the text, the inclusive position regarding matters of anguish is stated more emphatically than in the Tosefta, because of the addition of the word "any"—[*kol*] in three places. The Tosefta text states, "For a matter of anguish, a person who wants to declare himself an individual may do so. . . . For a matter of praise, any person who wants to declare himself an individual may not do so." The *P. Berakhot* text, though, has *any* (*kol*) instead of *a* (*be*) throughout: "For *any* matter of anguish, *any* person who wants to declare himself an individual may do so. . . . And for *any* matter of praise . . . ," thus stating the point in a stronger fashion, emphasizing that in *any* matter of anguish, *anyone* could declare himself an individual.[51] Any type of individual would, then, according to Rabban Simeon b. Gamaliel, be permitted to engage in any type of ascetic behavior.

The *P. Berakhot* Talmudic sugya, which (anonymously) quotes this Tosefta passage directly after the Mishnah, then turns to another situation, thereby illuminating how the Tosefta passage was understood by later generations:

V.   It was taught: "It is permitted to turn to [private] sidewalks
VI.  in order to avoid road pegs. And at a time when one would sink, even in a field that is full of saffron."

This statement is part of a baraita[52] listing the stipulations concerning public treatment of private properties that Joshua laid down when he entered the land of Israel. One of these stipulations was that when it was difficult to walk on the public road because of

---

51. The Rif (ed. Zaks) here has "a common person" (*am ha'aretz*) instead of "anyone" (*kol*), which also reflects this inclusive position. For more information on the term *am ha'aretz*, see A. Oppenheimer, *The Am Ha-aretz* (Leiden: Brill, 1977).

52. The baraita is also found in *P. Baba Batra* 5:1 and *B. Baba Kama* 81a.

the "road pegs," it was permissible to walk on the side of the road on private property. The "road pegs" were pits that developed in the roads during the warm summer months when the mud of the road dried up, leaving the footprints of animals and people as holes in the road.[53] When the pits in the road were so deep (or perhaps wet, after a rain) that one would sink into them, it was even permissible to walk on the side of a field full of saffron (which was very valuable and could be damaged by trespassers).[54]

The Talmudic sugya continues by relating the following incident:

VII.   R. Abahu said: "It happened that R. Gamaliel and R. Joshua were once walking on the road and they turned aside to the private sidewalks in order to avoid the road pegs,

VIII.   and they saw R. Judah b. Papus[55] sinking [walking with difficulty along the main road] and coming toward them."

IX.   R. Gamaliel said to R. Joshua: "Who is that, who is pointing a finger at himself?"

X.   He replied: "It is Judah b. Papus, and all his deeds are done in the name of heaven."

This incident represents a case of someone "declaring himself an individual" and imposing a stringency on himself. R. Judah b. Papus clearly had no obligation to sink into the muddy pits in the road, yet he chose to do so nevertheless. He had a clear mandate from the times of Joshua allowing him to walk on the private sidewalk when walking on the road was difficult, yet he chose the more difficult path. His actions were viewed as presumptuous by R. Gamaliel, whose question "Who is that, who is pointing a finger at himself?" means "Who is that showing his greatness (i.e., presumptuousness) in our presence?"[56]

---

53. Rashi, *B. Baba Kama* 81a, s.v. *mipnei yetedot haderakhim.*

54. *P. Baba Batra* 5:1, and *P'nei Moshe* ad loc.

55. The Paris and London manuscripts here have R. Judah b. Nekosa, which is the name found in the *B. Baba Kama* 81b parallel to this incident (*Synopse,* ad loc.).

56. See below *B. Baba Kama* 81b parallel and S. Lieberman's discussion

Judah b. Papus, in all likelihood, is the same as Papus b. Judah,[57] who is described as behaving in an extreme manner that differed from the norm in yet another area of Halakhah. The Tosefta records that Papus b. Judah would lock his wife in the house so that she would not talk to her neighbors or relatives, lest she come to commit adultery.[58] The questions that we need to address here are, Were his actions considered "matters of praise" or "matters of anguish"? Was he considered a scholar, or a common person?

The Talmudic sugya continues by quoting our Tosefta passage as a conversation between R. Gamaliel and R. Joshua regarding Judah b. Papus:

XI. [He said to him]

XII. "But did we not learn that in any matter involving praise, not everyone who wants to declare himself an individual may do so, a student may do so unless the court has appointed him as a community leader."

XIII. [He said to him, "But we learned that:]

XIV. For any matter that involves anguish, anyone who wants to declare himself an individual may do so, a student does so and is deserving of a blessing."

XV. R. Zera stated: As long as he does not shame others.

The Vilna Gaon emends the text and deletes the words in parentheses (sections XI and XIII). No evidence in the manuscripts appears for this emendation; all the manuscripts have both sections XI and XIII.[59] Ginzberg suggests[60] that he made this emendation since early Tannaim do not use phrases such as "but we learned that" (*veha ta-nei*). Furthermore, R. Gamaliel and R. Joshua would hardly have debated statements that were made and discussed by the following generation, by tannaim such as R. Meir, R. Yosi, Rabban

---

of this phrase in *Hellenism in Jewish Palestine* (New York: Jewish Theological Seminary, 1950), p. 15.

57. See L. Ginzberg, *Perushim VeHidushim BaYerushalmi*, (New York: Ktav, 1971), vol. I, p. 410 and Lieberman, *Toseftah Kifeshutah, Sotah* 5:9, pp. 178–179.

58. Tosefta *Sotah* 5:9, *B. Gittin* 90a, and *P. Kiddushin* 4:4.

59. *Synopse,* ad loc.

60. Ginzberg, *Perushim,* ibid., pp. 410–412.

Simeon b. Gamaliel, and later by R. Simeon b. Eleazar. Finally, Ginzberg also points out that the parallel to this incident, found in *P. Baba Batra* 5:1, ends with the words "all his deeds are done in the name of heaven" and does not contain this "conversation." The quoting of the Tosefta, then (or the discussion of the Tosefta, according to the printed text), took place among the amoraim composing the sugya, and not between R. Gamaliel and R. Joshua. These amoraim may have been R. Abahu and R. Zera, whose names are mentioned in the sugya, or others who arranged the Talmudic sugya, who lived in their generation or in succeeding generations.[61]

The purpose of quoting this baraita after the story of Judah b. Papus seems to have been to justify his actions. There are numerous ways of explaining how the baraita, in fact, accomplished this task. Assuming that Judah b. Papus was a scholar (he is called "rabbi"), then this baraita shows that he was permitted to do what he did, even if his actions were considered a matter of praise, since a scholar is permitted to take both matters of anguish as well as matters of praise on himself.[62]

A second way is to assume that walking on the road pegs was a matter of anguish and that the Tosefta teaches that Judah b. Papus was permitted to do this whether he was a scholar or a common person. (The word *rabbi* may be a scribal error; in *P. Baba Batra* 5:1 he is referred to as Judah b. Papus, and even in this passage, R. Joshua

---

61. R. Abahu is the amora who relates the story about R. Gamaliel and R. Joshua, and R. Zera later adds a limitation to when people can "declare themselves individuals." R. Abahu was a second-third-generation Palestinian amora, and R. Zera, who emigrated from Babylon to the land of Israel, was his student and later his learning partner (A. Hyman, *Toledot,* vol. 1, p. 67). See also Ginzberg, ibid., who suggests that the conversation took place between R. Abahu and R. Ila, whose name, as a result of a scribal error, was recorded as R. La. Lieberman, however, in his review of Neusner's translation of the Palestinian Talmud, writes, "Even a beginner of the study of TP knows that the name of R. Ila is often abbreviated and spelled 'La.'" No scribal error, then, would have occurred here. See Saul Lieberman, "A Tragedy or a Comedy," *Journal of the American Oriental Society* 104:2 (1984), p. 317.

62. This is how the Ra'avyah explains this section (*Sefer Ra'avya,* vol. 2, "Megilah" 597, p. 339).

did not refer to him as rabbi but rather simply as Judah b. Papus.[63])
For according to the baraita, any individual is allowed to take a
matter of anguish on himself. The baraita, then, may have been
brought by the Talmudic sugya as an objection to R. Gamaliel and R.
Joshua's assumption that his actions were justified only because "all
of his deeds are done in the name of Heaven." For the baraita does
not mention the special qualification of his deeds being in the name
of heaven; hence Judah b. Papus deserved no censure for taking a
matter of anguish upon himself. (The Talmudic sugya then goes on
to explain that because his actions were done publicly and had the
potential to embarrass other people, he would have been deserving
of censure had his motivations not been sincere.[64])

If, however, we follow the printed text (and all of the manuscripts) and read the passage as a conversation, and we assume that
he was not considered a scholar,[65] then the conversation can be
explained as follows: R. Gamaliel considered walking on the road
pegs to be an act of praise, since he is in public and will be seen by
other people who will think that he is exceptionally pious and
assume that he is a scholar. His gain, then, would be in reputation.[66]
R. Gamaliel, then, would be questioning R. Joshua, who had just
defended R. Judah b. Papus, by saying, "(Why are you defending
him)—did we not learn that if it is a matter involving praise (which
is the case here), not everyone who wants to declare himself an
individual may do so . . . (and therefore he should not have been
walking in the middle of the road)?"

R. Joshua's response, then, would be pointing out to R. Gamaliel
that walking on the road pegs and sinking in the road was, in fact, a
matter of anguish and not a matter of praise. (It is difficult, tiring,

---

63. Ginzberg, *Perushim,* vol. I, p. 410, quotes the *Kaftor VaFerach's*
reading, which is "Papus b. Judah," without the title "Rabbi." Yet eve.ɪ if
Judah b. Papus (or Papus b. Judah) did not have the title of rabbi, he may,
nevertheless, still have been a scholar.

64. This is how R. David Luria explains this passage, in his comments
on the Vilna Gaon's textual emendations (*Hagahot haGera,* ad loc.).

65. If we accept that he was a scholar, then the passage would make
no sense as a conversation, since as a scholar his actions are justified even
if they are considered matters of praise.

66. R. Shlomo Goren, *HaYerushalmi HaMephorash, Berakhot,* ad loc.
(Jerusalem: Mossad HaRav Kook, 1961).

time-consuming, and potentially embarrassing since it looks bizarre.) He therefore said to him, "But we learned that any matter that involves anguish, whoever wants to declare himself an individual may do so . . . (and, therefore, he was allowed to impose this stringency upon himself)."[67]

Since it was R. Gamaliel who was criticizing R. Judah b. Papus for "pointing a finger at himself," R. Gamaliel's attitude toward deviating from normative Halakhic practice is relevant here. The Mishnayot earlier in our chapter discuss three different cases in which R. Gamaliel himself went against the general practice:

1. He recited the "Shema" on his wedding night, even though he had taught his students that a groom is exempt from this commandment (*Berakhot* 2:5).

2. He bathed the night after his wife died, even though he had taught his students that bathing is forbidden to mourners (*Berakhot* 2:6).

3. He accepted condolences for his slave Tabi's death, even though he had taught his students that condolences are not accepted for slaves (*Berakhot* 2:7).

The first case (in which R. Gamaliel recited the "Shema" on his wedding night) is an example of a bridegroom reciting the Shema, thereby observing a commandment from which he was exempt. (In the other two cases, he was exempting himself from a prohibition,[68] i.e., doing something that he himself had ruled was forbidden, rather than doing something that he was not obligated to do.) R. Gamaliel explains his actions by saying, "I will not listen to you to remove from myself the yoke of heaven even for a moment."[69]

---

67. R. Moses Margaliot in the *P'nei Moshe* and R. Isaac Krasilchikov in the *Toledot Yitzhak*, ad loc., explain the passage in this manner.

68. In the case of his slave, it is not clear whether it was actually forbidden to accept condolences for a slave or simply "not done." If it was forbidden, then this case would be the same as the case of bathing when in mourning—R. Gamliel would be exempting himself from a prohibition. If it was simply "not done," then his actions would be less radical—he would simply be going against the general practice, and not against an actual prohibition.

69. This wording is odd—he was the one who taught the exemption, yet he says to his students, "I will not listen to *you*," as if they were the originators of the exemption.

R. Gamaliel's explanation of why he recited the Shema on his wedding night corresponds with R. Joshua's justification of Judah b. Papus's actions and R. Gamaliel's apparent acceptance of R. Joshua's justification. R. Joshua explains that Judah b. Papus was not arrogant and was not trying to appear haughty or "holier than thou" but rather had pure intentions of serving his Creator. This idea is the same as that expressed by R. Gamliel himself, when he explains that he recited the Shema for purely religious motives, namely, "not removing himself from the kingship of heaven even for a moment." These two incidents suggest, then, that according to these tannaim, it is permissible for an individual to impose stringencies on himself as long as his motivations are of a purely religious nature, namely, to serve God, and not due to arrogance and/or an effort to appear more pious than other people. The emphasis here appears to be on internal motivation rather than the reactions of other people.

There is a parallel to this story in *B. Baba Kama* 81b, in its discussion of Joshua's stipulation that "[i]t is permitted to turn to [private] sidewalks in order to avoid road pegs." A similar incident is related but with different individuals and dialogue:

I.   As R. Judah the Prince and R. Hiyya were once walking on the road they turned aside to the private sidewalks,

II.  while R. Judah b. Nekosa[70] went striding along the main road in front of them.

III. R. Judah the Prince thereupon said to R. Hiyya, "Who is that showing his greatness in our presence?"

IV.  R. Hiyya answered him: "He might perhaps be R. Judah b. Nekosa who is my disciple and who does all his deeds in the name of heaven."

V.   When they drew near to him they saw him and he said to him:

VI.  "Had you not been Judah b. Nekosa, I would have sawed your thighs with an iron saw."

In this passage, it is R. Judah b. Nekosa, and not R. Judah b. Papus, who insists on walking in the middle of the road, even when

---

70. The printed text has Kenosa, but the correct name is Nekosa (see *Dikdukei Soferim,* ad loc.).

he was permitted by Joshua to walk along the private sidewalks. R. Judah the Prince and R. Hiyya observe and react to his actions, instead of R. Gamaliel and R. Joshua of the *P. Berakhot* version. Whether it was R. Hiyya or R. Judah the Prince who spoke to R. Judah b. Nekosa is not totally clear, since the text states only "he said to him," with no name. It seems likely, though, that it was R. Hiyya, since he identified "the offender" to R. Judah the Prince and claimed him as "my disciple."[71]

The statement made to R. Judah b. Nekosa (presumably by R. Hiyya), "Had you not been Judah b. Nekosa, I would have sawed your thighs with an iron saw," has been explained in different ways. Rashi writes that it is a metaphor for excommunication. The Arukh, on the other hand, gives two other possible explanations:[72]

1. I would question you until I would break your thighs—presumably, a figurative description of very difficult questions challenging his actions.
2. I would use actual metal tools—literally, "I would cut off your thighs."

How this statement is understood is important for determining R. Hiyya's attitude toward Judah b. Nekosa's behavior, and, consequently, his attitude toward self-imposed stringencies in general. According to Rashi's explanation, R. Hiyya spoke very seriously, and held that if anyone else had done the same action, it would have been an offense deserving of excommunication. The strength of the rebuke implies that although he was not going to excommunicate R. Judah b. Nekosa (since his motivations were "in the name of heaven"), he certainly did not approve of his behavior.

The Arukh understands the offense as being of a less serious nature than does Rashi. According to the Arukh's first explanation—namely, that if he were anyone else, he would challenge his actions with questions—then R. Judah b. Nekosa's actions were acceptable for him because he did everything "in the name of heaven," but they

---

71. There are textual variants of this passage, however, that leave doubt as to who initiated the conversation (R. Hiyya or R. Judah the Prince) and whose student R. Judah b. Nekosa actually was—see *Dikdukei Soferim,* ad loc., note 5.

72. *Arukh HaShalem,* vol. I, s.v. G.Z.R. II.

would have been unacceptable for someone else. According to the second explanation, "If you were anyone else, I would have sawed off your thighs," R. Hiyya's rebuke is worded in such a grotesque manner that it seems almost comical. He may, in fact, have viewed R. Judah's actions as being improper and was actually saying to him, "I won't cut off your thighs since I know you are sincere, but I still think that you are wrong."

This conclusion differs from the *P. Berakhot* sugya, for in the *P. Berakhot* sugya, R. Joshua's affirmation that R. Judah b. Papus acted "in the name of heaven" was accepted as justification for his behavior. In this source, however, R. Judah b. Nekosa is still rebuked, even though his rebuke was far more mild than it would have been for someone else. R. Hiyya, then, still held that R. Judah b. Nekosa was wrong for having done something that he was exempt from doing. This may be related to the position stated by Hizkiyah, R. Hiyya's son, later in the sugya (and discussed later), "Whoever fulfills a commandment from which they are exempt is called a commoner." If in fact it was R. Hiyya talking to R. Judah b. Nekosa (and not R. Judah the Prince), then R. Hiyya, like his son Hizkiyah, seems to have opposed public supererogatory behavior, even if one's motivations were sincere.

In the case of sinking into the road pegs, the Tosefta seems to have been quoted by the *P. Berakhot* sugya after R. Joshua's defense of R. Judah b. Papus to justify R. Judah b. Papus's actions in the face of R. Gamaliel's disapproval. Assuming that he was considered a scholar, then the Tosefta justifies his actions, whether they be classified as anguish or gain, since a scholar is permitted to take both matters of anguish as well as matters of praise on himself. If we assume, alternatively, that he was not a scholar, then his actions were still justified as long as they were matters of anguish. The Talmudic sugya, then, by quoting the Tosefta here, is following R. Simon b. Gamaliel, who is "liberal" in that he allows even common people to engage in supererogatory behavior, as long as they are matters of anguish.

The Talmudic sugya in *P. Berakhot* 2:9 continues by quoting R. Zera, who adds a condition to the baraita (section XV earlier):

I.  "R. Zera stated: As long as he does not shame others."

R. Zera's understanding, then, of the baraita is that common people may not accept "matters of praise on themselves," while scholars may do so as long as they do not shame others by their actions. Common people, though, as well as scholars, may accept "matters of anguish" on themselves, as long as, once again, they will not embarrass anyone else. According, then, to R. Zera, the baraita allows supererogatory behavior only when the individual who is accepting the extra religious obligation will not shame anyone else by doing so. This could only occur, then, in a situation when others would not see him and feel as if they are not sufficiently pious.

R. Zera's statement is similar to R. Hiyya's rebuke of R. Judah b. Nekosa in the *B. Baba Kama* (81b) version of the R. Judah b. Papus incident. R. Hiyya felt that "walking on the road pegs" still deserved a rebuke even though R. Judah's intentions were sincere. Likewise, R. Zera held that although Judah b. Papus was, theoretically, allowed to do what he did (based on the baraita), his behavior was, nevertheless, improper, since it was done publicly. When R. Gamaliel saw him, he felt that Judah b. Papus was embarrassing other people by showing off his own piety—that is, he was "shaming others."[73]

Following R. Zera's statement of "As long as he does not shame others," the Talmudic sugya continues:

XVI.   It occurred that[74] R. Miyasha[75] and R. Samuel b. R. Isaac were sitting and eating in one of the upper rooms of a synagogue.

XVII.  The time for prayer arrived, and R. Samuel b. R. Isaac got up and prayed.

XVIII. R. Miyasha said to him: But didn't Rebbe teach us "If one already started (eating), one is not required to stop (in order to pray)?

---

73. See P'nei Moshe, ad loc.

74. According to Lieberman, the word *dilma* is the Greek and Syriac word *drama*: a story (*HaYerushalmi Kifeshuta*, p. 24).

75. The printed text of *Berakhot* as well as many manuscripts have R. Yosa (Yosi) here. R. Miyasha, however, appears to be the correct reading, since his name appears below in the continuation of the incident in section XVIII. The Rome manuscript in *Berakhot* here, in fact, has R. Miyasha instead of R. Yosa, as does the parallel passage in *P. Shabbat* 1:2. (The Paris and London manuscripts, though, have R. Yosi both in sections XVI and XVIII.)

XIX.    And Hizkiah has stated: "whoever does something
         from which he is exempt is called a commoner"
         (*hedyot*).

The Talmudic sugya continues (lines xvi–xviii) by quoting
another related incident, concerning a scholar who stopped eating to
pray the afternoon prayer (*minhah*) when he was not required to do
so. The amoraim mentioned in this account are R. Miyasha and R.
Samuel b. R. Isaac, third-fourth-generation Palestinian amoraim.[76]
When R. Miyasha said to R. Samuel b. R. Isaac, "But didn't Rebbe
teach us . . . ," he was referring to R. Judah the Prince, since he
then quotes a Mishnah.[77] R. Samuel b. Isaac's action constituted a
supererogatory act of praise. It involved praying even when not
obligated to do so and is identical to the case of the bridegroom's
recital of the Shema. It would, presumably, increase the respect of
his colleagues, who would admire his dedication. R. Samuel b. Isaac,
however, did not gain the respect of his colleague when he interrupted his meal; instead, he was challenged by R. Miyasha.
         R. Miyasha questioned his actions by quoting *M. Shabbat* 1:2,
which states that one is not required to interrupt his meal to pray
*minhah:*

I.     One must not sit down before a barber near *minhah* until he
       has prayed, nor may he . . . eat . . . ,
II.    yet if they began (eating), they need not break off. . . .

R. Miyasha (or the Talmudic sugya) then added further strength
to his question, by quoting the baraita in the name of Hizkiyah,
stating that "whoever does something from which he is exempt is
called a commoner" (section XIX). Hizkiyah was one of R. Hiyya's
sons, and is considered a last-generation tanna (his statement here

---

76. Hyman, *Toledot,* vol. III, pp. 881, 1139.
77. Hyman quotes this passage as evidence that R. Miyasha was R.
Samuel b. Isaac's student, since he referred to him here as "Rebbe" (vol. III, p.
881). Ginzberg also claims this to be true, writing that those who say that R.
Miyasha referred to R. Judah the Prince are mistaken. He writes that the term
"*lo ken alphan rebbe*" is the language used by a student to question his own
teacher (*Perushim, Berakhot* vol. I, p. 413). The fact, however, that R. Miyasha
quotes a Mishnah indicates that he was, in all likelihood, referring to R. Judah
the Prince.

and in other places are introduced by the word *tani*).[78] Hizkiyah's
baraita is worded as a blanket statement, meant to apply to all
situations. It may, though, have been formulated in response to a
specific situation or type of situation and simply worded in a
hyperbolic fashion.[79]

R. Samuel then replied to R. Miyasha's question by quoting a
different Mishnah in support of his actions, namely, the Mishnah in
*Berakhot* 2:9 that states that a bridegroom may recite the Shema even
though he is exempt. There are three different textual versions of the
continuation of the "conversation" between R. Miyasha and R.
Samuel.[80] These textual variants totally change the meaning of the
text. One is the text found in our sugya (*P. Berakhot* 2:9) and is too
unclear to interpret:

XX.    He (R. Samuel) said to him: But we learned: "A bride-
       groom is exempt, a bridegroom if he wishes."

XXI.   He (R. Miyasha) said to him: "And isn't this according to
       R. Gamaliel?"

XXII.  He (R. Samuel) said to him: "I can explain this ac-
       cording to R. Gamaliel, for R. Gamaliel said, 'I won't
       listen to you to remove from myself the yoke (of
       heaven).'"

A second textual version, found in the Paris, London, and
Amsterdam manuscripts and in *P. Shabbat* 1:2, does not have section
XXI. Section XXII, then, would constitute R. Miyasha's reply to R.
Samuel:

XX.    He (R. Samuel) said to him: But we learned: "A bride-
       groom is exempt, a bridegroom if he wishes."

---

78. Hyman, vol. II., p. 419.

79. If R. Miyasha was indeed R. Samuel b. R. Isaac's student (as
Hyman and Ginzberg claim), then this quotation seems rather brazen, since
he was basically insulting his teacher. While, on the one hand, this could
simply reflect a very open and comfortable teacher-student relationship, it
is also possible that the Talmudic sugya, and not R. Miyasha, quoted
Hizkiya's baraita in criticism of R. Samuel b. R. Isaac.

80. While this conversation may have actually occurred, it may also
have been inserted by the Talmudic sugya, in which case "He said to him"
would really mean "He would have said to him."

XXI.   (missing)

XXII.   He (R. Miyasha) said to him: "I can explain this according to R. Gamaliel, for R. Gamaliel said, "I won't listen
to you to remove from myself the yoke (of heaven)."

According to this textual version, the conversation is as follows:
R. Samuel defends himself by quoting the Mishnah in *Berakhot* 2:9
regarding the Shema, which states that a bridegroom *may* recite the
Shema if he so desires. R. Miyasha then retorts that the Mishnah
about the Shema does not in fact support his interrupting his meal to
pray, since the Shema is the one exception to Hizkiah's ruling
because it contains the very essence of Judaism, namely, acceptance
of "the yoke of heaven." In R. Samuel's case, though (and, presumably, in all other areas of Halakha), Hizkiah's statement—namely,
that he who does something from which he is exempt is called a
commoner—would still apply.[81]

The Talmudic sugya thus ends, according to this textual version,
with R. Miyasha's criticism of R. Samuel, who imposed a stringency
on himself (in front of someone else). This ending to the Talmudic
sugya thus negates the position of the baraita with which the sugya
begins. For the baraita holds that "in any matter involving
praise . . . a student may do so (declare himself an individual)." R.
Samuel was a student (scholar), imposing a matter of praise upon
himself, an act that is permissible according to the baraita. The
Talmudic sugya, however, concludes that in fact, it is unacceptable
behavior and that reciting the Shema is the only matter of praise that
a scholar is permitted to observe even when exempt.

The *P. Berakhot* sugya, then, according to this textual emendation, holds that for a matter involving praise, neither a common
person *nor* a scholar may declare himself an individual, except in the
case of a bridegroom reading the Shema. This is a very strong
limitation of the right of scholars to impose extra religious obligations on themselves; the *P. Berakhot* Talmudic sugya, in other words,
is more stringent than the baraita, since it limits that which the
baraita permitted.

Perhaps for this very reason, a third textual version of this text

---

81. The *P'nei Moshe* and the *Toledot Isaac* both explain the text in this
manner.

is found in the *Ra'avyah* and R. Isaac b. Moses *Or Zarua*.[82] They change section XXI as follows:

XXI.   He (R. Miyasha) said to him: "And didn't R. Simeon b. Gamaliel teach, 'Not everyone who desires to take the name (of a scholar) may do so.'"

No manuscripts are available to us today with this text, and we have no way to determine whether the *Ra'avyah* relied on a manuscript or emended the text on the basis of his own logical reasoning—that is, in order to have the Talmudic sugya accept the baraita. The Talmudic sugya according to the *Ra'avyah's* text essentially ends in exactly the opposite manner, namely, with R. Samuel's defense of his actions.

The *Ra'avyah* explains the conversation as follows: R. Samuel defends himself by quoting the Mishnah in *Berakhot* 2:9 regarding the Shema. R. Miyasha then retorts by quoting Rabban Simeon b. Gamaliel's ruling in the Mishnah, since the law is according to Rabban Simeon b. Gamaliel whenever he states a position in the Mishnah. He ruled that not everyone was permitted to "take the name" (i.e., to call himself a scholar and recite the Shema). R. Samuel then defends himself against this claim by stating that even Rabban Simeon b. Gamaliel agreed that a scholar is permitted to take on extra religious obligations without the fear of appearing conceited, as can be seen from the example of R. Gamaliel. (The *Ra'avyah* assumes that R. Simon b. Gamaliel agreed with his father.[83]) R. Gamaliel's recital of the Shema, thus, was not an exception to a rule but rather simply an example of a scholar taking on an extra religious obligation.

The *P. Berakhot* Talmudic sugya thus ends, according to this textual variant, with R. Samuel defending his actions and claiming that a scholar is, in fact, permitted to impose supererogatory matters of praise on himself. This textual emendation concurs with the baraita quoted at the beginning of the sugya. R. Samuel thus refutes Hizkiyah's

---

82. *Sefer Ra'avya,* ibid., pp. 339–340, R. Isaac b. Moses, *Sefer Or Zarua* (vol. 1, Laws of *Keriat Shema,* 84).

83. *Ra'avyah,* ibid.

claim that he is considered a "commoner."[84] Assuming that all the attributions here are correct, then R. Samuel may have been aware of R. Zera's warning "as long as he does not shame others," for R. Samuel b. R. Isaac and R. Zera lived during the same time period, though R. Samuel was the older man.[85] R. Samuel might have held that his actions would not embarrass others.

## CHAPTER SUMMARY

This chapter began by proposing two possible definitions of the term *an individual*. One was the inclusive definition: that anyone who wished to fast could do so and is then considered "an individual." The second was the exclusive definition—namely, that only members of a special, elite, and explicitly defined group of people may fast, for only they (i.e., scholars or community leaders) are the true "individuals."

Assuming that "the individuals"—as defined by the exclusive definition—were the only ones permitted to fast, then there would be an actual rabbinic prohibition of supererogatory behavior for the rest of the population. If, though, the sources were actually mandating fasting for the scholarly population rather than simply permitting it, then the option of imposing supererogatory fasts would be left open to the rest of the population; the nonscholarly but especially pious members of the community would be allowed to fast and thus express their piety.

Tosefta *Ta'anit* 1:7 was presented, and it was found that both R. Simeon b. Eleazar and Rabban Simeon b. Gamaliel belong to the "exclusive" school of thought with regard to matters of praise. That is to say, both limit this behavior to scholars and community leaders. Concerning matters of anguish, though, Rabban Simeon b. Gamaliel represents the "inclusive" school of thought; he holds that supererogatory matters of anguish are permissible for any individual and are considered praiseworthy behavior for scholars. In the parallel to the Tosefta passage found in *B. Ta'anit* 10b, the Talmudic sugya (in

---

84. Leiberman writes that this is the correct explanation of this Talmudic sugya (*HaYerushalmi Kifeshutah*, p. 25). Ginzberg, however, holds that the *Ra'avyah* had a mistaken text that could not possibly be correct (*Perushim*, vol. I, p. 415).

85. Hyman, *Toledot*, vol. I, p. 394.

the printed text) erases the conflict between R. Simeon b. Eleazar and Rabban Simeon b. Gamaliel and ends with them both agreeing that limitations were placed only on supererogatory matters of gain, but not on matters of anguish.

From the *P. Berakhot* 2:9 sugya's quotation of Rabban Simeon b. Gamaliel, we see that it accepted his differentiation between matters of anguish and matters of praise. Any type of individual would, then, according to Rabban Simeon b. Gamaliel, be permitted to engage in any type of ascetic behavior. This baraita is then quoted a second time in the same *P. Berakhot* sugya, perhaps to justify the behavior of R. Judah b. Papus, who engaged in public supererogatory behavior. A crucial point made in this Talmudic sugya is that it is permissible for individuals to impose matters of anguish on themselves as long as their motivations are of a purely religious nature, namely, to serve God, and not to appear more pious than other people. As long as one's motivations are sincere and nobody else will be ashamed by the individual's stringency (R. Zera's addition), then supererogatory anguish would be permissible. This point, however, is complicated by Hizkiya's statement: "Whoever does something from which he is exempt is called a commoner (*hedyot*)." These ideas will be explored further in later chapters.

According to these sources, the following key issues need to be considered in an assessment of when and why supererogation is criticized:

1. whether the individual is a common person, a scholar, or a community leader;

2. whether the behavior involves matters of anguish or matters of praise;

3. whether the individual's motivations are sincere;

4. whether the individual's actions would shame other people (which is integrally related to whether the actions are done in public or in private); and,

5. when an individual who does something from which he is exempt is considered a "commoner" (*hedyot*).

# 2

# Criticism of Ascetic Behavior

In Chapter 1, various positions regarding self-imposed religious stringency were explored. It was established that according to some tannaim, anyone can declare himself an individual when it involves ascetic behavior (matters of anguish), while scholars who adopted ascetic practices were even "deserving of a blessing." This means that any person who so desired could take upon him- or herself extra fast days or other ascetic practices.

Ascetic behaviors, according to these tannaim, are legitimate forms of supererogation. The term *private fast* will be used synonymously with *supererogatory fast,* since private fasts were not explicitly required anywhere in the Talmud.[1] These fasts, thus, may have been

---

1. Maimonides, though, writes that just as it is a positive commandment for the community to fast when faced with calamity, so should an individual fast in such a case (*Yad,* Laws of *Ta'anit* 1:9). R. Joseph Karo, *Masgid Mishneh,* ad loc., understands that Maimonides is obligating the individual to fast, even though he has no explicit Talmudic source stating that individual fasts are obligatory. Maimonides, then, according to Karo's understanding, would be removing individual fasts in the face of tragedy or danger from the realm of the supererogatory and placing them in the realm of the obligatory. Similarly, R. Yehiel Michel Epstein writes that "the ruling

adopted by people who desired to "go beyond what is commanded or required."[2]

This inclusive view of matters of anguish (as opposed to the position that limited matters of anguish to an exclusive group of people) corresponds with the fact that private fasts seem to have been commonplace in Talmudic Judaism. They are mentioned in the Talmud in a matter-of-fact way, and rules and regulations were established for individuals involved in these private fasts. For example, the Talmudic sugya in *B. Ta'anit* 10b, immediately following the quote of the Tosefta passage discussed earlier, describes two different reasons for these fasts:

> The Rabbis taught: "Someone who was fasting because of a sorrow, and the sorrow passed, for a sick person, and the person was healed, he still completes the day's fast."

This source instructs anyone who is fasting because of a sorrow or for a sick person to complete the day's fast even if the sorrow or sickness has passed, thus establishing policy for what seems to have been a common occurrence. There is no evidence that the "someone" must have been a scholar. In all likelihood, the common practice of individual fasts preceded R. Yose and R. Simeon b. Gamaliel, and they were just echoing and reinforcing the accepted practice.

People fasted for many reasons, including to avert a tragedy or heal a sick person (as can be seen from the baraita quoted earlier), as a plea for rain, as a method of repentance or a plea for atonement, and to cancel a bad dream (*ta'anit halom*). Some tannaim even permitted dream fasts on the Sabbath, as long as one made up for it

---

that the individual is obligated to fast for personal sorrow is not explained anywhere in the Talmud, and Maimonides stated this based on his own logical reasoning (R. Yehiel Michel Epstein, *Arukh HaShulhan Orah Hayim* 578). A question that remains, though, is if Maimonides held that an individual must fast when faced with danger, then why does he permit only scholars to fast (before the month of Kislev) in the case of an impending drought? Perhaps he differentiated between private troubles, and public troubles, hence ruling differently in the two cases.

2. *The Oxford Dictionary*, s.v. *supererogatory.*

by fasting on another weekday.[3] Whether R. Simeon b. Gamaliel's confirmation (or perhaps formulation) of the permission for the common person to engage in supererogatory fasts influenced this custom or not, though, is difficult to determine.

With regard to scholars fasting individual fasts, a great deal of evidence indicates that this was quite common. There are cases of individual tannaim and amoraim who fasted for very long periods of time, and these fasts even included the Sabbath and holidays.[4] According to some historians, the practice of fasting on Mondays and Thursdays year-round was already widespread in the Land of Israel during the tannaitic period and was practiced mostly by scholars.[5]

Evidence from early Christian writings supports the claim that fasting on Monday and Thursday was already a known Jewish practice in first century Palestine. In Luke 18:11–12, a Pharisee is quoted as saying, "God, I thank thee that I am not like other men, extortioners, unjust. . . . I fast twice a week."[6] In the Didache, written in Syria at the end of the first century by Christians with a Jewish background,[7] Christians are told, "But do not let your fasts be with the hypocrites [Jews]; for they fast on Monday and Thursday; but you shall fast on Wednesday and Friday."[8]

---

3. *B. Ta'anit* 12b; *B. Berakhot* 31b.

4. Isaac D. Gilat, "Ta'anit beShabbat," *Tarbiz* 52(1) (1982), p. 5.

5. See G. Alon, "LeYishuvah shel Baraita Ahat," *Tarbiz* 4 (1932), pp. 285–291. Louis Ginzberg claims that "there is no doubt that the hasidim of the land of Israel used to fast (on Monday and Thursday) already in the days of the early tannaim; *Genizah Studies* (New York: Hermon, 1969), vol. I, p. 483, par. 6. Both of these scholars claim that these fasts were limited to Palestine. For information on "the hasidim of the land of Israel," see Buchler, *Types of Jewish Palestinian Piety,* and Samuel Safrai, "Teaching of Pietists in Mishnaic Literature," *Journal of Jewish Studies* XVI (1965), pp. 15–33.

6. *The New Oxford Annotated Bible* (New York: Oxford University Press, 1977).

7. Helmut Koester, *History and Literature of Early Christianity* (Philadelphia: Fortress, 1982), vol II, p. 158.

8. "Didache—Teaching of the Twelve Apostles" in *The Fathers of the Church: The Apostolic Fathers,* trans. Francis X. Glum, Joseph M. Marique, and Gerald G. Walsh (Washington, D.C.: Catholic University of America Press, 1969), 8:1. Both Alon and Ginzberg argue that these Christian sources

Although individual fasts thus seem to have been an accepted practice, among both scholars and common people, there were still tannaim and amoraim who criticized fasting and other ascetic practices and attempted to limit them, as did R. Meir and R. Simeon b. Eleazar in the Tosefta. Within the sources criticizing ascetic behavior, two major trends of thought can be found. One trend is to limit or forbid these activities because of their negative results—such as physical weakness caused by excessive fasting (not, though, because there is anything wrong with the behavior in and of itself). According to these sources, supererogatory anguish is wrong only in certain contexts. This school of thought will be labeled as "contextually negative."

The second trend found within the literature is to criticize self-denial because the behavior in and of itself is viewed as negative. This trend will be labeled as "inherently negative." This chapter will focus on both of these trends criticizing ascetic behavior.

## ASCETIC BEHAVIOR AS CONTEXTUALLY NEGATIVE

*Fasting in Times of Danger*

The community's response to times of danger involved blowing the shofar, fasting, and praying. These endeavors were undertaken to encourage repentance and God's forgiveness, in the hope of averting the impending tragedy. *M. Tanit* 3:7 lists the dangers for which the shofar is blown even on the Sabbath:

I.   For these (dangers), the shofar is blown on the Sabbath:
II.  A city that is surrounded by gentiles
III. or a river (which threatens to flood the city),
IV.  and for a boat which is in danger of being shipwrecked.
V.   R. Yose says: (The shofar is blown) as a call (to other people) for help, but not as a plea to God."

---

prove that the Jews commonly fasted on Monday and Thursday already in the first century. Although these sources certainly demonstrate that some Jews fasted on Monday and Thursday, it does not prove that this was common or widespread, as Alon claims.

While the Mishnah discusses blowing the shofar for people in danger,[9] *T. Ta'anit* 2:12 discusses a second response to danger, namely, whether someone in a dangerous situation is permitted to fast:

I.     A city surrounded by gentiles, or a boat about to be shipwrecked, or an individual being chased by gentiles or bandits or evil spirits;

II.    are not allowed to afflict (*lesagef*) themselves by fasting,

III.   so as not to lose their strength.

IV.    And this is just what[10]

V.     R. Yose said:

VI.    An individual is not permitted to afflict himself by fasting,

VII.   lest he become a burden onto the community

VIII.  and they will need to support him.

The beginning of the passage relates to dangerous situations and instructs people not to fast when in danger, lest it weaken their strength. The wording of "are not allowed to afflict *themselves* by fasting so as not to lose their strength" indicates that the Tosefta is addressing the people who are actually in danger themselves (who need to keep up their strength), and not necessarily others who hear about the danger but are not subject to it themselves. Supererogatory fasting, then, would be forbidden when it could endanger one's life.

R. Yose is then quoted as a supporting opinion. His reason, though, for prohibiting individuals to "afflict themselves by fasting" is lest they become a financial burden on the community. He was not referring only to dangerous situations; his statement appears to be a general prohibition due to the negative consequences resulting from excessive fasting in everyday existence. His statement, which may have been made in a different context, was juxtaposed to the anonymous Tosefta because it also discouraged fasting, albeit in

---

9. "The shofar is blown on the Sabbath" was interpreted symbolically by the amoraim as meaning reciting the special prayer of *Anenu* and not actually blowing the shofar, since the shofar is not blown on the Sabbath (*B. Ta'anit* 14a). *P. Ta'anit* 3:8, though, raises the possibility that the anonymous Mishnah meant it literally.

10. Line IV—"And this is just what" (*vekhen haya*)—is missing from the London manuscript of the Tosefta (*Tosefta,* ed. Leiberman, ad loc.).

different circumstances.[11] R. Yose's position, then, would be that afflicting oneself with fasting was always prohibited, while the anonymous Toseftah held that it was prohibited only to people whose lives were in danger.[12]

R. Yose, who permitted supererogatory fasting in *B. Ta'anit* 10b (discussed in Chapter 1), thus places limits on this behavior in this source. He seems to differentiate between an occasional fast, which he permitted and even encouraged, and afflicting oneself with fasting, which he forbade. He does not say "the individual is not permitted to fast"; he says "the individual is not permitted to *afflict* himself with fasting." Although we do find the concept of self-affliction used in association with just the one Day of Atonement,[13] R. Yose here is clearly referring to "afflicting oneself with fasting" as a habit. We know this because he prohibits "afflicting" oneself with fasting so that the individual will not damage his health and hence his livelihood. This would be a concern only if one made fasting a way of life, and not if one fasted for merely one day.

A parallel to this passage, found in *B. Ta'anit* 22b, contains a marked difference from the Tosefta passage. While in the Tosefta everyone agrees that the individual should not afflict himself by fasting, in the *B. Ta'anit* passage only R. Yose maintains this opinion:

I.      The Rabbis taught:

II.     "A city which is surrounded by gentiles, or a river, or a ship lost at sea in a storm, or an individual being pursued

---

11. The London manuscript's text of the Tosefta that does not have the phrase "and this is just what" (*vekhen haya*) would then be correct, since R. Yose did not hold the same position as did the anonymous Tosefta.

12. Leiberman understands R. Yose as expanding the prohibition of the anonymous Tosefta. He writes that while the anonymous Tosefta spoke of the people actually in danger, R. Yose is forbidding even the individuals who are outside of danger from fasting (*Tosefta Kifeshuta Ta'anit*, p. 334, lines 76–79). Nevertheless, he limits R. Yose's comments to times of danger and does not read his statement as does this writer, namely, as a general prohibition of fasting excessively.

13. The wording of *veinitem et nafshotekhem* is used in Leviticus 23:27, and *inuy* is synonymous with *lesagef*, which is used here (*Arukh*, vol. IV s.v. S.G.F.).

by the gentiles or by bandits, or by evil spirits,[14] [they blow the shofar on the Sabbath]:[15]

III. for all of these, an individual is allowed to afflict himself by fasting."[16]

IV. R. Yose states: "the individual is not permitted to afflict himself by fasting

V. lest he need help from other people

VI. and other people will not show him mercy."

VII. R. Judah said in the name of Rab:

VIII. "What is R. Yose's reasoning? It says, 'And Adam became a living spirit' (Gen. 2:7)—the spirit which I have given you—keep it alive."[17]

The anonymous baraita here appears to be the opposite of the anonymous Tosefta. While the Tosefta prohibited fasting for people in dangerous situations, the *B. Ta'anit* baraita permitted it. The phrase "for all of these" (*ve'al kulan*) means "in all of these cases"; that is, in all of these cases, an individual may afflict himself by fasting.

---

14. Malter's edition of *Ta'anit* here has "a wild animal" (*haya ra'ah*) instead of "evil spirits" (*ruach ra'ah*) (*Ta'anit*, ed. Henry Malter, p. 94, cf. *Dikdukei Soferim,* ad loc., note 70). The danger to a person being chased by "evil spirits" is explained by Pseudo-Rashi as a fear that he will drown in a river or fall into a dangerous place while running away (*B. Ta'anit* 22b, s.v. *mipnei ruach ra'ah*). The *Meiri* (*Ta'anit* 3:5) interprets the "evil spirits" in a more rationalistic way, as being a product of the person's imagination. He writes, "An individual being chased . . . by an evil spirit which frightened him and runs away because he imagines that a person is running after him."

15. The phrase "they blow the horn on the Sabbath" from the preceding Mishnah, though not found in the printed text of this baraita is found in the Munich manuscript, in Malter's edition of *Ta'anit* (p. 94) and in most of the readings of this text, according to Lieberman (*Toseftah Kifeshutah*, *Ta'anit*, p. 334, lines 76–77; cf. *Dikdukei Soferim,* ibid.).

16. The Rosh and the Rif here also rule that the individuals are permitted to afflict themselves by fasting; the Ran, though, has "the individuals are *not* permitted to afflict themselves by fasting," a reading that follows the Tosefta.

17. Sections VIII and IX will be discussed later in the section regarding fasting as inherently negative.

This baraita, then, does not limit supererogatory fasting as did the anonymous Tosefta passage.[18]

R. Yose's position, though, is consistent in both texts; he limits the individual's right to fast excessively, since excessive fasting will hurt him. (Just where he would draw the line, though, between permitted supererogatory fasting versus forbidden "excessive" fasting, is not mentioned.) In the Tosefta passage, the reason given for R. Yose's position is "lest he become a burden on the community and they will have to support him," with the emphasis being placed on the negative consequences that his behavior will create for the community. In the *B. Ta'anit* 22b parallel, however, the reason given is "lest he need help from other people *and other people will not show him mercy.*" The emphasis here is on the negative consequences that his fasting will create for himself; if other people will not show him mercy, then he will live in wretched poverty or even possibly die of hunger.

*Fasting that Interferes with Job Performance*

Another area of halakhah in which fasting was criticized because of its negative results was business ethics, when fasting detracted from one's ability to work. Tosefta *Baba Metzia* 8:2 contains a string of statements, all echoing the same theme:

I.    A worker is not allowed to do his own work during the night and then hire himself out [to work for someone else] during the day,

---

18. Another interpretation of this baraita harmonizes the two baraitot, by explaining that the *B. Ta'anit* 22b baraita refers only to people who were not in danger themselves but who were praying and fasting for others. The phrase "for all of these" (*ve'al kulan*), then, would mean "for all of these people." While the Tosefta forbidding fasting referred to the people actually at risk—to those captured within the city or trapped on the boat—the *B. Ta'anit* anonymous baraita permitting fasting refers to Jews outside of the scene of danger who wished to fast for their brethren (R. Yesha'aya Aharon, *Piskei Ri'az,* in *Piskei HaRid, Piskei Ri'az* (Jerusalem: Machon haTalmud HaYisraeli, 1971), vol. III, *Ta'anit* 3:7, also quoted in the *Shiltei Giborim,* "*Leshon Riaz*" printed with the Rif (*Ta'anit* 3:5). Lieberman, who favors this interpretation, also differentiates between an individual and the community in these cases. He writes that while the individuals were permitted to afflict themselves by fasting, the community may only fast occasionally (ibid., lines 76–77).

II. or to plow with his cow in the evening and then hire it out in the morning.

III. He may not starve and afflict himself

IV. and feed his food to his children,

V. because he will be stealing labor from his employer.

Sections I and II of this passage deal with simple business ethics: a person may not exhaust himself (or his animal), and then hire himself out for work the next day, since he would then be cheating his employer. Section III deals with the same concern, of cheating one's employer, but focuses on fasting as being the potential cause of the breach of business ethics. The term *afflict* himself in this context may be a synonym for starving himself, since it means causing oneself to suffer.[19] It could mean causing oneself to suffer in other ways as well, but these are not delineated.

While "starving himself and afflicting himself" usually connotes ascetic piety, the phrase "and feed his food to his children" sounds more like a situation of severe economic distress. One does not imagine a person feeding his food to his children as an act of piety. Instead, the image evoked is one of extreme poverty in which the father is trying to feed his children, at the cost of his own hunger.[20] Even if this is the case, the halakhah is that he is not allowed to do this.[21] This ruling refers both to the food that the employer provides

---

19. *The Arukh*, vol. 4, s.v. *sagaf*.

20. Jacob Neusner, in fact, translates this sentence as follows: "Nor may he deprive himself of food and starve himself *in order* to give his food to his children." He thus translates "and feed his food to his children" (*u-ma'achil*) as "in order to. . . ." (*The Tosefta*, trans. Jacob Neusner [New York: Ktav, 1981], ad loc.)

21. Maimonides quotes lines I through IV of this passage in the *Mishneh Torah*, Laws of Sekhirut 13:6. He adds the following explanations: A person should not starve himself and afflict himself and give his food to his children, because he would be stealing the labor he owes his employer. For he will lose his strength, and his mind will weaken, and he will not be able to do his work with strength. R. Moses of Coucy, the *S'MaG*, quotes the same passage (Tel Aviv: Opst Brody-Katz), Positive Commandment 92.

for him at his job[22] and his own food at home,[23] since the prohibition of starving oneself is stated as a general prohibition and is not limited only to starving oneself while "on the job."

There is a parallel to the Tosefta passage found in P. _Demai_ 7:3 (26b),[24] which is basically the same in sections I through III, but lacks section IV ("and he is not allowed to feed his children") and contains an additional passage in sections V through VIII.[25] According to this parallel, there is a definite connection here between business ethics and supererogatory anguish. The employee in this parallel is not starving himself to feed his children; he is fasting for ascetic reasons:

I.     A man should not plow with his cow at night, and then rent out the cow to others during the day.

II.    And he should not do his own work at night and then hire himself out to work for someone else during the day.

III.   He should not starve himself or afflict himself,

IV.    because he then takes away from the work [he owes] the landlord.

V.     R. Johanan came to a certain location and found a children's school teacher in a drowsy state.

---

22. The issue of whether an employee may use his employer's food to feed his family is debated at length in B. _Baba Metzia_ 92a–93a. The law according to the _Shulhan Arukh_ is that it is forbidden (_Hoshen Mishpat_ 337:15).

23. R. Joshua Falk of the sixteenth century (the _Perishah_ and the _Me'irat Einayim_), the _Tur, Shulhan Arukh_ 337:19, and Lieberman (_Tosefta Kifeshutah Baba Metzia_ 103:7, p. 260) all hold that the food being discussed here must be the food found in the worker's own house and not that which is provided for him by his employer during work hours. The Perishah argues his case, though, from the wording of the _Tur_ and _Shulhan Arukh,_ and not from the Tosefta. For the _Tur_ (earlier in the paragraph) and _Shulhan Arukh_ (par. 16) both state explicitly that an employee may not feed the food given him by his employer to his wife and children. Since that was already stated, the Perishah assumes that par. 19 is referring to the employee's own food.

24. This passage is not found in the Babylonian Talmud, though the sentences immediately following it in the Tosefta passage are found in B. _Baba Metzia_ 89a. It is quoted, though, in the Rif (_B.M.,_ chap. 7, p. 52b), the Rosh (ibid., chap. 7, par. 3) and Maimonides quoted earlier, and later in the _Tur_ and _Shulhan Arukh, Hoshen Mishpat_ 337:19.

25. This is true in all the available manuscripts of P. _Ta'anit,_ according to the _Synopse zum Talmud Yerushalmi,_ ad loc.

VI.   He asked them: "Why is he like this?"
VII.  They said to him: "He has been[26] fasting."
VIII. He said to him: "This behavior is forbidden to you. For when one labors for a human being, this [fasting excessively] is forbidden; all the more so when one labors for the Holy One Blessed be He.

Lines IV through VIII relate an incident recorded in the name of R. Johanan, involving a schoolteacher who was in a drowsy state. Rather than *ayenus* (found in the printed text) or the suggested emendation *atomos,* which means extremely weak or sickly,[27] the correct word here seems to be *ayenim* from the root *N.U.M.,* meaning to drowse or to sleep. This is, in fact, the word found in the Krotoschin edition of the *P. Ta'anit.*[28] R. Johanan then informs this sleepy teacher that his actions are forbidden, for he is cheating his employer, who in this case happens to be God Himself, since he is teaching God's Torah. The Talmudic sugya is giving an example of the principle it had just established, namely, that a person may not impose fasts on himself, if it will interfere with his ability to work.[29] R. Johanan emphasizes that a teacher of Torah must be especially vigilant about doing his work properly.

---

26. The *S'MaG* explains that *dehava tzayem* means that he fasted regularly (Positive Commandment 92).

27. *The Arukh HaShalem,* vol. I, s.v. *ayenus.* Alexander Kohut suggests that the correct word could be *atomos,* which means languid or feeble in Greek (cf. Marcus Jastrow, *A Dictionary* [New York: Judaica, 1975], s.v. *ayenis).* He suggests this emendation based on R. Moses Padua, *Hagahot Maimoniyot,* who writes *safra atimus* and explains that he was as weak as a sick eye (*Yad,* "Laws of Sechirut," 13:6) and on the Rash's text. The *S'MaG* (ibid.) also has *atimus* and explains it the same way (as meaning sick—he uses *ayin atum).*

28. Michael Sokoloff, *A Dictionary of Jewish Palestinian Aramaic of the Byzantine Period* (Ramat Gan: Bar Ilan University Press, 1990), s.v. *num,* p. 344b, and note 6 in *Mar'eh Mekomot veHagahot* in the margin of the Krotoschin edition of *P. Demai* 26b (written by R. Zalman Braun, Yudel of Slobodka and R. Mordechai Wiseman Chajes).

29. R. Moses of Padua (the *Hagahot Maimoniyot,* ibid., and the *Or Zarua* (section III, *Baba Metzia* 246) both quote the Avi Ezri, who wrote the following in his book *Aviasaf:* "A teacher is not allowed to stay up at night later than his usual bedtime, because the next day he will be too lazy to teach well. He should not deprive himself of food and drink if he is self

As was discussed in Chapter 1, scholars were permitted to impose "matters of anguish" on themselves; some opinions even encouraged scholars to do so (*T. Ta'anit* 1:7, *B. Ta'anit* 10b). Fasting (as has been noted) constitutes a clear example of matters of anguish. Sources in both the Babylonian and Palestinian Talmuds describe both tannaim and amoraim who fasted severely and were admired for their extreme piety.[30] These scholars lived according to the policy delineated by R. Yose and R. Simon b. Gamaliel (in *B. Ta'anit* 10b) that stated that a scholar may impose "matters of anguish" on himself and is remembered positively for his actions.

Yet just as there were those who opposed self-imposed "matters of anguish" for the general population, there were critical voices raised specifically against scholars who engaged in self-imposed fasts. R. Johanan's position (*P. Demai* 7:3 [26b]) just decribed represents one such opinion. R. Johanan was a first-generation Palestinian amora.

Two statements in *B. Ta'anit* 11b confirm that this same attitude was known in Babylonia as well. The first Babylonian statement (to be cited later) is attributed to R. Jeremiah b. Abba in the name of Reish Lakish. R. Jeremiah b. Abba was a third-generation Babylonian amora who moved to Israel.[31] Reish Lakish was a first-generation Palestinian amora:

I.   R. Jeremiah b. Abba said in the name of Resh Lakish:
II.  A scholar may not fast excessively because he lessens thereby his heavenly work.

Although the schoolteacher discussed by R. Yohanan did not necessarily have the status of the scholar mentioned here by R. Jeremiah b. Abba (in the name of Resh Lakish), the same principle was applied to both of these professions. Both are considered "employees" of God Himself, doing the heavenly work of teaching and studying Torah. Just as a scholar may not fast excessively, because then he will become too weak to study,[32] so too a

employed since he will not be able to study, and, similarly, he should not eat and drink too much."

30. S. Lowy, "The Motivation of Fasting in Talmudic Literature," *Journal of Jewish Studies* 9 (1958), pp. 22–23.

31. Hyman, *Toledot,* vol. II, p. 813.

32. Rashi, ad loc., s.v. *shememaet bimlekhet shamayim.*

schoolteacher may not fast excessively, because then he will not be able to teach.[33] Limitations were, thus, placed on supererogatory anguish for teachers (according to R. Johanan) and scholars (according to Reish Lakish) when it would interfere with their primary goal of studying and teaching.

The prohibition for scholars to fast excessively, though, does not contradict the Tosefta's encouragement of scholars to fast (T. Tosefta *Ta'anit* 1:7 discussed in the previous chapter). For the Tosefta passage that encouraged the individuals (who were identified as the scholars) to fast was dealing with public fasts in times of trouble, when the community suffered from lack of rain. R. Johanan and Reish Lakish, on the other hand, demanded that scholars limit their private, personal fasts.[34]

The second Babylonian statement (in *B. Ta'anit* 11b) criticizing scholars for excessive fasting (i.e., "matters of anguish") is attributed to R. Shesheth, a third-generation Babylonian amora:

R. Shesheth said: The young scholar who fasts excessively, let a dog devour his meal.

R. Shesheth here condemns excessive fasting for a young scholar in no uncertain terms. (Presumably, he would feel the same way about the same behavior in an old, hence weaker scholar.) He declares "let a dog devour his meal," thus rendering his fast meaningless, since then his fast would have the same (non)status as someone who fasts because they have nothing to eat.[35] He does not explain why he is so opposed to excessive fasting for a young scholar, but this will be explored later when the Talmudic sugya in which this statement appears is discussed. There are, thus, statements attributed to both Palestinian and Babylonian amoraim,

---

33. The Tur, in fact, connects both these sources, writing that both the scholar and the children's teacher may not fast excessively (*Orah Hayim* 571).

34. While the Tur (*Orah Hayim* 571) writes only that the scholar and the children's teacher should not fast, R. Yosef Karo in the *Shulhan Aruch,* ibid. (571:1,2), adds that scholars must fast in times of trouble. The Vilna Gaon (s.v. *ela im ken*) points out that "the individuals" (i.e., the scholars) fast even before the public in times of drought and continue to fast even after the public has finished.

35. Rashi, ad loc., s.v. *sheirutei.*

ranging from the first through the third generations, that criticize excessive fasting for teachers or scholars.

## Imposing Fasts on Children

*T. Yoma* 4:1–2 discusses how Shammai the Elder went against the accepted practice of permitting minors to eat on the Day of Atonement and did not want to feed his child. He was, however, forced to do so by the other sages:

I,1.   On the Day of Atonement, it is forbidden to eat, drink, wash. . . . [M]inors are permitted to do all of these. . . .

II,2.   Minors who are close to the age of maturity are taught [to fast] a year or two before [they mature], so that they will be accustomed to fulfilling the commandments.

III.   R. Akiba used to stop teaching in the study hall [on the Day of Atonement][36] for the minors, so that their fathers could feed them.

IV.   It happened that Shammai the Elder did not want to feed his son [on the Day of Atonement], and they decreed upon him and he fed him with his hand.[37]

We first have the explicit statement that children may eat on the Day of Atonement but should be trained to fast when they get close to maturity. We are then told that R. Akiba used to stop teaching in

---

36. There is another source, *B. Pesahim* 109a, which states that R. Akiba never said that it was time to stop studying in the House of Study except for on the eve of Passover, and on the *eve* of the Day of Atonement ("in order that they should give food to their children"). This Tosefta, nevertheless, refers to Yom Kippur itself, not the day before (*erev*) Yom Kippur (R. Tam, *Sefer HaYashar,* 631 [Vienna]; Meiri, *Eruvin* 40b; Lieberman, *Tosefta Kifeshuta Yoma* p. 249, pp. 812–813).

37. The Erfurt manuscript is significantly different, in that it reads, "He wanted to feed his son with one hand, and they decreed that he must feed him with two hands." This reading is closer to the reading in the sugya in *B. Yoma* 77b, which quotes the Shammai incident with a few significant textual variants and interprets it as being related to his reluctance to wash his hands on the Day of Atonement rather than his requirement that children fast.

the study hall, so that fathers could go home and feed their children. Shammai the Elder, however, did not want to feed his son on the Day of Atonement.

Shammai may have held that minors were obligated to fast on Yom Kippur, just as he held that they were obligated to sit in the sukkah.[38] This source, then, would be beyond the scope of this study, since it would then fall into the realm of stringency within the context of Halakhic debate, with the anonymous Mishnah ruling leniently and Shammai ruling in a stringent manner.

The wording of the Toseftah, however, may indicate a personal stringency, rather than an alternate Halakhic ruling. For the text (section IV) states that Shammai the elder "did not want to feed his son," not that he held it was forbidden. Assuming that Shammai did not actually rule that eating on Yom Kippur was prohibited for minors but rather chose to be stringent in how he personally raised his children, this source would then be directly relevant to this study. The issue at hand would be whether the rabbis permitted parents to force their young children to fast, a practice that is the equivalent of extreme self-denial for an adult. (The text indicates that the child was extremely young, since Shammai actually had to feed him with his hand.)

The rabbis, in this case, did not permit Shammai's stringency and insisted that he feed his son. The reason for the rabbis' insistence that he feed his son (and for R. Akiba's stopping the learning in the House of Study so that fathers could go home and feed their children) was, presumably, their concern lest fasting endanger the children's health.[39]

Saul Leiberman holds that this source is evidence for the existence of an ancient custom of having 1- and 2-year-old children fast on Yom Kippur.[40] He bases this argument on *Masekhet Soferim* 18:7:

I.   And there was a good custom in Jerusalem taught to young sons and daughters on a fast day:

---

38. *M. Sukkah* 2:8 and *B. Sukkah* 28b, Maimonides, *Commentary to the Mishnah* and the *Ran* ad loc., s.v. *nashim*.

39. Lieberman, ibid., p. 812.

40. S. Lieberman, "*Masekhet Soferim*," ed. Michael Higger, *Kiryat Sefer* XV (1938), pp. 56–57.

II.   at the age of 11 years, [they fast] till midday, at the age of
      12 years they fast the whole day,

III.  and afterwards they carry them and bring them close in
      front of every elder in order to be blessed."

This translation is based on the edition printed in the standard text
of the Talmud and on Michael Higger's critical version of the
tractate.[41] The Vilna Gaon emends the word "they carry them"
(*sovelo*) to "at the age of 13 they walk him (*molicho*) (meaning
accompany him) and bring him close."

Lieberman holds that Higger's text is wrong. He writes that six
out of seven of the manuscripts of this text have "at the age of 1 (*ben
shana*), they fast till midday, and at the age of 2, they fast all day." He
criticizes Higger for choosing to print the one text of the seven that
contains the ages of 11 and 12 rather than ages 1 and 2. He feels that
this text reflects an ancient custom of Jerusalem, to afflict 1- and
2-year-old children on Yom Kippur. He cites various sources as
evidence, including the previously cited Tosefta passage relating
how Shammai refused to feed his son. He also holds that the word
*sovelo* proves that a baby who is carried is being described.

Daniel Sperber agrees with Lieberman's assumption, writing
that "there is no place for these emendations" (of changing 1 and 2
years to 11 and 12 years),[42] and so does Isaac Gilat. To this writer,
however, Higger's emendations are valid. For while the sources
gathered by these scholars demonstrate that there was an ancient
custom for young children to fast, the children could not have been
as young as 1 and 2 years old. If the purpose, as the text states, was
to teach them how to fast, then the ages of 1 and 2 are extremely
young, since no education could take place with such little children.
Children of that age, most of whom were still being breastfed, are
too young to understand why food is being withheld from them; all
that would be accomplished is that they would cry incessantly,
because of their hunger and thirst. The Vilna Gaon's emendation of
"he accompanies him" may have been made precisely to prevent the

---

41. *Masekhet Soferim,* ed. M. Higger (New York: DeVei Rabban, 1937).

42. D. Sperber, *Minhagei Yisrael* (Jerusalem: Mossad HaRav Kook,
1991), vol. II, pp. 130–132, and note 12); I. Gilat, "Ben Shelosh Esreh
leMitzvot?" *Mehkerei Talmud* I, ed. J. Sussman and D. Rosenthal (Jerusalem,
Magnes: 1990), pp. 44–45.

misconception that a baby was being carried in to the elder for a blessing.

Although the specific ages of the children who fasted in Jerusalem remain unclear, what is clear is that the rabbis did not approve of the stringency that Shammai imposed on his son (*T. Yoma* 4:1–2). Their disapproval was expressed not merely in words but in action: "they decreed upon him" and thereby forced him to feed his son.[43]

## Stringency on the Sabbath That Endangers One's Life

The principle that danger to life overrides the restrictions of the Sabbath is the basis of the ruling that it is permissible to kill dangerous insects, snakes or scorpions on the Sabbath (*M. Shabbat* 16:5; *B. Shabbat* 121b; *P. Shabbat* 14:1). There is a debate in *B. Shabbat* 121b regarding which dangerous creatures should be killed automatically and which should be killed only when they are actually chasing someone and covered with a utensil if they are not chasing anyone. R. Joseph states that everyone agrees that all dangerous creatures may be killed if they are actively chasing someone, while the five extremely dangerous creatures that were enumerated by R. Joshua b. Levi may be killed automatically. Among those five to be killed automatically are a type of scorpion, a snake in the Land of Israel, and a certain type of wasp. The Talmudic sugya continues as follows:

I. A tanna recited before Rabba bar R. Huna:

II. He who kills snakes and scorpions on the Sabbath, the spirit of the hasidim is not pleased with him.

III. He said to him: And those hasidim—the spirit of the Sages[44] is not pleased with them (*ein ruah hakhamim nohah heimenu*).

IV. And this goes against R. Huna,

---

43. This ancient custom of parents forcing their young children to fast, either continued into medieval times or reemerged, only to meet rabbinic opposition once again (see Sperber, *Minhagei Yisrael*, vol. II, pp. 130–132, for references).

44. The Munich manuscript has "wisdom" (*hokhma*) here instead of "sages" (*hakhamim*).

V. [for R. Huna saw a man kill a wasp on the Sabbath, and he said to him:] "Have you finished [killing] all [wasps]?

According to this source, there were pietists who refused to kill snakes and scorpions on the Sabbath, contrary to Mishnaic halakhah. These pietists thus allowed their lives to be put into danger, rather than violate the Sabbath laws, and were displeased with the accepted halakhah which permitted the killing of dangerous creatures. Rabba bar R. Huna's response to the tanna, "and those hasidim—the spirit of the Sages is not pleased with them," expresses rabbinic disapproval of the practice of the hasidim, who endangered their lives by acting excessively stringent with regard to the Sabbath laws.[45]

According to Safrai, however, this whole debate was not an example of supererogatory piety to which the rabbis objected but instead was a halakhic dispute between the early pietists and the tannaim. He claims that this case demonstrates that the hasidic Halakhot represented a distinct Halakhic tradition, "which sometimes differs from the prevailing rulings," and are not simply "the practice of austerity."[46]

The debate found in this sugya, whether it be an actual Halakhic debate or an example of excessive "austerity," encompasses a vast period of time. For the hasidim that the tanna is describing lived in the Land of Israel during the first and second centuries, while Rabba bar R. Huna was a third-generation amora, living in third-century Babylonia. Although his disapproving comments refer back to a tannaitic practice, remnants of this practice apparently still existed, as we see from sections IV through V earlier that state that Rabba bar R. Huna's objection to the hasidim went against his father, who objected to someone who killed wasps on the Sabbath. When R. Huna said, "Have you finished [killing] all [wasps]," he was expressing his disapproval, since wasps are so numerous that nothing is accomplished by killing only a few.[47] According to this

---

45. Other sources related to the issue of endangering one's life on the Sabbath will be examined in Chapter 4's discussion of the foolish pietist.

46. Safrai, "Teaching of Pietists," pp. 24–25. Kampen challenges Safrai's theory, but his arguments are not very convincing (John Kampen, *The Hasideans*, pp. 199–200, 206–207).

47. Rashi, s.v. *shleimtinhu lekulhu*.

sugya, the permission to violate the Sabbath to kill dangerous creatures was not yet unanimously accepted, even during amoraic times.[48]

## Rabbinic Suspicion of Ascetic Behavior

Another source that is relevant here reflects rabbinic suspicion of the sincerity of someone acting in an ascetic manner. *B. Sanhedrin* 25a discusses a case of someone imposing a matter of anguish on himself to show that he has repented. The amoraim doubt his sincerity:

I.   A certain slaughterer was found to have passed a *terefah* (unkosher meat, as fit for food), so R. Nahman disqualified and dismissed him.[49]

II.  Thereupon he went and let his hair and nails grow.

III. Then R. Nahman thought of reinstating him, but Raba said to him: Perhaps he is only pretending [repentance].

IV.  What then is his remedy—The course suggested by R. Iddi b. Abin, who said:

V.   He who is suspected of passing *terefoth* cannot be rehabilitated unless he leaves for a place where he is unknown and finds an opportunity of returning a lost article of considerable value, or of condemning as *terefah* meat of considerable value, belonging to himself.

The butcher's choice of penitence—growing his hair and nails long—(self-affliction),[50] was not trusted by Raba, who felt that he might be insincere. Instead, the Talmud suggested a penitence that

---

48. There is a great deal of literature, both primary and secondary, regarding the killing of snakes and scorpions. See, for example, *Berakhot* 5:1, which states that "even if a snake was twisted about his heel, he may not interrupt his prayer," and Safrai, "Teaching of Pietists," pp. 28–32.

49. This is according to the printed text and the Munich manuscript. The Rif (ed. Zaks) here has "he excommunicated him." Maimonides may also have have "he excommunicated him," for the *Kesef Mishneh* on the *Yad*, "Laws of Talmud Torah" 6:14, gives this passage as Maimonides' source for stating that a butcher who passes *terefoth* to the public is excommunicated.

50. One of the features of the early Christian monks in Syria and Armenia was that they never cut their hair or nails (see A. Voobus, *History*

"fit the crime"—it required him to demonstrate that he would observe the law, even in the face of monetary loss. His "ascetic penitence" was not acceptable to Raba (although R. Nahman was prepared to trust that he was sincere).

This suspicious attitude is also found in the sources discussing the "ascetic woman" of *Sotah* 3:4 (see Chap. 3). Abstinent women, or women who fasted and prayed more than usual, were regarded suspiciously and their sincerity was questioned, since it was viewed as a pretense for piety, used as a cover-up for sin.

All of the categories of asceticism discussed here—namely, fasting in dangerous situations, fasting that interfered with one's job, imposing a fast on children, and ascetic behavior undertaken for insincere reasons—limited these practices because of the negative consequences that would result from this behavior, not because something is wrong with the anguish per se. Theoretically, if someone in danger would not become weak from fasting, then he or she was permitted to fast, and, even according to R. Yose, if an individual was wealthy and sure that he would not become a burden on the community, then he too could afflict himself by fasting. If a laborer or a teacher could fast and still function perfectly well the next day, then he also would be allowed to do so.[51] If someone grew his hair and nails as a sign of repentance and the rabbis had no reason to doubt his sincerity, then his behavior would also have been acceptable. Ascetic behavior, according to these sources, is negative only within certain contexts.[52] In the next section, sources from

---

*of Asceticism,* vol. II, p. 27). This source reflects rabbinic mistrust of this type of extreme behavior.

51. R. Nissim in *Ta'anit* 22b, s.v. *ve'al kulam,* makes precisely this point and writes that when Mar son of Rabina fasted all year long, he was allowed to afflict himself with fasting in this manner because he did not have to support himself.

52. The Sefer Hasidim (thirteenth century) spells out this attitude explicitly. While he writes that excessive fasting is recommended for someone who is tempted to sin, he also instructs many different types of people to avoid fasting too much. He instructs teachers, scribes, and workers not to fast excessively so that they do not become too weak to work (Wistineski edition 66; Margaliot ed. 617). As was mentioned in Chapter 1, he also instructs anyone whose fasting would endanger themselves or others not to fast. The examples he gives are people in a city

which we learn that ascetic behavior is inherently negative will be explored.

## ASCETIC BEHAVIOR AS INHERENTLY NEGATIVE

As mentioned, another theme found in the Talmudic sources relates to supererogatory anguish as wrong on an ideological level. Fasting, for example, is seen as problematic in and of itself and not only because of its negative consequences. The sources that demonstrate this theme criticize self-denial in general, holding that it goes against basic principles of Judaism.

### The Paradigm of the Nazirite

The issue of whether supererogatory anguish was criticized or praised is integrally connected with the debate concerning whether a nazirite (Numbers 6) was regarded as a sinner or as a holy person. This is because the nazirite practices certain forms of self-denial; he denies himself alcoholic beverages and wine products and avoids cutting his hair and having contact with dead bodies, even if they are family members. His reason for accepting these stringencies, presumably, is to express his piety. The nazirite wishes to do more, in a spiritual sense, than is required of the average Jew, and his vows thus fall into the category of supererogatory behavior.

Those who held that the nazirite was holy would also, presumably, have held that self-denial in general was positive.[53] Those, on the other hand, who held that he was a sinner would also, presumably, have criticized and limited the religious value of self-denial. The sources, in fact, reflect precisely this connection.[54]

---

surrounded by non-Jews and all types of people who are needed by other people, such as someone going to ransom captives or help save a life, a midwife, and someone who takes care of an elderly parent or of an ill person (Wistineski ed. 68; Margaliot ed. 618).

53. See, for example, the *Sifrei Zuta, Numbers* 6:8, which states that the nazirite is called holy "because he has decided to follow the way of abstinence and purity."

54. Steven Fraade, "The Nazirite in Ancient Judaism," *Ascetic Behavior in Greco-Roman Antiquity,* ed. George Vincent Wimbush (Minneapolis: Fortress, 1990), p. 219, note 16.

The classic debate regarding the nazirite appears in the *Sifre Numbers* 30:

I.   "And [the priest] shall make atonement on his behalf [for the sin that he committed through the corpse (*al hanefesh*): For he sinned through the corpse." [*Numbers* 6:11]

II.  R. Eleazar haKappar says: Against which soul (*nefesh*) did he sin that he needs atonement? For he denied his soul wine. And we can make this inference from a minor premise to a major premise: if one who denies his soul wine needs atonement, how much more so one who denies himself everything.

III. R. Ishmael says: "Scripture [in speaking of atonement] refers only to the impure Nazirite, as it says, 'And shall make atonement on his behalf for the sin that he committed through the corpse,' for he became impure through contact with the corpse."

When the nazirite becomes impure through contact with a corpse, he must bring a sacrifice. The Torah explains that he brings this sacrifice because he "sinned through the (*nefesh*)." R. Eleazar HaKappar translates the word *nefesh* here as soul rather than corpse, and explains that he sinned against his own soul by denying himself wine. R. Ishmael, on the other hand, translates the word *nefesh* as corpse—he sinned by becoming impure because of the dead body. This controversy represents a fundamental difference in outlook regarding self-imposed stringency. According to R. Eleazar HaKappar, naziritism is sinful; hence, self-denial of all sorts is sinful. According, though, to R. Ishmael, the verse says nothing of that sort, and the nazirite remains "holy unto the Lord" (Numbers 6:8).[55]

---

55. The question of the nazirite's motivations for taking his vows is another important issue to consider. David HaLivni Weiss claims that the practice of contracting nazirite vows for frivolous, nonreligious reasons, was already common in the times of Simon the Just and became even more prevalent in later times. For that reason, Simon the Just refused to partake of guilt offerings brought by nazirites and made an exception only in the

This same baraita (*Sifre Numbers* 30) is quoted in numerous other Talmudic sugyas. In three of these,[56] it is used as a source to condemn supererogatory behavior other than the nazirite vows. In other words, the debate regarding the nazirite (whether he is praised or criticized) serves as a paradigm for tannaitic and amoraic evaluation of self-denial in general.[57]

The first of the three citations of the nazirite paradigm is found in *B. Ta'anit* 11a–b, where this baraita is cited as a tannaitic source to support Samuel's criticism of excessive fasting:

I.   Samuel said: "Whoever (*kol*) sits and [afflicts himself with] fasts is called a sinner."

II.  He is of the same opinion as the following tanna. For it has been taught:

III. Eliezer HaKappar Beribi[58] says: "What is Scripture refer-

---

case of the shepherd who proved his sincerity. See *B. Nedarim* 9b; *P. Nedarim* 1:1; and Weiss, "On the Supposed Anti-Asceticism or Anti-Naziritism of Simon the Just," *Jewish Quarterly Review* 58 (1968), pp. 248–250.

56. This same baraita is also quoted in *B. Nedarim* 10a, after Abbaye lists three tannaim who all agreed that a nazirite is a sinner: "Abbaye said: Simon the Just, R. Simeon, and R. Eleazar HaKappar are all of the same opinion, viz. that a nazir is a sinner." The Talmudic sugya then quotes this baraita to demonstrate R. Eleazar HaKappar's opinion. In *P. Nedarim* 1:1, R. Eleazar HaKappar's position is attributed to R. Simeon, who held that the early hasidim sinned when they vowed to be nazirites.

57. Fraade, "The Nazirite," p. 215.

58. Many scholars hold that there were two tannaim (a father and his son) with similar names. The father was called R. Eliezer HaKappar, and the son was called either R. Eliezer HaKappar Beribi or Bar Kappara. Bar Kappara was an important tanna who lived during the times of R. Judah the Prince (Dan Urman, "R. Eliezer haKappar," *Be'er Sheva* II [1985], p. 8, note 7). Urman suggests that the opposite is true—that R. Eliezer HaKappar (the father) was really Bar Kappara, based on his analysis of sixteen cases which the names R. Eliezer HaKappar and Bar Kappara are used to express the same view, while the names R. Eliezer the son of R. Eliezer HaKappar is interchanged with R. Eliezer HaKappar Beribi (Urman, ibid., pp. 7–25). The case of the nazirite discussed here challenges his conclusion. For R. Eliezer HaKappar (in *Sifre Numbers* 30) and R. Eliezer HaKappar Beribi (in *B. Ta'anit* 10b) express the same view. Perhaps Urman's

ring to when it says [of the nazirite], 'And make atonement for him, for he sinned against the soul.' Against which soul did he sin? [It must refer to the fact that] he denied himself wine.

IV.     We can now make this inference from a minor premise to a major premise: "If this man [the nazirite] who denied himself only wine is called a sinner, how much more so he who denies himself the enjoyment of ever so many things."

V.      R. Eleazar says: "He is called 'Holy' as it is said, 'He shall be holy, he shall let the locks of the hair of his head grow long' (Numbers 6:5).

VI.     And if he, who only denied himself one thing, is called holy, so much more so someone who denies himself everything [will be called holy]."

VII.    And for Samuel, 'holy' refers to the long hair. And for R. Eleazar, his being called a 'sinner' refers to his having become ritually impure.

VIII.   But did R. Eleazar really say this?

IX.     For R. Eleazar said, "A person should always relate to himself as if the insides of his body are holy, since it is stated: "Within your midst, I am holy, and I will not come into the city" (Hosannah 11:9).

X.      This is not a contradiction. One [source] refers to someone who can fast easily [and is called "holy"], and the other refers to someone who can not fast easily (and is called a sinner).

XI.     Reish Lakish said: "He is called a Hasid, as it says, 'He who does good to his own soul is a merciful man (*ish hasid*): but he that troubles his own flesh is wicked'" (Proverbs 11:17).

XII.    R. Sheshet said: "The young scholar who sits and fasts, let a dog devour his meal."

XIII.   R. Jeremiah b. Abba said: "There are no public fasts in Babylonia, except for the ninth of Ab."

XIV.    R. Jeremiah b. Abba said in the name of Reish Lakish, "A

desire to solve the apparent contradiction between the archaeological findings at Dabbura and certain Talmudic statements led him to a premature conclusion that did not account for all of the sources.

scholar may not afflict himself by fasting because he lessens thereby his heavenly work."

Samuel's statement (section I) is clearly directed at anyone ("Whoever—*kol*"), be they scholar or common person. While Samuel gives no reason why he held that someone who fasts excessively is called a sinner, the Talmudic sugya (in section II) connects his opinion to that of R. Eliezer HaKappar, the tanna of the baraita who called the nazirite a sinner and then inferred that anyone who fasts excessively is also considered a sinner. This argument, then, reflects an antiascetic motif that can be found in various sources throughout Talmudic literature. The basic idea, which can be inferred from R. Eliezer HaKappar Beribi's statement, is that God gave the world to human beings to use and enjoy, and when they do not partake of God's creations, it is as if they are denying or scorning His gifts. The Talmud here understands Samuel's position as being based on this antiascetic school of thought.

This passage continues by questioning whether R. Eleazar really held that a nazirite is termed holy (section VII). R. Eleazar is quoted as having stated that a person should treat his body with respect and not afflict it, since it is as if God himself dwells within it. Afflicting the body by denying oneself wine should then be discouraged by him, for it shows that the person is not taking care of the body given to him by God to "house" the individual's God-given spirit. This antiascetic approach would thus go against his words that praised the nazirite's self-denial (section V).

The sugya resolves this difficulty by dividing people into two groups. If fasting is easy for someone, then he is deemed holy by R. Eleazar. If it is difficult and causes physical suffering, then he is deemed a sinner.[59]

Reish Lakish is then quoted as saying that "He" is called a hasid (section X). The verse "He who does good to his soul is a man of mercy (*hesed*)," according to this interpretation, refers to someone who fasts, and fasting is considered to be good for the soul.[60] Reish

---

59. The medieval commentators codified this subjective element. The *Tur* and *Shulhan Arukh* (*Orah Hayim* 571, 1) write that "Someone who sits and fasts—if his body can handle it easily, is called holy, and if not—then he is called a sinner."

60. R. Gershom, ad loc., s.v. *Reish Lakish*.

Lakish's usage of the term *hasid* to praise someone who fasts corresponds to the usage of the term *holy* immediately before, as a description of someone who fasts easily.[61]

It is in this context that the remark of R. Sheshet, in section XI, is quoted. Although he does not explain why the young scholar who fasted excessively deserved to have a dog devour his meal, he may have agreed with the position stating that self-denial was wrong and felt that a young scholar should be discouraged from engaging in this type of behavior. He may also, on the other hand, have agreed with Reish Lakish's position (quoted in section XIII) that forbade fasting for scholars because the fasting would weaken them and detract from their ability to study.[62]

The Talmudic sugya then ends by quoting Reish Lakish's comments advising the scholar not to fast, since he will lessen his ability to study. While Reish Lakish in section X described someone

---

61. A second and diametrically opposed interpretation of Reish Lakish's intent is that this verse refers to someone who does not fast and is thereby treating his soul in a respectful manner. Reish Lakish would then be supporting the second part of the conclusion here, namely, that someone who does not fast (because it is difficult for them) is doing the right thing (Tosafot, ad loc., s.v. *gomel nafsho*). Still a third explanation is that the first half of the verse "He who does good to his own soul is a merciful man" refers to someone who fasts, who is called merciful (*ish hasid*), and the second half, "but he that troubles his own flesh is wicked," also refers to someone who fasts, who is called wicked (Pseudo-Rashi, ad loc., s.v. *niqra hasid* and *veokher she'ero*). This latter explanation meshes perfectly with both parts of the sugya's conclusion—namely, that someone who can fast easily and does so is called holy (*ish hasid*), while someone who has difficulty fasting yet persists in doing so is called a sinner (i.e., wicked). The difficulty, though, with this explanation is that Reish Lakish prefaced his quote of the verse with only a positive statement of "He is called a hasid"; he does not say "he is also called a sinner."

62. Following R. Sheshet, the sugya quotes R. Jeremiah b. Abba saying that in Babylonia, there are no public fasts except for the ninth of Ab. (This statement is attributed to Samuel in *B. Pesahim* 54b and *B. Ta'anit* 12b.) This statement has been interpreted as a move to limit the number and strictness of public fasts by Samuel; see Lowy, "The Motivation of Fasting," p. 29. Lowy claims that in the amoraic period, private fasts amongst the scholars increased (pp. 22–23), while public fasts decreased (p. 29); his evidence for this distinction, however, is not convincing.

who fasts as a *hasid,* the statement attributed to him here contains the opposite message. We thus see within this passage a diversity of viewpoints regarding supererogatory anguish, with the vows of the nazirite being used as a paradigm for evaluating the value of fasting in general.

As noted, R. Eliezer HaKappar Beribi's baraita regarding the nazirite (*Sifre Numbers* 30) was used as a model for criticizing other supererogatory behaviors besides fasting. The second source which quotes this baraita (*P. Nedarim* 9:1 [41b]) uses it to support an amora who criticizes people who vow not to eat bread:[63]

I.  R. Hanina of Tzippori in the name of R. Pinhas . . .
II. "If one vowed not to eat bread, woe is to him if he eats, and woe is to him if he does not eat.
III. If he eats, then he is not keeping his vow.
IV. If he does not eat, then he is sinning against his soul (*hatei al nafshei*). . . .
V. R. Dimi in the name of R. Isaac: "It is not enough for you, whatever the Torah forbade you, that you go and look to forbid yourself other things,
VI. "To bind with a bond (*le'esor isar*) (Numbers 30:3)"[64] [to make a vow adding prohibitions to those that were already in the Torah is prohibited].[65]

---

63. As was discussed in the introduction, rabbinic criticism of vows in general will not be included in this study, since the criticism is usually directed toward the act of taking a vow and then, in all likelihood, having difficulty keeping it. When, though, rabbinic criticism of vows involving self-denial includes a condemnation of the content of the vow itself, then those sources will be examined. *P. Nedarim* 9:1 (41b) is an example of this type of source.

64. *Korban haEdah,* ad loc.

65. R. Dimi's statement sounds, at first glance, similar to the prohibition known as *bal tosif*—"Do not add" to the commandments of the Torah. This prohibition is derived from Deuteronomy 13:1, which states, "Regarding all the things which I command you, these you shall take care to observe; do not add to them and do not subtract from them." This prohibition of adding to the Torah could, theoretically, have been interpreted as forbidding all supererogatory behavior. However, no such link is

In this source, the baraita condemning the nazirite is cited in section IV as criticism of someone who vows not to eat bread. R. Hanina of Sephoris in the name of R. Pinhas (both Palestinian amoraim) holds that when someone makes a vow not to eat bread, he is committing a sin (of depriving himself of food) if he fulfills that vow. He uses the wording found in the verse quoted earlier, that a nazirite brings a sacrifice because "he has sinned against his soul."[66]

Following R. Hanina's statement, R. Dimi (one of the third-century *nehutei*[67] who moved from Babylonia to the Land of Israel), exclaims in utter annoyance: was it not enough for you to keep the prohibitions of the Torah that you need to add to them prohibitions of your own! He quotes part of a verse in Numbers 30:3 to support his point with a play on the words "to bind (*le'esor*) with a bond (*isar*)." He interprets those words as "to prohibit (*le'esor*) is prohibited (*isar* = *asur*)." A related statement is attributed to R. Dimi in *B. Nedarim* 77b that demonstrates his negative attitude toward vows in general:

---

made in the Talmudic sources between this prohibition and self-imposed stringency. Instead, the prohibition of *bal tosif* was applied to very specific and circumscribed situations, involving adding to a mitzvah that was already in the Torah and claiming the addition to be Pentateuchal (Maimonides, *Yad*, "Laws of Mamrim," 2:9). Some of these situations are the prohibition of adding a fifth compartment to the tefillin (four are understood to be prescribed in the Torah) (*Sanhedrin* 11:3), or of adding a fifth species to the lulav on Sukkot (*Sifre Re'eh* 82), or of a priest's adding a fourth blessing to the three Priestly Blessings (*Rosh Hashanah* 28b). All of these are examples of adding to pre-existent Pentateuchal laws. Supererogatory behavior, then, which did not involve such tampering and instead consisted of adding new expressions of piety, was not included in this prohibition. For a general overview of the laws of *bal tosif*, see *Encyclopedia Talmudit* (Jerusalem: Encyclopedia Talmudit, 1951), vol. 3, s.v. *bal tosif*.

66. This baraita is also found in *B. Nazir* 19a, to explain that R. Ishmael agreed with R. Eliezer HaKappar and held that making vows in general was a sin.

67. *Nehutei* were amoraim who traveled back and forth from Babylonia to Israel, spreading Torah teachings from location to location.

For R. Dimi,[68] the brother of R. Safra, taught: He who vows, even though he fulfills it is designated a sinner."[69]

R. Dimi's exclamation in *P. Nedarim* 9:1 (41B) demonstrates that he was against vowing to forbid behaviors that were permitted by the Torah (i.e. ascetic vows). This statement can be interpreted in a narrow sense, as meaning that the prohibitions of the Torah should not be added to specifically and only by making vows. It can also, however, be interpreted in a broader sense. His opposition to vows of self-denial may have extended to ascetic practices that people accepted even without the commitment of the vow (i.e., supererogatory anguish, which is the topic of this chapter). This inference is based on section V of *P. Nedarim* 9:1 (41b), where he states that the prohibitions already in the Torah are sufficient and should not be added to.

In a third source (*B. Baba Kama* 91b), the baraita of R. Eliezer HaKappar Beribi (*Sifre Numbers* 30) is quoted to provide a basis for the prohibition of hurting oneself. The passage begins with a controversy regarding whether a person is allowed to injure himself. M. *Baba Kama* 8:6 states that "where one injures oneself, though forbidden, he is exempt (from paying a penalty)." The Talmud then quotes Leviticus 5:4 implying that one could make an oath to harm

---

68. This position dates back to tannaitic times, to a debate between R. Meir and R. Judah: "For it was taught: 'Better it is that thou shouldst not vow, than that thou shouldst vow and not pay. Better than both is not to vow at all'; thus said R. Meir. R. Judah said: 'Better than both is to vow and repay'" (*B. Ta'anit* 9a). (The same debate is recorded in *P. Nedarim* 1:1, but the names are reversed.) R. Dimi follows R. Meir's position but elaborates on it by saying that someone who vows and fulfills that vow is actually a sinner.

69. This same statement is attributed to Samuel in *B. Nedarim* 22a, which is interesting, since Samuel also expressed anti-ascetic opinions such as "He who afflicts himself by fasting is called a sinner." While this negative attitude toward vows can be found in the sources, an equally positive attitude toward them can also be found, such as R. Judah's position quoted earlier, "Better than both is to vow and repay" (*B. Ta'anit* 9a) and R. Nathan's statement that "Whoever makes a vow, it is as if he built an altar" (*B. Nedarim* 22a, 59a, 60b). (Lieberman in "Oaths and Vows" stresses the Rabbis' negative attitudes toward vows; he does not discuss these positive statements—see pp. 115–116.)

himself. Samuel then states that the harm referred to in that verse was fasting, which harms a person yet is still permitted.[70]

Following Samuel's comment, the Talmudic sugya continues to discuss the different views regarding whether self-injury is permitted and searches for the identity of the author of the Mishnah forbidding it. It finally quotes the baraita of R. Eliezer HaKappar Beribi to prove that he is the tanna of the Mishnah who held that self-injury (an extreme form of self-denial) is forbidden.

The baraita of R. Eliezer HaKappar Beribi, stating that a nazirite is a sinner, is thus used as a source to criticize three other types of supererogatory anguish: fasting excessively, vowing not to eat bread, and injuring oneself. The idea uniting all of these sources is that just as the nazirite is considered a sinner because he denied himself wine, so all people who deny themselves food or who hurt their bodies in other ways are, likewise, sinning. Denying oneself food and hurting one's body were, undoubtedly, sometimes practiced by people for unknown reasons, or because of mental illness. These forms of self-denial, however, are classic examples of behaviors universally associated with ascetic piety—with a desire to renounce "immediate sensual or profane gratifications . . . in order to attain a higher spiritual state."[71] While people in Talmudic times often made vows out of anger or a flippant desire to prove a point,[72] vowing specifically not to eat bread, the main staple of the diet in Talmudic times, would, presumably, be undertaken only for the serious purpose of ascetic piety. For vowing not to eat bread was almost like vowing not to eat at all.

## Extreme Asceticism as a Response to the Destruction

In other sources, theological objections to self-denial are made without invoking the concept of the nazirite. As was discussed in the

---

70. This appears to contradict his statement in _B. Ta'anit_ 11b that someone who afflicts himself with fasting is called a sinner. Perhaps, though, Samuel used the word _sinner_ loosely, as a way of expressing his disapproval of fasting, even though it was not technically forbidden.

71. See Walter O. Kaelber, "Asceticism," _Encyclopedia of Religion,_ pp. 441–442.

72. See Lieberman, "Oaths and Vows," pp. 115–143, and Adin Steinsaltz, _Introduction to B. Nedarim_ (Jerusalem: HaMakhon HaYisraeli LePirsumim Talmudiyim, 1991), p. 7.

introduction to this study, Baruch Bokser writes that "the Temple's destruction initially posed a traumatic crisis. . . . Jews developed new forms of religiosity and piety" to overcome their crisis.[73] After the destruction (70 C.E.), segments of the community took on ascetic practices as a sign of mourning. Tosefta *Sotah* 15:11–12[74] describes this phenomenon, as well as the Rabbinic reaction it evoked:

11.

I.   When the Temple was destroyed for the second time, large numbers in Israel became ascetics, binding themselves neither to eat meat nor to drink wine.

II.  R. Joshua got into conversation with them.

III. He said to them: "My children, why do you not eat meat?"

IV.  They said to him: "[How could] we eat meat, which was always sacrificed upon the altar, when we no longer have an altar?"

V.   He said to them: "If that is your argument, then we can no longer eat bread . . . we can no longer drink water . . . we can no longer eat dates and grapes [since they were all used in the Temple ritual]."

VI.  They were silent.

12.

I.   He said to them: "My children, to mourn too much is impossible, and not to mourn is impossible,

---

73. Baruch M. Bokser, "Rabbinic Responses to Catastrophe: From Continuity to Discontinuity," *Proceedings of the American Academy for Jewish Research* 50 (1983), p. 61. The new forms of piety that Bokser discusses in this article, however, are the increased stress on the importance of prayer, charity, and acts of lovingkindness (p. 37); he does not discuss ascetic responses to the destruction.

74. *T. Sotah* 15:10, immediately preceding this passage, discusses R. Yishmael's refusal to legislate that these extreme ascetic practices become the law. This passage was not included in this study, since he agreed that these practices were appropriate in theory and may not have objected to individuals imposing these stringencies on themselves. His only objection was to legislating that extreme asceticism be mandatory for the whole nation, since "the court does not impose a decree on the community unless the majority can endure it."

II.  but instead, this is what the Rabbis said, 'A person plasters his house, and leaves a section (unplastered), in memory of Jerusalem.'"

R. Joshua appears to have held that excessive mourning was not an ideal.[75] For he states, "to mourn too much is impossible" after demonstrating that if meat and wine were to be restricted because they were used in Temple worship, then bread, water, dates, and grapes should likewise be forbidden, since they were also used in Temple worship. To be logically consistent, then all food staples, including bread and water, should likewise be denied; this would lead to massive starvation, obviously not an ideal response to anything. What R. Joshua meant by "to mourn too much is impossible" was that it was logically absurd and even dangerous for the Jewish people, since carried to its logical conclusions, virtually all food should be avoided in mourning for the Temple. Starvation, as a sign of mourning, is not an ideal according to R. Joshua but an absurd and dangerous situation that had to be prevented.[76] Instead, symbolic and more easily observable mourning rituals were legislated by the rabbis to commemorate the destruction of the Temple (such as leaving a section of one's house unplastered).

## Vows of Self-Denial

Within the laws of vows in general, we have clear evidence that the tannaim (expounding, in this case, on a verse in the Torah) tried to limit self-denial. *M. Nedarim* 11:1 states that a husband or father[77] can annul any vows made by his wife or daughter that involve

---

75. R. Joshua also objected to a fast decreed on Hanukkah in Lod after the destruction, against the specific instructions of *Megillat Ta'anit,* and publicly went to bathe on that day (*Ta'anit* 2:14; *P. Nedarim* 8:1; Urbach, "Iskizm VeYisurim," p. 55).

76. In the Talmudic sugya in *B. Baba Batra* 60b, however, R. Joshua is quoted as stating, "To mourn overmuch is also impossible, because we do not impose a decree on the community unless the majority can endure it." R. Joshua, according to this reading, agreed with R. Ishmael and held that ascetic denial was an ideologically correct response to the destruction but that it was too difficult for the nation as a whole to observe.

77. The law is equivalent for husbands and wives, and fathers and daughters (see *Sifrei Numbers* 144, ed. Horovitz, pp. 206–207).

supererogatory anguish. This law is based on the verse in Numbers 30:14, "Every vow, and every binding oath *to afflict the soul,* her husband may let it stand, or her husband may make it void." From this verse, the tannaim derive that the husband may not annul all vows made by his wife but may annul only vows of self-affliction.[78] The Mishnah codifies this law as follows:

I.   Now these are the vows which he can annul:
II.  Vows which involve self-denial [e.g.] "If I bathe," or "If I do not bathe," "If I adorn myself," or "If I do not adorn myself."
III. R. Yose said: These are not vows of self-denial, but the following are vows of self-denial: viz. if she says "Konam[79] be the produce of the [whole] world to me," he can annul,
IV.  "Konam be the produce of this country to me," he can bring her that of a different country,
V.   "[Konam be] the fruits of this shop-keeper to me," he cannot annul, but if he can obtain his sustenance only from him [this particular shop-keeper, then] he can annul: this is R. Yose's opinion.

The Talmudic sugya (*B. Nedarim* 79b) following this Mishnah explains the extent of this ruling, stating that while a husband can also annul vows that affect the sexual relationship between him and his wife, his annulment of her vows of self-denial are longer lasting:

I.   He can annul both, but vows of self-denial he can permanently annul;
II.  but if they involve no self-denial [but affect their relationship], the annulment is valid only so long as she is married to him, but if he divorces her, the vow takes effect.

This source demonstrates the negative attitude found in the Talmudic literature to vows involving self-denial. The husband (and father) were given permission to annul this specific type of vow, demonstrating that it was considered undesirable behavior. In this

---

78. *Sifrei,* ibid.; *B. Nedarim* 79b.

79. *Konam* is a term used to introduce a vow of self-denial (see *B. Nedarim* 10a).

source, however, the tannaim seem to be frowning specifically on female asceticism, whether the female be single or married. While the girl/woman's vow would be annuled by her caretaker (be it her father or her husband), the adult males were responsible for their own vows and had to go through a formal vow annulment ceremony. No such annulment ceremony is delineated for male ascetic vows, either in the Torah or in the Mishnah, and a woman is not permitted to demand that her husband go to court in order to annul his vows of self-denial. Although the many anti-nazirite and anti-ascetic views of the tannaim and amoraim quoted in this chapter clearly demonstrate that rabbinic criticism of asceticism applied to men as well as women, this Mishnah may be demonstrating that female asceticism was singled out for special censure.[80] The tannaim and amoraim may have been concerned lest the wife not be able to fulfill her marital obligations to her husband. While this same concern would apply to a man as well, it is not voiced.

Dead Sea Scroll passages discuss the husband's/father's rights to annul their wife's/daughter's oaths. *Zadokite Fragments* XVI, 7–13, states that a husband can annul a wife's oath. No mention is made there, however, of the specific type of oath that he can annul, and we cannot assume that the sect placed the same restrictions on taking vows as did the tannaim.[81] The author of the *Temple Scroll,* however (11QT LII, 11–LIV, 7) paraphrases Numbers 30:14 and singles out vows of self-affliction as a type of vow that a husband may confirm or annul:

I.   (As to) [any vow] or any binding o[ath to afflict oneself,]
II.  her husband may con[firm it] or her husband [may] annul it on the day when he hears it, in which case I will forgive [he]r.

The actual words "to afflict oneself," though, are missing from the scroll (as is most of section I) and are reconstructed by Yadin based

---

80. This discussion will be continued in Chapter 3's discussion of Mishnah *Sotah* 3:4, which also censures female asceticism in particular.

81. Lawrence H. Schiffman, "The Law of Vows and Oaths (Numbers 30, 3–16), in the *Zadokite Fragments* and the *Temple Scroll,*" *Revue de Qumran,* 57–58 (1991), p. 204.

on Numbers 30:14.[82] Assuming that his reconstruction is correct, how the Dead Sea Sect understood these words and whether their interpretation agreed with that of the tannaim still remains unknown.

While Qumran practices remain unclear, the exact opposite of the tannaitic-amoraic stance against female vows of self-denial can be found amongst the early Christians. Some Church fathers tried to preserve marriages, whereas other patristic writers "encouraged [even married] women to adopt ascetic lives—lives that would free them from submission to their husbands."[83] Virginity and abstinence were considered so holy a virtue by some that even women who were already married were urged to separate from their husbands. For example, the Acts of Judas Thomas (written in Syria, 220 c.e.), contains a dramatically told story of a woman portrayed as a model of virtue, who became celibate against her husband's will and to his terrible distress.[84] Parents were also counseled by some church fathers to encourage their daughters to adopt a life of virginity, to the extent that Ambrose, in the fourth century, even implies that "Providence arranged the death of a recalcitrant father who hindered his daughter's adoption of the ascetic life."[85] The tannaitic-amoraic position against women's vows of self-denial stands in direct contrast to this Christian phenomenon. This issue will be discussed further in Chapter 3.

## The Responsibility to Preserve Life

The idea that self-denial is inherently negative because a person is held responsible for the welfare of his own body and for preserving

82. Yigael Yadin, *The Temple Scroll* (Jerusalem: Israel Exploration Society, 1983), vol. II, p. 242. My translation, however, is taken from Schiffman, ibid., p. 207.

83. Elizabeth Clark, "Early Christian Women: Sources and Interpretation," in her *That Gentle Strength: Historical Perspectives on Women and Christianity* (Charlottesville: University Press of Virginia, 1990), p. 22.

84. *The Acts of Thomas,* Supplements to Novum Testamentum, trans. A.F. J. Klijn (Leiden: Brill, 1962), pp. 108–123; Peter Brown, *The Body and Society* (New York: Columbia University Press, 1988), pp. 97–98.

85. Elizabeth Clark, *Ascetic Piety and Women's Faith* (Lewiston, ME: Mellen, 1986), p. 178; Ambrose, "Concerning Virgins," *A Select Library of Nicene and Post-Nicene Fathers of the Christian Church*, vol. X (Grand Rapids, MI: Eerdmans, reprint 1983), book I, chap. 12, p. 373.

the life that God gave him is expressed in a number of sources. *B. Ta'anit* 22b concerns fasting in times of danger, as has been already discussed. After R. Yose states that an individual should not afflict himself by fasting lest he become dependent on other people for financial support, the sugya continues:

VII.    R. Judah said in the name of Rab:

VIII.   "What is R. Yose's reasoning? It says 'And Adam became a living spirit' (Genesis 2:7)—the spirit which I have given you, keep it alive."

Taking care of one's body to preserve one's God-given life is considered, by R. Judah in the name of Rab, to be the responsibility of every human being.[86]

The anonymous Mishnah in *Peah* 8:8 states that God will bless the poor who do not take charity because they trust in him, but the Talmudic sugya following this Mishnah states the exact opposite. The Mishnah is as follows:

I.      Anyone who needs to take (charity) but does not take will not die of old age until he (becomes wealthy enough to) support others,

II.     and regarding this it was stated, "Blessed be the man who trusts in God" (Jeremiah 17:7).

The Talmudic sugya (*P. Peah* 8:8 [21b]), following this Mishnah, quotes R. Aha in the name of R. Hanina as stating that a poor person who refuses charity is considered a killer, since he does not take care of his own body. After quoting this source (section II next), the Talmud then quotes the part of the Mishnah which conflicts with this statement (section III here):

I.      R. Aha in the name of R. Hanina: So is the Mishnah to be read (*keini matnita*):

---

86. Various other sources express this idea, such as *Aboth deRabbi Nathan* Version B, chap. 30, where Hillel states that taking a bath and using the bathroom are both fulfillments of the positive commandment to preserve your body (see A. J. Heschel, *Torah min haShamayim,* pp. 127–131 for further references).

II. "A person who should take [charity from others because he has no food] but does not take is considered to be a killer and it is forbidden to take pity on him. Since on his own life he does not take pity, on others all the more so. . . ."

IIIand "anyone who needs to take charity but does not will not die of old age until he (becomes wealthy enough to) support others . . . 'Blessed be the man who trusts in God'."

The difference between the Mishnah and R. Hanina's statement has been interpreted as dealing with different levels of poverty. The poverty of the person in the Mishnah is not so extreme. If the person works very hard and lives with very little, then he can survive and is blessed. The poverty described by R. Hanina, however, is so extreme that if he does not take charity, then he will not have enough to live on and will afflict himself, leading a terrible life,[87] or will be so poor that he will not be able to marry off or support his daughters.[88]

If, however, we follow the simple meaning of the words of the sugya without added interpolation, then two diametrically opposed viewpoints are presented here. The Mishnah praises someone for living an impoverished existence, whereas R. Hanina likens such a person to a killer. These two statements represent two totally opposite viewpoints regarding the same issue, a rather common phenomenon within the sources on this topic.

The phrase *keini matinita,* according to this interpretation, cannot be read as "so is the Mishnah to be read," or "thus the Mishnah taught," since R. Aha in the name of R. Hanina directly contradicts the Mishnah; he does not simply modify how the Mishnah is to be read. The word *matnita,* which is used in the *PT* to refer to either a Mishnah or a baraita,[89] would refer to a baraita, and the word *keini* would be used to introduce the baraita. Even though the printed text of the Palestinian sugya as well as all of the *P. Peah*

---

87. R. Samson of Sens, *Rash* on *Peah* 8:9; *Or Zarua,* vol. I, Laws of *Tzedakah* 16; Maimonides, *Yad,* Hilkhot Matnot Aniyim, 10:19.

88. R. Moses of Coucy, *S'MaG,* Positive Commandment 162.

89. Zekhariah Frankel, *Mavo HaYerushalmi* Reprint: Jerusalem: Opst HaOmanim, 1967 p. 12; H. Albeck, *Mavo LaTalmudim* (Tel-Aviv: Dvir, 1969), p. 20.

manuscripts[90] have *keini matni'*, the Vilna Gaon emends this phrase to *tani matnita*.[91] Following either the printed text of *keini matnita* or the Vilna Gaon's emendation of *tani matnita,* meaning "thus the baraita taught (in disagreement with the Mishnah)," then the sugya would flow in a logical manner.[92] The phrase would introduce a baraita that disagrees with the Mishnah; the Talmud's quotation of the Mishnah would then show the conflict between the two sources.

### Enjoyment of Food as a Religious Obligation

While the sources presented here demonstrated that preserving one's life was considered a religious obligation, other sources take this idea a step further and hold that actually enjoying the pleasures of God's world is a religious obligation. In *B. Bezah* 16a, Hillel and Shammai debate whether one is permitted to eat good food during the week or whether one should save it all for the coming Sabbath.[93] Hillel holds that one should eat it during the week, since "God is blessed every day, let all your deeds be done in the name of heaven." He is expressing the idea that pleasure in God's world ("all your deeds") can be a religious experience if approached with the mindset that it

---

90. The Vatican manuscript has *beini matnita* (*Synopse zum Talmud Yerushalmi,* ibid., ad loc.), which appears to be an error.

91. Albeck, *Mavo,* p. 21. Albeck suggests that the term "*bematnita tana*" in the Babylonian Talmud indicates a late baraita, often associated with names of amoraim, rather than tanaim. He does not discuss, however, whether this observation applies to the sources in the Palestinian Talmud as well or whether it would apply when the word order is reversed, as it is in our case (pp. 44–45). In our case, R. Aha may have been a tanna in the rabbi's generation (Hyman, vol. 1, p. 119), quoting R. Hanina, a second-century tanna who was a child during the times of R. Gamaliel of Yavneh (Hyman, vol. 2, p. 477). He also, however, may have been a fourth-generation Palestinian amora, who also quotes R. Hanina (Hyman, vol. II, pp. 119–120).

92. Adin Steinsaltz suggests that this is precisely why the Vilna Gaon changes the reading to *tani matnita* (*P. Peah* 8:8, *shitot,* ed. A. Steinsaltz (Jerusalem: Israel Institute for Talmudic Publications, 1987).

93. In Tosefta *Arakhin* 4:27 and *B. Hullin* 84a, R. Eleazar b. Azariyah states that a wealthy person may eat meat every day. This advice, however, seems to be based more on economics than on attitudes toward asceticism (cf. Urbach, "Iskizism," p. 56 and note 39).

is all a gift from God.[94] Shammai, on the other hand, limits pleasure to the Sabbath.

This idea is also found in *P. Kiddushin* 8:12 (66d):

R. Hezekiah the Priest in the name of Rav: "In the future, a person will be asked to give a justification for everything which his eye saw but which he did not eat."

R. Eleazar tried to follow this teaching carefully; he would collect coins in order to buy all new foods at least once a year.

According to this source, a person will actually have to explain why he did not allow himself pleasure when he had the opportunity to eat something he wanted. Rav in this statement is not simply criticizing people for denying themselves food which is life sustaining, like bread. Instead, he is actually criticizing people for not enjoying food whenever they wanted to.[95] This source represents antiasceticism to the extreme.

Rav's name (assuming correct attributions) is associated with another behavior that could, ostensibly, be seen as part of an extremely antiascetic approach to life in general. In *B. Yevamot* 37b and *B. Yoma* 18b, the Talmud records that:

Rav, whenever he happened to visit Dardeshir, used to announce, "Who would be mine for the day?" So also R. Nahman, whenever he happened to visit Shekunzib, used to announce, "Who would be mine for the day?"

Rav, according to this source, would marry a woman for the day (or few days) in which he stayed in Dardeshir.[96] Various apologetic

---

94. Hillel and Shammai's attitude toward taking care of the body expresses the same theme. While Hillel considered taking a bath and using the bathroom to be religious activities, Shammai's attitude was one of resignation or even annoyance—"let our obligations to this body be fulfilled" (both deRabbi Nathan version B, chap. 30).

95. Cf. Tosafot *Berakhot* 37a, s.v. *boreh nefashot,* who explains that the blessing of *boreh nefashot* gives thanks to God for the foods that humans need to eat to survive, like bread and water, as well as for those that were created solely for pleasure, such as apples.

96. Rashi, ad loc., s.v. *man havya leyoma.* R. Ya'akov Emden holds that

explanations for this passage have been suggested.[97] However, as Gafni points out, the Talmud itself was not at all disturbed by this behavior and understood these stories literally.

## CHAPTER SUMMARY

Many different sources have been discussed to analyze the reasons behind rabbinic criticism of ascetic behavior. What is evident is that there are two basic approaches to this issue. The first approach, discussed in the first section of this chapter, is based on the idea that self-denial is generally positive and is only criticized within certain contexts (contextually negative). These contexts are situations in which self-denial yields negative practical consequences. The specific negative consequences that have been discussed here were endangering one's life (or one's child's life), becoming a burden on the community, cheating one's employer, and not being able to study and/or teach Torah properly. Ascetic behavior that was suspected of being insincere has also been criticized.

The second approach, discussed in the second section of this chapter, is based on the premise that self-denial is not only contextually negative but inherently negative. According to this approach, supererogatory anguish is criticized because it is simply wrong to deny that which God permitted and because the Jew has been commanded to take good care of the body that was given by God.

This attitude is extended even further in some sources, where self-denial is criticized not only because it is wrong to deny that which is permitted, but because God wants human beings to actively pursue the enjoyment of the world that he gave them. These attitudes thus fit along a continuum that ranges from the position that self-denial is praiseworthy behavior, all the way to the opposite

---

they were not actually marrying these women but were taking them as concubines. He argues that the taking of concubines (*pilegesh*) is not only permissible but would actually be a positive practice (*She'elat Ya'aetz*) (Lemberg: Uri Ze'ev Wolf Salat, 1884), p. II, responsa 15.

97. See Leo Jung, in his notes to the Soncino ed. of *Yoma* 18b, note 7, and references in Isaiah Gafni, *Yehudei Bavel BiTekufat HaTalmud,* p. 272; Ephraim Urbach, *Hazal* (Jerusalem: Magnes, 1971), p. 422; and Daniel Boyarin, *Carnal Israel: Reading Sex in Talmudic Literature* (Berkeley: University of California Press, 1993), pp. 140–141 and note 13.

extreme that holds that enjoying all foods is actually a religious obligation.

No definitive historical or geographic trends can be traced here. Criticisms of ascetic behavior are found in tannaitic and amoraic sources of both early and late time periods. One interesting pattern, though, is that all of the amoraic sources stem from Babylonia except one (*P. Nedarim* 9:1 [41b]). A second is that the majority of the sources that find "supererogatory anguish" to be negative only within certain contexts are tannaitic, while the majority of sources that find this behavior to be inherently negative are amoraic and stem from Babylonia.

Certain specific ideas span the generations and the countries. One such idea is that scholars and schoolteachers should not indulge in private fasts. This idea is found in *P. Demai* 7:3 (26b), expressed by R. Johanan (a first-generation Palestinian amora), and in *B. Ta'anit* 11b, expressed by R. Jeremiah b. Abba in the name of Reish Lakish (a first-generation Palestinian amora) and R. Sheshet (a third-generation Babylonian amora). A second idea, which extends from the tannaitic to the amoraic time period, is that the enjoyment of food (as God's gift to the world) is actually a religious obligation. This idea is expressed by Hillel, the tanna (*B. Bezah* 16a), and R. Hezekiah the priest in the name of Rav, the first-generation Babylonian amora (*P. Kiddushin* 8:12 [66d]).

Assuming that the attributions are all correct, then the sources indicate that Rav had a very positive attitude toward the human body and physical pleasure. He held that every person is religiously obligated to keep his "living spirit" (i.e., his body) alive (*B. Ta'anit* 22b). In addition to stating that the enjoyment of food is a religious obligation, he appears to have extended this positive attitude to the area of human sexuality as well.[98]

---

98. *B. Yevamot* 37b. See also *B. Nedarim* 20b. For a discussion of the attitude of Rav (and of other amoraim as well) toward human physical drives, see Urbach, *Hazal,* pp. 421–422.

# 3

# *The Ascetic Woman (Ishah Perushah): Criticism of Super-erogatory Anguish in M. Sotah 3:4*

The Mishnah in *Sotah* 3:4 lists four categories of people who bring destruction on the world. Three of these categories are examples of people who impose religious stringencies on themselves:

   I.    R. Joshua says: A woman prefers one kab and sexual indulgence (*tiflut*) to nine kab and separation (*perishut*).

   II.   He used to say,

       A.  "A foolish pietist (*hasid shoteh*) . . .

       B.  a deceitful villain (*rasha arum*),[1]

---

1. The second category, "the deceitful villain (*rasha arum*)," is not identified with supererogatory behavior and is, therefore, not relevant to this study.

   Can ascetic woman (*ishah perushah*), and
   Dhe wounds of separatists (*makot perushim*),
III. behold these bring destruction upon the world" (*harei eilu mevalei olam*).

In section I of the Mishnah, R. Joshua states that a woman prefers a small amount of food but frequent sexual relations with her husband, to having a great deal of food but infrequent sexual relations.[2] In section II, four categories are introduced with the words "He used to say." "He" presumably refers to R. Joshua, to whom the immediately preceding statement is attributed. The connection between the two sections lies in the fact that category C—an ascetic woman—relates to R. Joshua's statement in section I regarding women's attitudes to sexual "separation"; category D—the wounds of the separatists—also deals with the phenomenon of separation (*perishut*).

R. Joshua lists four categories of people, all of whom "bring destruction upon the world" (*mevalei olam*). The root of the word *mevalei* is V.L, meaning to wear down and become old and ruined, as in Deuteronomy 29:4: "Your clothes are not worn old (*valu*)." In Mishnaic Hebrew, this same root is found in *Aboth* 5:22, which states that one should grow old while immersed in the study of Torah (*vesiv u'vleh vah*). An alternate reading of this word, found in the Kaufmann, Paris, and Parma manuscripts, is *mekhalei*,[3] from the root KH.L.H, which means to destroy. The word *olam*, which has been translated literally as "world," actually means society.

The next three chapters will focus on each of the relevant categories quoted here, defining each category and then examining why R. Joshua and other tannaim and amoraim felt that these people's behavior was so negative that they brought "destruction upon the world." The ascetic woman and the wounds of the separatists (categories C and D in the Mishnah) will be discussed first (in Chapters 3 and 4 respectively), since these both fit into the

---

2. Rashi and Tosafot, *Sotah* 21b, s.v. *rotza isha bekav vetiflut*. Maimonides, though, explains *tiflut* here as wickedness, as opposed to piety. He does not, then, interpret this phrase as dealing with sexuality (Commentary to the Mishnah, ad loc., s.v. *limdah tiflut*).

3. *Dikdukei Soferim, Sotah* 20a.

category of supererogatory anguish, the subject of the previous chapter. The first category of the Mishnah (the foolish pietist) will then be discussed in Chapter 5.

## TANNAITIC DEFINITIONS OF *ISHAH PERUSHAH*

The definition of the term *ishah perushah*[4] can be derived from the context of the Mishnah itself. R. Joshua in the Mishnah uses the term *separation (perishut)* as meaning separated from sexual relations in the immediately preceding section of the Mishnah (section I): "A woman prefers one kab and sexual indulgence (*tiflut*) to nine kab and separation (*perishut*)." Assuming that R. Joshua is the "He" who listed the four categories of the Mishnah, then we can assume that he used the term *separated (perusha)* in section II in the same way as he used it in the immediately preceding statement (section I), namely, as separated from sexual relations. Statement I is clearly criticizing women, since he uses the term *tiflut,* which means frivolity or licentiousness, in order to describe frequent sexual relations. The term *tiflut* is used earlier in this Mishnah by R. Eliezer, when he states, "Whoever teaches his daughter Torah, it is as if he has taught her obscenity (*tiflut*)." If one were to restate R. Joshua's position, then he would clearly be saying that separation = abstinence = *perishut* was a positive behavior, while licentiousness = frequent sexual relations = *tiflut* was a negative behavior. When, however, R. Joshua lists "an ascetic woman" *(isha perusha)* at the end of the Mishnah, he once again uses the root P.R.SH, but in this case it is used as a criticism. An internal contradiction is thus immediately apparent. For although R. Joshua in section I of the Mishnah criticized a woman for not wanting "separation" (infrequent sexual relations or perhaps abstinence), here he calls an ascetic woman a destroyer of the world.

Although this contradictory use of the same term suggests two

---

4. Abraham Geiger writes that he saw a manuscript of Maimonides in Paris that had *isha perutza* (a sexually promiscuous woman) instead of *isha perusha*. If this were indeed the correct reading, then, ironically, this woman would be the exact opposite of the "ascetic" woman who will be described below. (A. Geiger, in a letter to Ig. Blumenfeld, found in *Otzar Nekhmad* (Vienna: Blumenfeld, 1857), vol. II, p. 100.

different authors, the Mishnah's "He used to say" introducing section II clearly seems to attribute section II as well as section I to R. Joshua. This problem has two possible solutions. One is that the root P.R.SH. may have been used differently in the two sections. In section I, it meant sexual abstinence; in section II, it may have meant other types of separatist behavior.[5] This would be similar to section D of this Mishnah, "the wounds of the separatists" (*makot perushim*). The word *perushim* in this section is interpreted as meaning various kinds of separatist behavior, and not necessarily sexual abstinence (see chapter 4).

A second solution to the apparent contradiction between R. Joshua's statements in sections I and II is that although the root P.R.SH. means sexual abstinence in both sections, he may have, nonetheless, felt that while abstinence (*perishut*) was positive for men, it was negative for women. When he used the term as a positive trait in section I, he meant that in a general, generic sense (i.e., for men), abstinence is positive. In section II then, when he used the term in a negative sense, he was referring specifically to women. Having already described in section I how women preferred frequent sexual relations to an abundance of food, he may have held that abstinence went against women's nature,[6] and therefore felt that abstinence for women was abberant behavior that would yield only negative results. While category D, "the wounds of the separatists," presumably refers to male "separatists," R. Joshua condemns only certain aspects of these separatists, namely, their wounds, or their personality traits (see Chapter 4); he does not condemn "the ascetic man" (*ish parush*) in a general sense, as he does "the ascetic woman."

The idea that female asceticism received particular censure was discussed in Chapter 2, in reference to the permission for a husband

---

5. Maimonides, in fact, explains *perishut* in section I as separation from evil, rather than abstention from sexuality, and *tiflut* as frivolity, and later as wickedness (Commentary to the Mishnah, ad loc., s.v. *limdah tiflut*). He does not explain the term *ishah perushah,* but, based on his explanations of the above terms, he may not have understood the term as referring to sexual abstinence per se.

6. The Maharal of Prague states this idea explicitly in *Hiddushei Aggadot, Sotah* (Jerusalem: 1972), p. 62.

or father to annul a wife's or daughter's vows of self-denial, while no parallel procedure for the annulment of male vows of self-denial is found in the sources. Just what these negative results of female asceticism would be, though, is not defined by the Mishnah, but is elaborated on in both the *BT* and the *PT*.

Exactly what type of "ascetic woman" the Mishnah is referring to is also unclear. She could be a married woman, as is suggested by the word *ishah* (a grown woman, presumably married) who abstains from or limits sexual relations with her husband,[7] or else simply a grown woman who is either a virgin or a widow but pledges to remain abstinent.

The baraita quoted in *B. Sotah* 22a introduces two categories of women, the elucidation of which will help clarify the meaning of the Mishnah's ascetic woman:

I.   *Ishah Perushah*:
II.  Our Rabbis have taught: A praying virgin (*betulah tzalyanit*),
III. a gadabout widow (*almanah shovavit*) . . .
IV.  a minor whose months are not completed[8]
V.   behold these bring destruction upon the world.

This baraita states that a virgin who prays all the time and a "gadabout widow" destroy the world, echoing our Mishnah's statement that an ascetic woman destroys the world. The "praying virgin" is a young girl who continuously prays,[9] day and night.[10] One simple explanation of this part of the baraita is that it is criticizing this girl for her ascetic practice of praying all the time, just as R. Joshua had criticized the "ascetic woman."

A few explanations of the term "gadabout widow" have been suggested. Instead of the word *shovavit*, R. Nissim Gaon calls her

---

7. Albeck suggests a possible connection between the separated woman of our Mishnah and the nazirite woman who separated herself from wine and other worldly pleasures. This connection, while certainly possible, is conjectural, since naziritism is not linked to celibacy in the Talmudic sources. See Hanoch Albeck, *Mishnah Commentary, Nazir* (Jerusalem: Bialik Institute and Dvir, 1958), Appendix, Chap. 4, p. 374.

8. This category is not relevant to this study.

9. Rashi, ad loc.

10. Aruch, s.v. T.Z.L. #5.

*sovavit,* meaning someone who goes around and around (from the root S.V.V.), and explains that she is a woman who pretends to be very righteous and acts piously in front of other people but in fact practices witchcraft.[11] A similar explanation is that she constantly visits her neighbors and pretends to be very pious to hide her sinning. (The word *shavavta* in Aramaic means "neighbor.")[12] The word *shovavit* has therefore been translated as "gadabout," that is, "a person who moves restlessly or aimlessly about, especially for curiosity and gossip."[13]

R. Nathan b. Yehiel in the Arukh gives an alternate explanation to the term that is much closer in meaning to the ascetic woman of the Mishnah. He says that she is a widow who decides never to marry again and to devote her life only to God, declaring:

> "I have repented—I will never marry and I have given my soul up to God for the rest of my life." This is something with which she will not be able to live and when it becomes difficult for her she will commit many sins.

This declaration of the gadabout widow sounds exactly like the vows of a nun[14] and very much like the sexually abstinent ascetic woman described earlier.

---

11. R. Nissim Gaon, *Hibbur Yaffe Min HaYeshuah* (Amsterdam, 1746), p. 16, and quoted in *Otzar HaGeonim Sotah*, pp. 241–242. The theme of the gadabout widow being a witch in disguise will be elaborated below, in my discussion of *B. Sotah* 22a.

12. This explanation is given by Rashi and the Arukh. Rashi holds that both the gadabout widow and the praying virgin are merely pretending to be pious to hide the fact that they are really sexually promiscuous and practice witchcrat (s.v. *harei elu mevalei olam*). The Arukh gives a second explanation to the word *shovavit. Shovav* means wild and free spirited—this woman does not remain in her house modestly but instead goes out in the market and street. According to this explanation, her behavior would not be relevant to this study.

13. *Random House Dictionary of the English Language* (New York: Random House, 1981).

14. *Arukh,* s.v. SH.V. #8. Female monasteries were, in fact, quite common in the times of the Arukh who lived in Rome during the eleventh to early twelfth century. See Caroline Bynum, *Holy Feasts and Holy Fasts* (Berkeley: University of California Press, 1987), p. 15. While the Arukh's definition of the gadabout widow may, at first glance, sound anachronistic,

P. *Sotah* 3:4 (19a) contains a passage that is very similar to the *B. Sotah* baraita discussed previously:

I.    They added to them:
II.   a fasting virgin (*betula tzaymanit*);
III.  fasting all the time causes her to lose her virginity.
IV.   And a gadabout widow (*almanah shovavit*):
V.    Who? Hogla, who got a bad name (or "because she was a gadabout, she got a bad name").

The *P. Ta'anit* sugya lists these two categories right after it discusses the fourth category in the Mishnah, "the wounds of the separatists." They belong, however, to the *PT*'s discussion of the ascetic woman since they are both women and are nearly identical to the categories in the baraita quoted the *BT* as examples of an ascetic woman. The identity of "they" in the phrase "They added to them" is unclear, and there is no other introductory phrase that tells us whether this passage is tannaitic or amoraic. This passage may have developed in two stages, with the original core baraita containing only sections II and IV, or perhaps II, III, and IV. Section IV, which switches from Hebrew to Aramaic, is amoraic and will therefore be discussed later when the *PT* Talmudic sugya as a whole will be analyzed. What is important, however, at this point, are the original core phrases of "a fasting virgin" and "a gadabout widow," and the explanatory phrase in section III.

The fasting virgin (from the root TZ.M) is parallel to the praying virgin of the *BT*. This source, like the baraita of the praying virgin and the Mishnah of the ascetic woman, would thus be criticizing ascetic women. This "fasting virgin" of the *PT*'s baraita completes the picture drawn earlier of the ascetic behavior that the tannaim are censuring; abstinence and excessive praying and fasting were frowned on for women. (It should be noted that the term *fasting* (*metzaymah*) here may actually mean sexual abstinence, for the opposite term—*eating* is, in fact, used as a euphemism for sexual relations in both Mishlei 30:20 and in *M. Ketubot* 5:11.)[15]

Section III explains why the fasting virgin is condemned:

---

the fact is that the phenomenon of abstinent women did already exist in tannaitic times, as will be discussed at length later.

15. See *P. Ketubot*, ad loc., and *B. Ketubot* 65b. For further references, see

"fasting all the time causes her to lose her virginity." The fasting virgin then is a girl whose constant fasting results in the loss of her virginity. Both terms, *fasting* and *her virginity,* are meant literally here—that is, that when she does get married, her hymen will fail to bleed because of her emaciated state. The problem then is not her fasting per se but rather the results of her fasting—the loss of her hymen.[16] While this idea sounds medically unsound to a modern person, it appears to have been an accepted belief in Talmudic times. In *B. Ketubot* 10b, a case in which this is reported to have happened is discussed. A couple came to R. Judah the Prince after the bride did not bleed when their marriage was consummated. The bride claimed that she had been a virgin but that there had been a time of drought, and her consequent hunger and thirst (i.e., fasting) had caused her hymen to disappear.[17] This claim was confirmed when the bride did bleed after R. Judah the Prince gave them food and drink and she had relations with her husband.[18]

The fasting virgin, according to this explanation, is doing

---

Meir Minkowitz, "Ishah Perusha, Utzevuim Shedomim LiPerushim, *HaDoar* 54 (1975), p. 136.

16. A second explanation of this passage is that fasting is a euphemism for celibacy. Since this girl is celibate and will not get married, she will not receive the financial reward for her virginity that she would get if she were to marry (Minkowitz, ibid., p. 136). The word may have been used in this manner in Judges 11:29, when Jephte's daughter cries over her virginity (*betulehah*). She was mourning that she would either die as a virgin or be forced to live a celibate life and never get married. The word *betulehah* (*her virginity*) would then mean the extra *ketubah* money that a virgin receives, (*M. Ketubot* 1:2) rather than the literal meaning of the word (i.e., "her hymen"). A third explanation of section III is that the fasting virgin was lying; she claimed that her fasting caused the loss of her virginity, when in fact she had sinned. She was, then, using her religiosity as a cover-up for her sins. Tosafot explains that this fasting virgin is the same as the praying virgin of the *BT*, who uses her piety as a cover-up for sin (*B. Sotah* 22a, s.v. *kol*). This theme will be developed further in my discussion of the *BT* sugya; it is a recurrent theme among the medieval commentators on this topic.

17. Tosafot's first explanation in *Sotah* 22a,. s.v. *kol*, is that due to all of the fasting, her hymen really disappeared.

18. What may have happened in this case was that the marriage had not yet been consummated since the young couple was so weak from hunger that they did not have the strength with which to complete sexual

something in the name of piety that in fact causes harm to herself. Although her motivation for fasting may have been sincere, the tanna of the baraita is criticizing her for the negative external effect that her behavior has on her own body (and consequently on her ability to find a worthy husband), namely the loss of her virginity. This example would then fit into the viewpoint discussed in Chapter 2, in which the rabbis view asceticism as negative only within certain contexts, such as when excessive fasting causes personal injury.

Since the concept of abstinent women (or "Jewish nuns") as a Jewish phenomenon seems, a priori, foreign to Judaism, an investigation into whether we have evidence other than that found in the Mishnah and Talmud for Jewish abstinent women (as well as ascetic women in general) is in order at this point.

The Essenes were an ascetic group, who generally lived in communities of continent Jewish men.[19] Josephus, though, speaks of an order of Essenes which did marry in order to have children. They considered procreation to be the only legitimate justification for marital life and consequently avoided intercourse with their wives during pregnancy.[20] Since, in principle, "the restriction of marital relations during pregnancy should apply with equal force to men and women past their childbearing years," the marrying Essenes, (both men and women) who already had a child or children, or who were past their childbearing years, would have lived celibate lives.[21]

---

intercourse. After R. Judah the Prince provided them with food, they were able to consummate their marriage. The bride though, nevertheless, thought that the drought had caused her lack of "virginity." (See Julius Preuss, *Biblical and Talmudic Medicine,* trans. Fred Rosner (Northvale, NJ: Aronson, 1993), p. 479.)

19. Josephus, *Jewish Antiquities,* XVIII, 19–22, trans. Louis H. Feldman, The Loeb Classical Library (London: Heinemann, 1965), vol. IX; Emil Schurer, *The History of the Jewish People in the Age of Jesus Christ,* ed. Geza Vermes, Fergus Millar, and Matthew Black (Edinburgh: Clark, 1979), vol. II, p. 565.

20. Josephus, *Jewish War,* ed. Loeb, vol. II, pp. 159–163, 385.

21. Joseph Baumgarten, "The Qumran-Essene Restraints on Marriage," *Archaeology and History in the Dead Sea Scrolls,* ed. Lawrence H. Schiffman (Sheffield: J.S.O.T. Press, 1990), pp. 16–17, and note 14. A Syriac source

Many scholars assume that the Qumran community was Essene, male, and celibate. There is, however, reason to question this assumption. Both textual and archaeological findings suggest that women lived at Qumram and that the sect, or perhaps part of the sect, was not necessarily celibate.[22] Some of the women at Qumran may have been married, others may have been celibate. There may also have been "marrying Essenes" or their equivalent at Qumran, in which case the women (as well as the men) may have become celibate after having children.

Besides for the Essenes, another first-century Jewish community that was pledged to celibacy is known to have included both men and women. This community, described by Philo in his *De Vita Contemplativa,* was known as the Therapeutaue. This Jewish sect of ascetics lived near Alexandria, Egypt, and had some connection to the Essenes.[23] These Therapeutaue renounced their property and left their families either after or before marriage to devote their time to study and spiritual contemplation. They lived in seclusion for six days a week and ate very little.[24] On the seventh day, they gathered

---

states that the Essenes separated from their wives permanently once they became pregnant (James H. Charlesworth, "The Origin and Subsequent History of the Authors of the Dead Sea Scrolls: Four Transitional Phases among the Qumran Essenes," *Revue de Qumran* 10 (1980), p. 216, note 19). The reliability of these sources, though, is questionable (Baumgarten, ibid., p. 16). On a practical level, it seems highly unlikely that a group that wanted to procreate would have limited themselves to only one (as yet unborn) child, given the high infant mortality rates in ancient times.

22. Baumgarten, ibid., pp. 13–14, 19; Schurer, *The History of the Jewish People,* vol. II, p. 578; Todd S. Beall, *Josephus' Description of the Essenes Illustrated by the Dead Sea Scrolls* (Cambridge: Cambridge University Press, 1988), pp. 38–39.

23. Schurer, ibid., vol. II, pp. 596–597.

24. As alluded to earlier, the Arukh's description of the gadabout widow, resembling as it does the vows of a nun, bears a striking resemblance to the Theraputae described by Philo. (The only difference is that the Theraputae were a group, while the gadabout widow was an individual.) The Arukh, however, was not familiar with Philo's writings. They were preserved by the church and were not "rediscovered" by Jewish scholars until the sixteenth century by Azarya dei Rossi. See Hans Lewy, Introduction to 'Philo," *Three Jewish Philosophers* (New York: Atheneum, 1977), p. 8. Another medieval commentary, the Abravanel, in his commen-

for a general assembly in which they studied, prayed and sang, and ate a "feast" consisting only of bread, salt and water. Philo, describing the Sabbath feast, portrays the women of the sect:

> The feast is shared by women also, most of them aged virgins, who have kept their chastity not under compulsion, like some Greek priestesses, but of their own free will in their ardent yearning for wisdom. Eager to have her [wisdom] for their life mate they have spurned the pleasures of the body.[25]

Since the Therapeutaue lived in Alexandria and not in the Land of Israel, we do not know whether the tannaim were even aware of their existence. However, evidence suggests contact between the Alexandrian Jewish community and the community in the Land of Israel. There was even a synagogue in Jerusalem of Alexandrian Jews. Possibly, R. Joshua's denunciation of the ascetic woman in the Mishnah may, then, have been aimed at women like the Therapeutaue or the (possibly) celibate Essene women of Temple times, assuming that they were known to him.

In the religions surrounding the Jewish people during tannaitic and amoraic times, the phenomenon of "holy virginity" was very common and was found in varying degrees depending on the religion. The Greco-Roman religions had virgin priestesses. The vestal virgins in Rome, for example, were responsible for the public worship of Vesta, the goddess of the hearth, and served for thirty years under a vow of chastity.[26] These priestesses, however, were the exception rather than the rule.[27] Prolonged virginity within Greco-Roman religions was a rare requirement expected only of

---

tary to Judges 11, also uses the concept of a nun and the term *ascetic* to describe what happened to Jephte's daughter. He says that she became *perusha* in a house that she never left—and that the non-Jews learned from this to have cloisters (*batei perishut*) for women, where women stayed all their lives and never saw a man.

25. Philo, "The Contemplative Life," trans. F. H. Colson, *The Loeb Classical Library* (Cambridge, MA: Harvard University Press), vol. IX, p. 155.

26. Robin Lane Fox, *Pagans and Christians* (New York: Knopf, 1986), pp. 347–348.

27. Gillian Clark, *Women in the Ancient World: Greece and Rome,* New Surveys in the Classics No. 21 (Oxford: Oxford University Press, 1989), p. 34.

some priestesses; it was never enjoined on the general population.[28]

In early Christianity, however, virginity and fasting were considered tremendous virtues and were not limited to a select few. As Peter Brown writes, "From the second century onward, and almost certainly from an earlier, less well-documented period, little groups of men and women, scattered among the Christian communities throughout the eastern Mediterranean and in the Near East, as far as the foothills of Iran," lived lives pledged to abstinence.[29] For early Syrian Christians, virginity was considered "a prerequisite for the adoption of the Christian faith"; early Christians, therefore, are simply referred to as "virgins"—*betula* (masculine) and *betulta* (feminine) in some early sources.[30]

The usage of this term in these early Christian sources as well as in the baraitot of the *BT* and *PT* (*betulah tzalyanit* and *betulah tzaymanit*) suggest that the baraitot were actually referring to these early Christians, many of whom were Jews. One such person may have been "the prophetess Anna," described in Luke 2:36–7 as an elderly widow who could be found, day and night, fasting and praying in the Temple. Perhaps R. Joshua, who lived during the second half of the first century C.E., and the tannaim of the baraita wanted to condemn this type of behavior by stating most forcefully that Judaism considered this to be a force leading to the destruction of the world. "The destruction of the world" here can be understood both figuratively and literally—figuratively in that it destroys marital life, and literally in that abstinent women would, obviously, not be able to have children.[31]

While early Christian leaders encouraged both men and women to become celibate, the Mishnah and baraitot focus their criticism only on the women. This could, however, have been because more Christian women may have engaged in this type of activity than did men, and R. Joshua may have been reacting to that reality. With regard to fasting, female ascetics were famous for their ability to endure especially long fasts, and "Exceptional, even extreme and

---

28. Fox, *Pagans and Christians,* pp. 347–348.

29. Peter Brown, *The Body and Society: Men, Women and Sexual Renunciation in Early Christianity* (New York: Columbia University Press, 1988), p. 85.

30. Voobus, *History of Asceticism,* vol. I, pp. 103–104.

31. Brown, *Body and Society,* p. 61–63.

punitive fasting is commended to Christian women by their male advisors, and heroic examples of 'fasting women' are held up for emulation by other Christians, especially virgins."[32]

Early Christian women in particular were similarly encouraged to become sexually abstinent. A whole genre of literature, celebrating female chastity, was produced by the early Christian community. In this genre of "Chastity Stories" beautiful women, influenced by wandering ascetics, "renounce sexual relations with husbands, masters and fiancés."[33]

An example of this type of story can be found in the *Acts of Judas Thomas*, which appeals specifically to women who were already married to reject their husbands.[34] This source, stemming from Syria, is dated at the end of the tannaitic period (approximately 220 C.E.),[35] but the behavior it encourages may have already been taking place in certain communities. For although "Fasting and abstinence emerged as extensive corporate practices among Christians in the third and fourth centuries,"[36] these practices did not emerge overnight. Fasting and sexual abstinence may not have been initially *extensive*, but these practices most certainly existed in earlier times that were not as well documented.[37]

Another source of information about the "ascetic woman" may be the *Didascalia Apostolorum*, a third-century Christian work[38] written by an author who seems to have had a Jewish background.[39] This work deals with widows who pledge themselves to chastity

---

32. Gail Paterson Corrington, "The Defense of the Body and the Discourse of the Appetite: Continence and Control and the Greco-Roman World," *Semeia* 57 (1992), pt. I, p. 71.

33. Karen Jo Torjesen, "In Praise of Noble Women, Asceticism, Patronage and Honor," *Semeia* 57 (1992), pt. I, p. 58.

34. Brown, *Body and Society,* p. 98.

35. Helmut Koester, *History and Literature of Early Christianity* (Philadelphia: Fortress, 1982), vol. II, p. 208.

36. Bynum, *Holy Feasts,* p. 38. These practices became institutionalized in a later time period. By the late fourth to early fifth century, there were two women's monasteries in the Land of Israel (one on the Mt. of Olives and another in Bethlehem), and another in Constantinople; Torjesen, "In Praise of Noble Women," p. 50.

37. Brown, *Body and Society,* p. 85.

38. John P. Meier, *A Marginal Jew* (New York.: Doubleday, 1991), p. 391.

39. It was probably written in northern Syria, by an author who may

and views them as a holy order. The holy widow "who wishes to please God sits at home and meditates upon the Lord day and night, and without ceasing at all times offers intercession and prays with purity before the Lord."[40]

This source demonstrates the phenomenon of widowed women pledged to remaining abstinent, becoming especially pious and ascetic; and engaging in constant prayer, study, and fasts. This behavior reminds us of the praying and fasting virgin and the gadabout widow according to the Arukh's explanation. There seems to be a blurring of distinction in the Christian sources between virgins and widows, since abstinence was the ultimate goal. In fact, during the second and third centuries, many of the "holy virgins" were indeed widows: "The normal continent woman was not a virgin girl, dedicated to a pious seclusion from childhood up. Rather, she was a woman who had been the head of a Christian household and the mother of Christian children."[41] This blurring of distinction would correspond to the Talmud's inclusion of both virgin and widow in the definition of the "ascetic woman."

Exactly how these Christian sources are connected to the Jewish sources is very hard to determine.[42] But what is evident is that the phenomenon of abstinent, ascetic women found in the Mishnah and the baraita can certainly also be found in Philo's

---

have been a convert from Judaism, since whenever he enters into a doctrinal discussion, it is in refutation of Judaism. J. Quasten, "Didascalia Apostolorum," _The New Catholic Encyclopedia_ (New York: McGraw-Hill, 1967), vol. IV, p. 860.

40. _Didascalia Apostolorum_, The Syriac Version, trans. R. Hugh Connolly (Oxford: Clarendon, 1929), p. 136.

41. Brown, _Body and Society_, p. 150. This suggestion has been made with regard to the Therapeutaue as well. See Dorothy Sly, _Philo's Perception of Women_, Brown Judaic Studies 209 (Atlanta: Scholars, 1990), p. 209.

42. The Ethiopian Jews had male monks and female nuns, both of whom lived apart from the community. This practice was, though, probably a result of Christian-Ethiopic influence, rather than being a remnant of an ancient Jewish practice. The Ethiopian Jews themselves attribute its origins to the fifteenth century, a period of intense Jewish-Christian contacts, when the Ethiopian king's son converted to Judaism and instituted monasteries. See Wolf Leslau, _The Falasha Anthology_ (New Haven, CT: Yale University Press, 1951), pp. xxv, xxvi; James Quirin, _The Evolution of the Ethiopian Jews_ (Philadelphia: University of Pennsylvania, 1992), p. 66.

Therapeutaue,[43] Greco-Roman religious practices, and especially among the early Christians. While Philo and the early Christians thought of this phenomenon as highly commendable, extra-pious behavior, R. Joshua and the tanna of the baraita felt that it was so negative as to be classified as "destroying the world." Perhaps they were reacting to a growing phenomenon of female asceticism, and/or to a fear that such a phenomenon would grow in Jewish circles, as a result of the influence of the early Christians.

Tannaim were not the only ones who criticized this type of asceticism. Some of the early Christians themselves voiced condemnation of such asceticism. In the New Testament, Paul writes, for example, "It is better to marry than to burn with passion" (I. Corinthians 7:9). Clement of Alexandria, a late second-century Christian preacher, speaks out against two extreme groups in the Christianity of his day.[44] The first group that he opposes were "licentious" Christians who believed that women were created by God in order to be shared among the men (and acted upon this belief).[45] The second group consisted of Christians who shunned marriage;[46] Clement quotes Paul as support for his claim that marriage is holy.[47] Clement's position, though "moderate" among the Christians of his time, is still radically different from that of rabbinic Judaism. For in Judaism, marriage is the ideal state, whereas Paul and Clement held it to be a compromise that still contained holiness.

Another voice heard against abstinence is that of second-century Irenaeus. He castigates those Christians known as Encratites who preached abstinence from marriage and animal food. Irenaeus' position is more similar to Judaism, in that he does not see

---

43. For further discussion of Philo's views on asceticism, see Fraade, "Ascetical Aspects," pp. 263–266.

44. For further references on this topic, see Henry Chadwick, "General Introduction," *Alexandrian Christianity,* ed. John Oulton and Henry Chadwick (Philadelphia: Westminster, 1965), pp. 30–31; and Dominic J. Junger, "Introduction to Irenaeus," *Against the Heresies* (New York: Paulist, 1992), pp. 254–255, note 3.

45. Clement of Alexandria, *Stromateis,* trans. John Ferguson (Washington, D.C.: Catholic University of America Press, 1991), book 3 (8:1, 10:1).

46. Ibid., 45:1, 49:1.

47. Ibid., 68:1.

marriage as a compromise but rather as a fulfillment of God's creation, since God made male and females in order to generate the human race.[48]

Returning to the tannaitic literature, the reasons for the tannaim's severe criticism of the ascetic woman can now be summarized. R. Joshua may have denounced her internal motivations. He may have denied legitimacy to the very idea that female abstinence contributes in any manner or form to the worship of God, and he may have held that the ascetic woman was simply mistaken in her ideas of piety.

A more likely explanation, though, is that R. Joshua may have maintained that despite legitimate internal motivations (i.e., she felt that she could truly best serve God in this manner), her behavior must, nonetheless, be condemned. This condemnation would be warranted due to the negative external effects that her actions would have on herself and society. These negative effects could be multiple in nature.

He may have held that sexual abstinence would be extremely difficult for her and would, consequently, lead her to sin. For, as he states earlier in our Mishnah, he holds that an abstinent existence is abnormal for a woman, going against her very nature. Second, if she were married, then her decision would destroy her marriage and possibly even lead her husband to sin as well.

Third, in a more literal reading of "destroying the world," an abstinent woman could never have children, who, obviously, ensure the continuity of the world.[49] The need to have children was felt very acutely by the rabbis. R. Eliezer, for example, expresses this idea in very strong terms by stating, in a baraita, "He who does not engage in propogation of the race is as though he sheds blood" (*B. Yebamot* 63b).

Rabbi Joshua is quoted elsewhere in the Talmud as emphasizing the importance of having many children, stating, "If a man has children in his youth, he should continue to have children in his old age." R. Mattena, the amora, confirmed his opinion by stating, "The

---

48. Irenaeus, *Against the Heresies,* 28:1.

49. See Salo Baron's discussion of the great importance attached by the rabbis to orderly family life and intensive procreation: *A Social and Religious History of the Jews* (New York: Columbia University Press, 1952), vol. II, pp. 217–221.

Halakhah is in agreement with R. Joshua" (*B. Yebamot* 62b). If the attribution is correct here and refers to Rabbi Joshua of *M. Sotah* 3:4, then the same Rabbi Joshua who condemned the ascetic woman in the Mishnah also emphasized the importance of having many children. His condemnation of the ascetic woman, then, may very well have been linked to his sense of the importance of a high birth rate, which would ensure the continued survival of the Jewish people.

The pressing need to "propogate the race" was also felt in those days in the Roman Empire in general:

> Citizens of the Roman Empire at its height, in the second century A.D., were born into the world with an average life expectancy of less than twenty-five years. Death fell savagely on the young. Those who survived childhood remained at risk. Only four out of every hundred men, and fewer women, lived beyond the age of fifty. . . . Whether through conscious legislation, such as that of Emperor Augustus, which penalized bachelors and rewarded families for producing children, or simply through the unquestioned weight of habit, young men and women were discreetly mobilized to use their bodies for reproduction. The pressure on the young women was inexorable. For the population of the Roman Empire to remain even stationary, it appears that each woman would have had to have produced an average of five children.[50]

One can certainly assume that the Jews felt this need for children even more acutely than did the average Roman, since in addition to fearing natural death, they were also, ironically, in danger of death at the hands of their Roman rulers.[51]

---

50. Brown, *Body and Society,* p. 6.

51. According to this theory, an abstinent man (*ish parush*) should have been condemned by R. Joshua as well, especially since one man could marry more than one woman, and since the Halakhic obligation to procreate was assigned to the man. Perhaps, though, the reason that R. Joshua singled out the abstinent woman for condemnation was because, as Brown writes, the pressure on young women to have many children was relentless, since they were primarily responsible for childbearing. Widespread female abstinence, therefore, would have posed a grave danger to Jewish population growth.

## AMORAIC DEFINITIONS OF *ISHAH PERUSHAH*

*B. Sotah* 22a

Until this point, "the ascetic woman" who brings destruction upon
the world has been defined primarily as a sincere, albeit misguided,
female ascetic. The Talmudic sugya of *B. Sotah* 22a, however, views
the ascetic woman as evil only when she pretends to be pious, by
using ascetic behavior as a camouflage for her sins.

I.   Our Rabbis have taught: A praying virgin . . . brings
     destruction upon the world.
II.  But it is not so;
III. for R. Johanan has said: We learned fear of sin from a virgin
     and confidence in the bestowal of reward from a widow!
IV.  Fear of sin from a virgin—for R. Johanan heard a virgin fall
     upon her face and exclaim, "Lord of the Universe! Thou
     hast created Paradise and Gehenna; Thou hast created
     righteous and wicked. May it be Thy will that men should
     not stumble through me."
V.   Confidence in the bestowal of reward from a widow—a
     certain widow had a Synagogue in her neighborhood; yet
     she used to come daily to the School of R. Johanan and
     pray there. He said to her, "My daughter, is there not a
     Synagogue in your neighborhood?" She answered him,
     "Rabbi, but have I not the reward for the steps!"
VI.  When it is said [that they bring destruction upon the
     world] the reference is to such a person as Johani the
     daughter of Retibi.

The Talmudic sugya begins with the baraita discussed earlier,
and then questions the baraita's condemnation of the praying virgin
and the gadabout widow, by saying "but it is not so!" It then quotes
a statement by R. Johanan that seems to contradict the baraita. R.
Johanan states that we have learned fear of sin from a virgin and
confidence in the bestowal of reward from a widow. This statement
in and of itself need not be contradictory to the baraita, for R.
Johanan does not use the term "a praying virgin" or a "gadabout
widow"; he just mentions a virgin and a widow. The Talmudic
sugya, though, sees it as a contradiction and emphasizes this in its

explanation of R. Johanan's statement. It provides the examples of the specific virgin and the specific widow to which R. Johanan was referring; the virgin is in fact a praying virgin, and the widow is in fact a widow who goes away from her own neighborhood. R. Johanan himself could not be the narrator of this section, since the source refers to what R. Johanan heard the virgin praying for, and what he said to the widow.[52] The Talmudic sugya thus brings this story told by or about R. Johanan, which contradicts the baraita in the following manner: he praises a praying virgin for her extra carefulness (*yir'at het*) with regard to sexual matters, for she prays that no man be caused to sin on her account, presumably by being sexually attracted to her.[53] His story, then, would contradict the baraita's criticism of the praying virgin.

He then praises an extremely pious widow, who was, presumably, a gadabout widow—an *almanah shovavit*. The Talmud states that a certain woman had a synagogue in her neighborhood (*beshivevutah*), yet she walked great distances in order to pray in R. Johanan's synagogue. He asks her, "My daughter, is there not a synagogue in your neighborhood (*beshivevutech*)?" and she replies that she walks the greater distance to get a reward for her efforts. Her wandering about, then, is not for purposes of curiosity and gossip (as the gadabout widow is generally assumed to do); instead, she had a specific religious goal in mind. R. Johanan, then, according to the sugya's understanding, used a praying virgin and a gadabout widow as examples of model religious behavior, exactly the opposite of the "destroyers of the world" of the baraita.

The Talmudic sugya then goes on to solve this contradiction by saying that the baraita (and presumably the Mishnah) referred only to a certain specific type of woman, namely, someone like Johani the

---

52. R. Nissim Gaon, though, has R. Johanan himself narrating this story (*Hibbur Yaffeh*, p. 242). Given the narrative nature of this entire book, though, it is certainly possible that he was quoting from memory and that his version does not represent an actual textual variant. Lieberman discusses the phenomenon of medieval commentators who paraphrase the Palestinian Talmud rather that actually quoting from it in "Al HaYerushalmi," *Talmud Yerushalmi Codex Vatican* (Jerusalem: Makor, 1970), p. 41.

53. R. Nissim Gaon (ibid.) adds another line to the virgin's prayer, in which she prays that she herself will also be able to avoid sinning: "and that I will not stumble with people and inherit Gehenna."

daughter of Retibi, and not simply to any praying virgin or gadabout widow. The talmudic sugya does not explain who this Johani was; perhaps she was so notorious that no explanation was deemed necessary. R. Nissim Gaon and Rashi[54] explain that she was a widow who used witchcraft in order to make childbirth difficult for women, and then would offer to pray to help them deliver their babies. In fact, rather than really pray, she would use her witchcraft to then allow them to give birth. "Gadabout" (*shovavit*) would then mean someone who goes around, from house to house, ostensibly to pray. The "praying virgin" and the "gadabout widow," then, according to the Talmudic commentators, pretended to be pious to cover up some other sin, be it witchcraft[55] or sexual promiscuity.[56]

The earliest source for this specific midrash is R. Nissim Gaon. The generalized phenomenon, however, of using magic to help women having difficulties in childbirth is found in earlier sources. *Sefer HaRazim,* written in Palestine between the first and fourth centuries,[57] contains a magical formula to recite in order to ward off evil spirits that attach themselves to women in childbirth and kill their babies.[58] Magical bowls found in Nippur, Babylonia, from the fifth-sixth centuries contain incantations to help women in childbirth.[59] There are also fragments from the Cairo Genizah belonging to earlier books of magic, as well as amulets texts, which contain incantations and magic recipes for all sorts of occasions; one of the

---

54. R. Zvi Hirsch Chajes, in his novella, ad loc., cites this midrash as an illustration of the fact that Rashi had many aggadot that have now been lost, since this midrash is not in any of our midrashim or in the Palestinian Talmud.

55. According to R. Nissim Gaon and Rashi.

56. According to Rashi, s.v. *harei eilu.*

57. Baruch Levine states that the linguistic criteria favor a date closer to the beginning of that period, rendering it a tannaitic work. See "The Language of the Magical Bowls," appendix to Jacob Neusner, *A History of the Jews in Babylonia* (Leiden: Brill, 1970), vol. V, p. 344.

58. *Sefer HaRazim,* ed. Mordechai Margaliot (Tel-Aviv: Yedi'ot Aharonot, 1967), p. 23.

59. See bowls 24, 39, and 42 in Montgomery, *Aramaic Incantation Texts from Nippur* (Philadelphia: University of Pennsylvania, Museum Publication of the Babylonian Section, 1913).

dominant themes found in these fragments is aid for a woman giving birth (*le-isha hamaksha leyled*).[60]

The Talmudic sugya thus connects the ascetic woman (*ishah perushah*) with the praying virgin (*betula tyzalyanit*) and the gadabout widow (*almana shovavit*). It does not distinguish between the three terms and explains that they all destroy the world when they are like the infamous Johani bat Retibi. As already noted, the Talmud, though, does not explain why Johani was in fact so infamous. According to the Talmudic commentators, however, the issue of internal motivation was of crucial importance here. For according to these commentators, the women condemned in the Mishnah and baraita are not sincerely religious. Instead, they are fraudulent pretenders, using exaggerated outward piety in order to hide their sins.

The effects that these behaviors would have on other people are also negative: by their pretended piety, they trick people into trusting them and respecting them. If the sin they are hiding is of a sexual nature, this could certainly deceive a present or future husband. If the sin they are hiding is witchcraft, then anyone who comes into contact with these women is in danger of joining them in sin or simply of being deceived, especially since their virtuous reputation would trick people into trusting them. In the case of Johani the daughter of Retibi, for example, according to the Geonic legend, the women trusted her to pray for them to ease their labor pains. When they found out that they were being deceived, she was driven from the town.[61]

Thus, although the Mishnah and the baraita appear, at first glance, to condemn the ascetic woman unequivocally, the Talmudic sugya qualifies the condemnation found in these earlier sources. It concludes that the baraita and the Mishnah criticized only praying virgins and gadabout widows who were like Johani bat Retibi, and not just any praying virgin and gadabout widow. An ascetic woman who was not like Johani, then, was praiseworthy. The Talmudic commentators explain that women who had pure and sincere

---

60. Peter Schafer, "Jewish Magic Literature in Late Antiquity and Early Middle Ages," *Journal of Jewish Studies* 41 (1990), p. 88; Lawrence H. Schiffman and Michael D. Swartz, *Hebrew and Aramaic Incantation Texts from the Cairo Genizah* (Sheffield: Sheffield Academic Press, 1992), p. 32.

61. R. Nissim Gaon, p. 242.

religious motivation for their actions, like the virgin and widow in R. Johanan's example, were considered to be models of piety.[62]

P. *Sotah* 3:4 (19a)

P. *Sotah* 3:4 (19a) explains *Isha Perusha* as follows:

I.   An ascetic woman (i.e., *isha perusha*)—is she who sits and ridicules the words of Torah:

II.  "And she said, 'Come to me' and he lay with her that night" (Genesis 30:16).

III. R. Abbahu said: "She must have only thought this (*kiveya-khol haya bemachshavah*).

IV.  He alone knew that she did this only in order to establish tribes."

---

62. A. Rapaport-Albert cites this Mishnah and Talmudic sugya, as well as the Maharal (*Hiddushei Aggadot, Sotah*, p. 62) as evidence that within Rabbinic tradition, female ascetic piety was granted no legitimacy, since it was viewed "as inherently false, hyocritical or self-deluding." Male asceticism, on the other hand was "in certain circumstances . . . accorded full legitimacy and even sanctity." See Ada Rapaport-Albert, "On Women and Hasidism: S. A. Horodecky and The Maid of Ludmir Tradition," *Jewish History: Essays in Honour of Chimen Abramsky*, ed. Ada Rapaport-Albert and Steven J. Zipperstein (London: Peter Halban, 1988), p. 507, and notes 72 and 19. Though her point certainly has some validity, it is overstated. For the Talmudic sugya itself limits the criticism of the Mishnah to women who were "not like Johani" and actually praises women who are like those described by R. Johanan. And while Rapaport cites the Maharal (whose views on women appear, at times, to be extremely derogatory—see Maharal, ibid., pp. 62, 64–65), she does not refer to the Meiri, who specifically states that the Mishnah condemning the separated woman did not refer to all women. He states explicitly that women whose piety is proper and who have good intentions should not be criticized or questioned, "and there are some who are fearful of sin and even more careful in their observance than men" (*Beit HaBehirah, Sotah*, p. 46). Thus, the Meiri, following the B. *Sotah* sugya, accepts the legitimacy of the "ascetic woman" who has sincere motivations. See also the introduction of R. Joshua Falk (the *Drishah uPerishah*) to *Tur Yoreh Deah*, where he praises the ascetic piety of his mother. My thanks to Rabbanit Chana Henkin for this reference.

The verse quoted here is part of the exchange between Leah and Jacob in Genesis 30:16. Leah had mandrakes (*dudaim*) that her son, Reuben, had collected. Rachel wanted Leah to give her the mandrakes and Leah refused. Leah then agreed after Rachel promised her that in exchange for the mandrakes, Jacob would sleep with her that night instead of with Rachel. The verse then says, "And Jacob came home from the field in the evening and Leah went out to him and said, 'Come to me, for I have rented you with the *dudaim* of my son,' and he lay with her that night (*balayla hu*)"; (the PT quotes only part of the verse).

This passage needs to be divided into two parts. First we have sections I and II, which are anonymous. We then have sections III and IV, quoted in the name of R. Abbahu, or R. Johanan according to the Rome manuscript. Sections III and IV explain how the verse that the ascetic woman was mocking was to be properly understood.

In section I, the "ascetic woman" apparently ridicules Leah for telling Jacob to sleep with her. Perhaps this woman is "separated" in the sense of being either celibate or extremely reticent about sexual issues, and she belittles Leah for being so "brazen." She puts herself on a pedestal and belittles Leah for being so forward in sexual matters as to actually "buy" her husband for the night.[63] She finds it difficult to explain how this "indecent" verse could be written in the Torah and therefore ridicules it, feeling herself to be exceptionally

---

63. The Halakhic recommendation that a woman not make verbal requests of her husband for sexual relations ("*haisha tova'at balev veha'ish tove'a bape zo hi midah tovah banashim*") might be involved here. If that recommendation had already been formulated and was well known, then this very modest woman would be belittling Leah by saying, "Leah did not keep this law, she was so immodest" (*Korban haEdah*, ad loc.). The dating of the formulation and teaching of this recommendation, however, is not known. There is an opposing tradition attributed to R. Yohanan in *B. Nedarim* 20b indicating that the law was not formulated until after his times. It is also found in *B. Eruvin* 100b, in the name of R. Isaac b. Abdimi. R. Isaac b. Abdimi, though, could either have been the tanna in the house of Rabbi Judah the Prince (which would date the source as tannaitic) or a third-generation Babylonian amora (Hyman, *Toledot*, vol. II, pp. 784–786). Yet even if the "recommendation" had not yet been formulated, it may have reflected normative social behavior of that time period, which Leah's behavior did not follow—hence the ascetic woman's discomfort (cf. Boyarin, *Carnal Israel*, pp. 129–130).

modest.[64] This ascetic woman, then, is being criticized for being more modest with regard to sexuality than the Torah; feeling herself to be especially chaste, she mocked Leah's behavior.[65] The reason for the Rabbi's criticism of this woman would then be that her internal motivations are arrogant and haughty—she is belittling either the Torah itself or Leah's actions as they are reflected in the Torah.

R. Abbahu in section III then justifies Leah's actions. While the exact meaning of *kiveyakhol haya bemahshavah* is unclear, it may mean "as if to say,[66] her thoughts [i.e., her intentions] were pure." "He," meaning either God or Jacob, knew that her intentions were only to establish tribes and, therefore, her actions were justified.[67] It should be noted that even R. Abbahu seems to find Leah's request difficult to understand. For according to his position, had her motivation for "buying" Jacob been simply to be together with her

---

64. *P'nei Moshe,* ad loc. See *B. Eruvin* 100b, where this verse is quoted by R. Samuel b. R. Nahmani in the name of R. Yonatan to praise Leah and explain why she merited having wise children.

65. Following the manuscript of Maimonides, which was found by Geiger that has "a sexually promiscuous woman" (*isha perutza*—see earlier discussion), this *P. Sotah* sugya would be explained quite differently. The sexually promiscuous woman would then be ridiculing the words of the Torah by quoting this verse to justify, perhaps, her sexual misconduct; she may have jokingly wanted to show how Leah too was "forward" sexually. R. Abbahu would then be justifying Leah's actions by explaining that her motivations were not sexual but only to establish the tribes.

66. The term *kiveyackhol,* meaning "as if to say," is generally used to apologetically introduce an anthropomorphism; see Benjamin Z. Bacher, *Erkhei Midrash,* trans. A. Z. Rabinowitz (Tel Aviv: Ahdut, 1923), s.v. *kiveyakhol,* p. 50.

67. *P'nei Moshe,* ad loc. According to the *Korban haEdah,* though, R. Abbahu's *kiveyakhol haya bemachshava* means that she never actually said the words "Come to me" and it was all a thought. The word *He* refers to God, since God alone knew that her intention was to establish the tribes, and He wrote down her thoughts in the verse. (This certainly goes against the simple contextual meaning [*peshat*] of the verse, for how would Jacob have known to go to her tent if she had not asked him to do so?) R. Abbahu's defense of Leah's actions shows that he felt a need to justify what she did, perhaps to counteract the ascetic woman's difficulty with the text.

husband that night and not to establish tribes, then her actions would not have been justified.[68]

The *P. Sotah* sugya then turns to the next phrase in the Mishnah, "the wounds of the separatists." It then quotes the passage discussed earlier regarding the fasting virgin, which will be quoted again here for the sake of clarity and to explain sections IV and V, concerning the gadabout widow:

I.   They added to them:
II.  a fasting virgin,
III. fasting all the time causes her to lose her virginity.
IV.  And a gadabout widow (*almanah shovavit*):
V.   Who? Hogla, who got a bad name (or Because she was a gadabout, she got a bad name).

In section I, the "They" of "They added to them" appears to refer to the tannaim, who added two categories to the list in the Mishnah: the categories of the fasting virgin and the gadabout widow. These categories, though, are, in all likelihood, examples of the ascetic woman, since they are discussing women.

Sections I to III were explained earlier, since they are tannaitic. While the plainest meaning of the text (*peshat*) is that the fasting virgin literally loses her hymen by fasting excessively, some Talmudic commentators, as was already mentioned, explain that the fasting virgin uses fasting as a camouflage for promiscuity.[69] The PT here, then, would be parallel to the BT Talmudic sugya's conclusions regarding the praying virgin and the gadabout widow. They too were only pretending to be pious in order to cover up for

---

68. Lieberman suggests that this ascetic woman "who sits and ridicules the words of Torah" had in fact committed adultery and was now pregnant. Like the fasting virgin and gadabout widow, she had sinned and was trying to cover up her sin. She therefore quotes the verse in the Torah about how Jacob had relations with Leah on that night, ostensibly to claim that it was really her husband who had relations with her. Lieberman's explanation for this is certainly creative, but it lacks actual textual evidence "Tikunei HaYerushalmi," *Tarbiz* V (1934), p. 101.

69. Tosafot, *B. Sotah* 22a, s.v. *kol*.

their sins. According to the Talmudic commentators on *B. Sotah* 22b, the sin was witchcraft,[70] while here the sin was premarital sex, and the Rabbis were criticizing their fraudulent behavior.

The word *shovavit* was explained above as "always visiting her neighbors." The *P. Sotah* here, in section V, defines the gadabout widow by asking, "Who?" (*Mi*), meaning, "who is this widow?" and then answering, "Hogla, who got a bad name." Perhaps Hogla is the equivalent of the notorious Johani bat Retibi.[71]

In all likelihood, though, since the names are so different, *P. Sotah* is probably describing another person. The root H.G.L may be the same as A.G.L (*agol*—round),[72] meaning going around and around,[73] and Hogla would then refer to someone who is in constant movement, always going to visit her neighbors.[74] This explanation is consistent with a second possible translation for the entire phrase, namely, "Because of (*mi*) her frequent visits (*hogla*), she acquired a bad name."[75] According to this translation, no name is being given

---

70. R. Nissim Gaon and Rashi.

71. R. David Frankel (*Korban HaEdah*) in fact explains the *PT* as being the same as the *BT* and quotes the story of the widow who practiced witchcraft on women in labor.

72. The *ayin* and *het* sometimes interchange in Talmudic literature. For example, in Tosefta *Makkot* 5(4):15, the Erfurt manuscript has the word *mitalfin,* whereas the Vienna manuscript and the editio princeps have *mithalfin* (*Tosefta,* ed. Zuckermandel [Jerusalem: Wahrmann Books, 1963], p. 445, note to line 8) and *B. Sanhedrin* 103a, where the *ayin* of our Biblical text (of 2 Chronicles 33:13) is interchanged with a *het*. This phenomenon is also found in Qumram Hebrew, see Lawrence Schiffman, *The Halakhah at Qumram* (Leiden: Brill, 1975), p. 32, note 73, for further references.

73. *Arukh,* s.v. S.V.L.

74. *Pnei Moshe,* ad loc. He then says that this woman creates a bad name for her neighbors, whom she constantly visits and spreads gossip from one to another. He suggests emending the text to *Mirgila,* from the root R.G.L., meaning someone who is used to spreading gossip.

75. Lieberman suggests this, explaining that she claims to have received a bad reputation because she "went around" too much, when in fact she was always visiting her neighbors only to give charity to the poor and not to sin; "Tikunei Yerushalmi," *Tarbiz* V (1934), p. 101. The Arukh's second explanation of *shevavit* is the same: she does not remain in her house modestly but instead goes out in the market and street. He quotes *P. Sotah* as *"almanah shovavit mishum denisveit shum bish."* Instead of *mi hogla,* he

here; instead, a type of behavior is being described. Why her frequent visits gave her a bad name, though, is not discussed.

An interesting parallel within Christian sources to the phenomenon of the gadabout widow who acquires a bad name can be found in the *Didascalia Apostolorum* discussed previously. Within its instruction as to how holy widows should behave, it contains a warning as to how not to behave:

> A widow must not therefore stray or run about among the houses. For those who are gadabouts and without shame cannot be still even in their houses; . . . And because they are gossips and chatterers and murmurers, they stir up quarrels; and they are bold and shameless. [76]

The similarity between these criticisms and those of the *P. Sotah* sugya and its interpreters is remarkable. The gadabout widow was criticized in both Jewish and Christian sources for visiting neighbors excessively, gossiping, and generally being bold and shameless. This same theme will surface again, in the later discussion of the midrash found in *P. Hagigah* 2:2 (77d).

While the Mishnah and baraitot appear to express a general condemnation of the ascetic woman, both the *B. Sotah* and *P. Sotah* Talmudic sugyot qualified this condemnation. The *B. Sotah* sugya understood it as limited to women who were like Johani bat Retibi, and the *P. Sotah* sugya states that the ascetic woman is one who mocks the words of the Torah because of her excessive modesty. Presumably, if she were extremely modest, or even actually sexually abstinent, but did not have an arrogant attitude, then she would not have been condemned. One may conjecture that the amoraic limitation of R. Joshua's condemnation, in both the *B. Sotah* and *P. Sotah* sugyot, may have been due to the decreasing influence of Christianity on the Jews in amoraic times in Babylonia (and perhaps also in Palestine—see the introduction to this study).

As discussed earlier, Aphrahat's "Demonstrations" show that the Christians in fourth-century northern Mesapotamia felt the need to defend themselves against Jewish criticism. Aphrahat, in

---

simply has *mishum*—because she gets a bad name, due to her immodest behavior.

76. *Didascalia Apostolorum*, pp. 133–134.

fact, devotes his Eighteenth Demonstration to defending the Christian ideals of virginity and celibacy against Jewish criticism of those practices.[77] This demonstrates that the Jews, at least in northern Mesapotamia, were openly critical of Christian asceticism in the fourth century. Furthermore, the phenomenon of ascetic women in Babylonia was, in all likelihood, not at all popular, for marriage and sexuality were regarded extremely positively in Babylonian culture.[78] The idealization of abstinence was most likely limited to the persecuted Christian minority and, consequently, not likely to attract Jewish women.

## The Vision of Gehenna in P. Hagigah 2:2 (77d)

Another source, found in *P. Hagigah* 2:2 (77d) and in an abridged parallel in *P. Sanhedrin* 6:6 (23c),[79] is relevant to this study of the ascetic woman. It is an Aggadic passage, containing a dream in which a pious man has a vision of Gehenna. In his vision:

I. He also saw Miriam "of the onion bulbs" (*berat alei betzalim*)[80]

II. R. Eleazar b. Yosi said: She was hanging by the nipples of her breasts.

III. R. Yosi b. Hanina says, the hinge of the gate of Gehenna was set in her ear.[81]

---

77. *Aphrahat,* "Demonstration XVIII, against the Jews and on Virginity and Sanctity," trans. Neusner in *Aphrahat,* pp. 76–83.

78. Gafni, *Yehudei Bavel,* app. II, pp. 266–273; and Daniel Boyarin, "Internal Opposition in Talmudic Literature: The Case of the Married Monk," *Representations* 36 (Fall 1991), pp. 87–113, note 13.

79. Six different versions of this midrash are reprinted in "Ma'aseh HaMokhes veHaTalmid," *Tosefta Atikata,* ed. Chaim M. Horowitz (Israel: 1970), section V, pp. 66–75.

80. The parallel in *P. Sanhedrin* 6:6 also has this name. A different parallel, in "Midrash Aseret HaDibrot" has "Miriam daughter of Manilay" (*Beit haMidrash,* ed. Adolph Jellinek [Jerusalem, Bamberger & Wahrmann, 1938], vol. 1, p. 89). Lieberman, though, rejects this version in his discussion of this text. See "On Sins and Their Punishments," *Texts and Studies* (New York: Ktav, 1974), p. 35, note 48.

81. Jellinek's version of this midrash differs slightly here in that it

IV.     Said the Hasid to his comrade: Why is she thus being punished?

V.      He answered: Because she fasted and publicized it (*dehava tzayma umefarsema*).

VI.     Others say that she fasted one day and calculated it (*umakza ley*) as a two-day fast."[82]

VII.    He said to him: How long will she remain like this?

VIII.   He answered him, "Until Simeon b. Shetah comes and we remove the hinge from her ear and place it on his."[83]

Lieberman dates this text as being very early.[84] While this certainly may be true about parts of the passage, other parts are later. For R. Eleazar b. Yosi may either have been the Tanna R. Eleazar b. R. Yosi b. Halafta, or he might have been a fifth-generation Palestinan amora with the same name.[85] R. Jose b. Hanina was a second-generation Palestinian amora, a student of R. Johanan.[86]

This passage is fascinating, on many accounts. First, while it does not state that it is discussing a "fasting virgin," it may provide

---

reads, "R. Eliezer bar Yosi said, 'The hinge of the gate of Gehenna was set in her ear'"; it deletes the line "She was hanging by the nipples of her breasts," and R. Jose b. Hanina is not mentioned. In the version of this midrash found in R. Nissim Gaon's *Hibbur Yaffe* (reprinted in *Tosefta Atikata*, pp. 69–70), all mention of the woman is deleted. Rashi also records a version of this midrash in *B. Sanhedrin*, 44b s.v. *deba'ya mukhsa*, which also deletes all mention of the woman. Instead, the pious man sees a man (a former tax collector) with the hinge of the door to Gehenna in his ear and asks, "How long will *he* have to endure this harsh punishment," and he is told, "until Simeon b. Shetah dies."

82. Once again, Jellinek's version of the midrash differs slightly. Here it has "Because she fasted and publicized it to her neighbors." And others say, "Because she had two and said three" (Jellinek, p. 89).

83. This translation is taken from Lieberman, "Sins," pp. 33–34, with my own additions.

84. Lieberman, "Sins," p. 34. While he dates it as "very early," he does not suggest any precise time period.

85. Hyman, *Toldot*, vol. I, pp. 177–178.

86. Ibid., vol. II, p. 723.

us with an example of just such a woman (*betulah tzaymanit*).[87] According to section V, this woman's sin was to fast and then publicize her piety. Her piety, then, was insincere, since she was not fasting out of sincere religious conviction but rather so that people would respect her. According to the second explanation (section VI), she was deceptive—she fasted for one day and then counted it as two days of fasting.[88] The common denominator in both explanations is that this woman fasted for insincere reasons (just like the fasting virgin of *P. Sotah* 3:4 (19a), according to the medieval commentators).

The extreme severity of the punishment given to this woman seems shocking, in relation to the crime she committed. One would have expected that she had committed some gruesome murder or at least transgressed one of the more serious sins in the Torah. Instead, her sin was religious insincerity and hypocrisy.[89] This must be understood, as Lieberman points out, as typical of the embellished and exaggerated style found especially in Talmudic midrashim of an apocalyptic nature. He explains this phenomenon as follows: "It is indeed difficult to condemn the pious scribes who poured oil on hell-fire and invented all kinds of odd tortures for the wicked and the transgressors; for theirs was the best of intentions, to frighten the masses and drive them away from sin."[90]

There are many parallels within the New Testament Apocrypha

---

87. Lieberman calls the *betulah tzaymanit* "a self-afflicting girl" ("Sins," p. 35).

88. R. Samuel Jaffe Ashkenazi, in his commentary to the *P. Hagigah*, explains that she would fast for one day and pay herself back for two days; that is, she would eat and enjoy herself for two days in exchange for her one-day fast (*Yefei Mareh P. Hagigah* 2:2 (Venice: 1590)).

89. Lieberman understands her very odd name "of the onion bulbs" or "daughter of the onion bulbs" as a symbol for hypocrisy, since onion bulbs, which cover the bitterness of the onion, serve as a symbol for hypocrisy ("Sins," pp. 35–36). We find this idea in *Genesis Rabbah* 82:12 (ed. Theodore Albeck [Jerusalem: Wahrmann, 1965], p. 990): "I have searched Esau and revealed his secrets" (Jeremiah 49:10). R. Simon said, "I peeled his onions . . . in order to reveal the *mamzerim* in his lineage." R. David Frankel (*Korban HaEdah*), s.v. *vehama leMiryam*, suggests that her father's name was, actually, "Onion Bulbs."

90. Lieberman, "Sins," p. 31.

to the punishment described in this passage.[91] A variety of sources describe people in Gehenna who are hanging by various body parts, including their ears and their genitalia. The exact details of the punishment in our source, namely, the hinge of the gate of Gehenna being fixed in one's ear and hanging by the nipples, though, seem to be unique to the Jewish sources.[92]

The continuation of the passage, which is not quoted due to its length, contains an account of how Simeon b. Shetah deserved punishment because he had not fulfilled his promise to kill all witches, and then describes how he did indeed kill the eighty witches in Ashkelon. This is interesting in light of the Geonic connection between the ascetic woman and witchcraft; B. *Sotah* 22a concludes its discussion of the praying virgin and the gadabout widow by saying that the Mishnah meant a woman like Johani daughter of Retibi, whom the Geonim describe as a witch. There seems, thus, to be a connection in both the Geonic literature and the *P. Hagigah* sugya here between this ascetic woman, who prayed or fasted more than other women and was seen as being insincere, at best, or a witch, at worst. Although the *P. Hagigah* source does not claim that this Miriam "of the onion bulbs" was herself a witch, the juxtaposition of her story with the killing of the witches suggests such a connection.[93]

---

91. See ibid., pp. 36–51.

92. Ibid., p. 36.

93. There are other versions of this story that attribute still other sins to this woman in Gehenna, which remind us not only of the "fasting virgin" but also of "the gadabout widow." One of these is a parallel to this midrash found in the appendix to Rabbi Meir of Rothenburg's responsa (reprinted in *Tosefta Atikata* V, p. 71). This source clearly originates in the *P. Hagigah* passage quoted earlier, but contains detailed elaborations which originated in some other unknown source. In this expanded version of the midrash, the pious man in Gehenna is shown a woman, "upon whose ear the hinge of the door of Gehenna opened and closed, and he showed him men hanging by their male organs and he showed him women hanging by their breasts . . . and Elijah told him that the woman upon whose ear the hinge of the door of Gehenna opened and closed used to fast all her days and would say that her heart hurt from fasting, but when she heard gossip and insulting words she listened attentively in order to tell her husband and fill him with hatred of others; it is that ear which suffers the punishment of Gehenna. . . . [T]hose hanging by their breasts used to suckle their

## THE TARGUMIM OF EXODUS 38:8

Other sources related to the topic of the ascetic woman are found in the Targumim to Exodus 38:8, which describes the construction of the sink for the tabernacle:

> And he made the laver of brass, and its pedestal of brass, of the mirrors of the women assembling, who assembled (*hanashim hatzove'ot asher tzave'u*) at the door of the Tent of Meeting.

The root TZ.V.A in the phrase *hatzove'ot asher tzave'u* suggests a very large assembly of women who gathered at the door of the Tent of meeting. The simplest contextual meaning is that they gathered to donate their mirrors to the tabernacle. The biblical translators, though, explain this verse differently. First among these translations is the Septuagint, which has "of the mirrors of the women that fasted, who fasted by the doors of the tabernacle of witness" in Exodus 38:26.[94] The Septuagint's mention of fasting recalls the

---

children publicly so that men saw their breasts." In this source, the woman suffering in Gehenna was also a woman who fasted—though clearly not a virgin, since she was married. This woman (the Miriam of *P. Hagigah* 2:2?) also fasted for personal gain and behaved hypocritically. Although she used to fast and complain about how her heart hurt from all of her fasts (similar to fasting and publicizing it), she was a gossip and purposely tried to fill her husband with hatred of others. The theme of gossiping is reminiscent of the "gadabout widow" (*the almanah shovavit*). The "female gossip," condemned to torture in Hell, is also found in a Christian Apocryphal source, the *Apocalypse of the Virgin (or Mary):* "And she saw a woman hanging by both her ears . . . and she is the one who eavesdrops at other houses and the houses of her friends and increases gossip in order to cause dissension" (trans. Lieberman, *Texts and Studies,* p. 41; also found in *The Apocryphal New Testament,* trans. Montague R. James [Oxford: Clarendon, 1975], p. 563). The New Testament Apocrypha in general is dated as approximately the second century by Koester, vol. II, p. 13, but this work in particular is considered early medieval (ninth century) by James H. Charlesworth, *The New Testament Apocrypha and Pseudepigrapha* (Metuchen, N.J.: American Theological Library Association and Scarecrow Press, 1987), pp. 36–37.

94. *Septuaginta,* ed. Alfred Rahlfs (Stuttgart: Privilegiert Wurttembergische Bibelanstalt, 1935); *The Septuagint Version: Greek and English,* trans. by

"fasting virgin" of *P. Sotah.*[95] Since the Torah itself speaks of gathering, and not of fasting, it is possible that the Septuagint's translation reflected a practice of its time period[96] rather than being a mere translation.

Onkelos translated this as "with the mirrors of the women who came to pray in front of the Tent of Meeting." Once again, since the text itself speaks only of gathering, Onkelos's addition to the text may have reflected a practice of his time period.[97] Alternately, Onkelos may be reflecting some ancient tradition about a group of especially pious women who assembled at the Tent of Meeting in order to pray. This is suggested by the root TZ.V.A., which as previously explained, suggests a large group of people.[98] Onkelos's translation, in any event, recalls "the praying virgin" of the *B. Sotah* sugya.

---

Sir Lancelot C. L. Brenton (Grand Rapids, Michigan: Regency Reference Library, 1970).

95. Later commentaries expand on what may have been an ancient tradition concerning these women, hints of which appear in the targumim (but do not appear in any midrashim available to us). Ibn Ezra, for example, writes that "there were women in the desert who would remove themselves from the pleasures of this world and come to the Tent of Meeting every day to pray and to hear the commandments of God" (Exodus 38:8). Nachmanides and Seforno are two other commentators who mention this tradition (see *Torah Shelemah,* ed. Menahem Kasher (Jerusalem: Makhon Torah Sh'lemah, 1969), vol. 23, p. 50, note 4, for further references).

96. The Septuagint was not, however, reflecting the realities of tannaitic times, since it was written in a much earlier time period. The writing of this work (the Hellenistic Greek version of the Bible, used by the Alexandrian Jewish community), began in the third century B.C.E. (see L. H. Schiffman, *From Text to Tradition* (Hoboken, NJ: Ktav, 1991), p. 92).

97. Onkelos's translation, though, was written in Talmudic times. See Philip Alexander, "Jewish Aramaic Translations of the Hebrew Scriptures," *Mikra* (*Compendium Rerum Iudaicarum ad Novum Testamentum,* ed. Martin Jan Mulder [Philadelphia: Fortress, 1988], pp. 217–218. Cf. Luke 2:36–37's description of Anna (discussed earlier), who lived, presumably, in tannaitic times and spent days and nights fasting and praying in the Temple.

98. Roland de Vaux questions whether the *nashim hatzove'ot* (the "women who assembled") were women who served in the Tent (and later the Temple) in some capacity, perhaps as did the Bedouin women who looked after the Bedouin holy tent. See *Ancient Israel,* trans. John McHugh (London: Darton Longman & Todd, 1961), pp. 383–384; cf. Nahum Sarna's note on *Exodus* 38:8 where he refutes de Vaux's suggestion in *The Jewish*

Targum Pseudo-Jonathan gives an expanded and somewhat different description of the character of this "assembly of women":

*Neshaya tzeniyuta*—the modest women, and during the time when they came to pray in front of the Tent of Meeting they would bring a sacrifice . . . and return to their husbands and have pious children.

The modesty of these women clearly had nothing to do with sexual abstinence, since after returning from their prayers they go back to their husbands and have pious children.[99] Other Targumic texts also translate "the women who assembled" as "the modest women"—[*neshaya tzeniyata*],[100] and still others have "the just women"—[*neshaya tzadikata*.][101]

A connection can thus be made between the Septuagint's and Onkelos's translations of this verse and the Talmud's "ascetic woman." While the Septuagint and Onkelos refer to "fasting" and "praying" women in general, and not specifically to virgins, this is

*Publication Society Torah Commentary* (Philadelphia: Jewish Publication Society, 1991), p. 230. The question, though, remains a valid one since Lieberman discusses sources that describe a group of noble virgins below the age of puberty who participated in the weaving of the veil of the Temple (*Hellenism in Jewish Palestine* [New York: Jewish Theological Seminary, 1950], pp. 167–168).

99. The most well-known midrash on this verse contains an extremely antiascetic motif—it describes how the women in Egypt used these mirrors to seduce their husbands and thereby become pregnant, thus ensuring the continuity of the Jewish people by creating the "armies"—that is, hordes (*tzeva'ot*) of the Jewish people. These mirrors, considered holy by God, were then used to create the *laver* in the Tent of Meeting. See *Midrash Tanhuma* with commentary of H. Zundel [reprint, Jerusalem: Lewin-Epstein, 1962], Pikudei 9, quoted by Rashi Exodus 38:8.

100. This term is found in the printed Targum Yerushalmi, in three texts of the Fragment Targum (in *The Fragment Targums of the Pentateuch* [Analecta Biblica 76, ed. M. Klein: Rome: Biblical Institute Press, 1980], and in a variant or marginal gloss of Neophyti I (*Neophyti I, Exodo,* ed. Alejandro Diez Macho [Madrid: Consejo Superior de Investigaciones Cientificas, 1970]).

101. This is found in a manuscript of the Targum Yerushalmi and in the main text of Neophyti I.

not a significant difference. For, as noted, the distinctions between "woman" and "virgin" are blurred in the Talmudic sources themselves. These Targumim, however, reflect a totally different attitude toward the women's behavior than do the Talmudic sources discussed here. For the women who either fasted according to the Septuagint or prayed according to Onkelos were being praised for their piety and generosity; they were not criticized.

## CHAPTER SUMMARY

The "ascetic woman," in the context of the Mishnah, was a sexually abstinent woman. The praying virgin of the *B. Sotah* baraita and the fasting virgin of the *P. Sotah* baraita, when added to the sexually abstinent woman of the Mishnah, complete the portrait of an ascetic woman, condemned by the tannaim as a destroyer of the world. The Mishnah's wording of "an adult woman" (*ishah*) suggests that the "ascetic woman" may have been married but separated from her husband, and the two baraitot add a virgin and a widow as further examples of the ascetic woman. All different types of women are thus included in the tannaitic condemnation of the female ascetic— a married woman, an unmarried virgin, and a widow.

An investigation of whether the phenomenon of Jewish abstinent women can be found in extra-Talmudic sources of roughly the same time period has demonstrated that there may have been abstinent women among the Essenes and the Qumran sect. Likewise, Philo reports that there were Jewish abstinent women among the Therapeutaue living in Egypt in the first century B.C.E.—early first century C.E.

In the religions surrounding the Jewish people during tannaitic and amoraic times, the phenomenon of "holy virginity" was very common and was found in varying degrees depending on the religion. The Greco-Roman religions, for example, had virgin priestesses. Nonetheless, prolonged virginity within these religions was never considered to be "human nature at its peak" or the ideal state of being for the general population.[102]

In early Christianity, however, virginity was considered a tremendous virtue and was not limited to a select few. Likewise,

---

102. Brown, *The Body and Society*, p. 8.

extensive fasting was highly valued. Young girls and widows were encouraged to be "holy virgins" and "holy widows," and even married women were encouraged by some Christian preachers to separate from their husbands. The usage in some early Syrian sources of the masculine and feminine terms for "virgins"—*betula* and *betulta,* respectively—as a reference to early Christians[103] suggests that the baraita, which uses the same term (*betulah*) in its description of the ascetic woman as a praying or fasting virgin, may have been referring to early Christian "holy virgins."

Exactly how these Christian sources are connected to the Jewish sources is very hard to determine, but what is evident is that the phenomenon of ascetic women certainly existed, and it was emphatically opposed by the tannaim. While Philo and many early Christians thought of this phenomenon as highly commendable, extra-pious behavior, R. Joshua and the tanna of the baraita felt that it was so negative as to be classified as "destroying the world." Perhaps they were reacting to a growing phenomenon of female asceticism or to a fear that such a phenomenon would grow in Jewish circles, as a result of the influence of the early Christians.

The *P. Sotah* baraita regarding the fasting virgin condemned her for one of three possible reasons: for being celibate, for fasting so much that she actually loses her hymen, or for using fasting as a cover up for her promiscuity. The gadabout widow, according to the *P. Sotah,* is accused of immodestly "going around and around" and thereby acquiring a bad name.

*P. Hagigah* 2:2 (77d) provides an example of what the *P. Sotah* baraita might have meant by a fasting virgin (*betulah tzaymanit*).[104] The sin of the woman hanging in Gehenna was to fast and then publicize her piety. Her piety, thus, was deemed insincere, since she was not fasting out of authentic religious feeling but rather so that people would respect her.[105]

---

103. Voobus, *History of Asceticism,* vol. I, pp. 103–104.

104. Lieberman calls the *betulah tzaymanit,* "a self-afflicting girl" ("Sins," p. 35).

105. There seems to be a connection in both the Geonic literature and this *P. Hagigah* sugya between the ascetic woman and witchcraft. According to the Geonim, Johani b. Retibi in *B. Sotah* 22a was actually a witch, and *P. Hagigah* 2:2 juxtaposes the story of the woman who fasted insincerely with the killing of the witches in Ashkelon.

The B. *Sotah* Talmudic sugya significantly limits the Mishnah's criticism of the female ascetic. After discussing cases of an extremely pious virgin and widow, it concludes that only a certain type of ascetic woman was condemned by the tannaim, namely, women like Johani bat Retibi. The Talmud itself does not explain what type of woman she was; the Geonim explain that she was a fraudulent pretender to piety who used her piety to conceal her witchcraft. It is conceivable that there was a historical change in attitude between the tannaim and amoraim vis-à-vis the ascetic woman. The Babylonian amoraim may have no longer felt the need to criticize the female ascetic so severely, for two reasons. First, the threat of Christian influence was not as strong in amoraic Babylonia as it had been in tannaitic times in the land of Israel. Second, since marriage and sexuality were viewed favorably in Babylonian culture, sexual abstinence in general may not have been very prevalent in amoraic Babylonia.

The *P. Sotah* Talmudic sugya also qualifies the Mishnah's condemnation of the ascetic woman, by defining the ascetic woman as someone who is intent on mocking the words of the Torah, by acting as if she is more modest than the biblical heroes themselves. This woman is called a destroyer of the world, then, because she is "modest" in an arrogant and haughty manner. If she did not belittle the Torah then, presumably, her ascetic behavior would not be problematic.

Another example of the ascetic woman may be provided by the Targumim to Exodus 38:8, who speak of women who prayed or fasted. These women, however, were being praised for their piety and generosity and not criticized.

Two major themes thus emerge from the sources regarding the ascetic woman. The first, found in the Mishnah and baraitot in B. *Sotah* and *P. Sotah* (as understood independently of the amoraic interpretation), appears to be that the rabbis criticized her self-imposed religious stringency in no uncertain terms, because they felt that this type of behavior would destroy the world both figuratively and literally. Not only was it unnatural, but it would also lead to sin, the breakdown of Jewish families, and a lower Jewish birthrate. According, then, to these tannaitic sources, the ascetic woman was always to be condemned; no matter how sincere her intentions, her chosen spiritual path was never to be accepted as an optional lifestyle.

The second theme to emerge from these sources, which is found explicitly only in the amoraic passages, is that only a certain type of ascetic woman was criticized, namely, those like Johani bat Retibi. While the *B. Sotah* sugya does not explain who Johani bat Retibi is, the Talmudic commentators hold that she pretended to act in an exceptionally pious manner (praying and fasting excessively) only to hide her actual evil intent—witchcraft or promiscuity. The *P. Sotah's* definition of the ascetic woman as someone who arrogantly mocks the words of the Torah implies that an ascetic woman who is not arrogant is not to be condemned. A variation on this theme (found in *P. Hagigah* 2:2 [77d]) is the condemnation of the woman who fasts in order to publicize her piety or deceitfully states that she fasts more than she actually does.

According to this second theme, a sincerely religious ascetic woman would be allowed to follow her chosen spiritual path without being criticized or condemned as a "destroyer of the world." For according to the *B. Sotah* sugya, the Mishnah and the baraita were condemning only women like Johani bat Retibi who, according to the commentators, were not sincerely religious women like the pious virgin and widow described by R. Yohanan. While this position is more fully developed in *B. Sotah*, it is not, however, limited to the Babylonian amoraim.

According to the *P. Sotah* sugya, for example, the ascetic woman of the Mishnah was arrogant and irreverent. If she had been sincere, then she would not, presumably, have been criticized. Furthermore, the statement in *B. Sotah* that praises a virgin and a widow as models of piety is attributed to R. Yohanan, a Palestinian amora. Assuming that the attribution is correct, then *B. Sotah's* "softening" of the Mishnah's criticism of the ascetic woman may have actually originated in Palestine.

An ascetic woman per se, then, according to the amoraim, was not to be automatically censured. Evaluation of her chosen lifestyle was dependent on her motivations; if she were sincere, then she would not be condemned. If she were not like Johani bat Retibi, then her behavior was actually deemed praiseworthy.

# 4

# The Wounds of the Separatists (Makot Perushim)

*M*. *Sotah* 3:4 lists "the wounds[1] of the separatists" (*makot perushim*) after "the separated woman" in its list of people who bring destruction on the world. The word *perushim* will be translated literally as "separatists." Lieberman suggests that the word is actually *paroshim*, the active form of the root P.R.SH., meaning people who separate from the community.[2] The word Pharisees will not be used, since that term usually refers to the pre-rabbinic Pharisees as a movement and not to the individuals or small groups of individuals being discussed here.

The name Pharisees, in all likelihood, originally meant something like "separatists," because they were exacting and hence

---

1. The text of the Mishnah found in the Meiri has *midot* instead of *makot*, meaning "the characteristics of separatists." Lieberman quotes the Mishnah as "the *kat* of perushim" ("Tikunei Yerushalmi," *Tarbiz* V [1934], p. 101).

2. Leiberman, *Tosefta Kifeshutah, Berakhot* 3:25, p. 18. In the context of this Toseftah passage, the separatists (*paroshim*) separate from the community specifically in times of trouble and sorrow.

somewhat separatist in their study and observance of the Torah.[3] Although they ceased to exist as a separate group after the destruction of the Temple, the ideal of separation (*perishut*) was still considered a positive value in rabbinic literature. The separation (*perishut*) encouraged by some rabbis involved being separate from other nations and abstaining from physical pleasures.[4] Yet despite separatism being considered an ideal, R. Joshua condemned individuals, or perhaps small groups of people who became separatists (*perushim* or *paroshim*). The nature of their separation, why they separated, and why R. Joshua condemned them cannot be determined from the Mishnah itself. The discussion of "the wounds of the separatists" in P. *Sotah* 3:4 following the Mishnah is not relevant to our topic, since the examples all involve using legal means for the purposes of financial trickery. The discussion of "the wounds of the separatists" found in B. *Sotah* 22b, though, is directly related to this study.

## THE SEVEN SEPARATISTS: *B. SOTAH* 22B:

I.  Our Rabbis have taught: There are seven types of separated people:[5]
    1. the *shikmi* separatist,
    2. the *nikpi* separatist,
    3. the *kizai* separatist,
    4. the *medukhya* separatist,
    5. the "What is my duty that I may perform it" separatist,
    6. the separatist from love,
    7. and the separatist from fear.

---

3. Fraade, "Ascetical Aspects," p. 269, note 63. For a more complete discussion of the relationship between the Pharisees and "separatists," see pp. 269–272 and notes ad loc.

4. See, for example, *Mekhilta* Jethro (Bahodesh) 2 (ed. Horowitz, p. 209), B. *Abodah Zarah* 20b, and Fraade, ibid., p. 270, notes 66 and 68 for further references.

5. The words [who bring destruction on the world] are added in R. Nissim Gaon's *Hibbur Yaffe min HaYeshuah,* printed in *Otzar HaGeonim Sotah*, p. 243, and in the version of this passage found in the *Midrash HaGadol* on Genesis 34:24. This addition strengthens the connection between the baraita and the Mishnah, but the earliest source containing this phrase is Geonic.

II.

    1. the *shikmi* separatist—he is one who performs the action of Shechem.

    2. the *nikpi* separatist—he is one who knocks his feet together.

    3. the *kizai* separatist—R. Nahman b. Isaac said: He is one who makes his blood flow against walls.

    4. the *medukhya* separatist—Rabbah b. Shila said: [His head] is bowed like [a pestle in] a mortar.

    5. the "What is my duty that I may perform it?" separatist. But that is a virtue!

    No, what he really says is, "What further duty is there for me that I may perform it?"

    6–7. The separatist on account of love and the separatist on account of fear:

III.    Abbaye and Rabbah said to the tanna [who was reciting this passage], "Do not include the separatist on account of love and the separatist on account of fear"; for R. Judah has said in the name of Rav: A man should always engage himself in Torah and the commandments even if it is not for their own sake (*lo lishma*), because from [engaging in them] not for their own sake, he will come [to engage in them] for their own sake.

IV.    R. Nahman b. Isaac said: What is hidden is hidden, and what is revealed is revealed; the Great Court will exact punishment from those who rub themselves against the walls.[6]

Section I of this passage contains the anonymous baraita that briefly lists the seven separatists but does not explain them. Section II, which is amoraic, explains the categories of the baraita. While the

---

6. The final section of this Talmudic sugya contains King Jannai's instructions to his wife on his deathbed. This section of the text, though, switches from use of *perushim* as individuals who separate themselves from the general community to *perushim*, i.e., Pharisees as a political movement in the first century B.C.E., and is, therefore, not relevant to this study. For further information see Josephus, *Antiquities of the Jews*, XIII:XV; and E. Schurer, *The History of the Jewish People in the Age of Jesus Christ*, ed. G. Vermes, F. Millar, vol. I (Edinburgh: Clark, 1973), pp. 220–30.

term *separated* when used in reference to the ascetic woman (*isha perusha*) meant separated from sexual relations, in this context it connotes a more general and varied separation. These separatists (*perushim*) set themselves apart from the general population by acting more pious than the average person in many different ways, all of which will be discussed later. Parallels to both the baraita and the ensuing Talmudic discussion quoted are found in *P. Sotah* 5:5 (20c) and *P. Berakhot* 9:5 (14b) and will be included in this discussion.[7] As noted earlier, this baraita and its explanation is not quoted in *P. Sotah* 3:4's discussion of the Mishnah; only *B. Sotah* connects the two sources. According to the *P. Sotah*, "the wounds of the separatists" that destroy the world are unrelated to the seven separatists of the baraita.

## 1.THE *SHIKMI* SEPARATIST

"The *shikmi* separatist—he is one who performs the acts of Shechem." Shechem, after raping Jacob's daughter, Deena, then circumcised himself and all the members of his household, so that he could marry her (Genesis 34). The act of Shechem that the sugya, in all likelihood, is referring to is the circumcision that he performed for his own personal gain, and not for the sake of God. The *shikmi* separatist, then, is being criticized by the rabbis for the insincere internal motivation for his behavior. He is someone who behaves in an especially pious way for his own personal gain: i.e., for material gain

---

7. There are also parallels to the baraita alone, without the Amoraic embellishment in *Aboth deRabbi Nathan*, Versions A and B. The text in Version A, while similar to the *B. Sotah* 22b and the *P. Sotah* 5:5, contains many errors, and the text in Version B is basically the same as the list in the *P. Sotah*. See Schechter's notes to Aboth de Rabbi Nathan (New York: Feldheim, 1967), Version A, chap. 27, p. 109, note 4; and Version B, chap. 45, p. 123, note 1. Several other parallels to this passage also exist. One, which is basically parallel to the *P. Sotah*, is found in the *Yalkut HaMakhiri, Tehilim,* 109:17 (ed. S. Buber; Jerusalem: Opst, 1964). Others are found in R. Nissim Gaon's *Hibbur Jaffe,* in *Midrash HaGadol* Genesis 34:24 and *Midrash haGadol* Numbers 5:28 (Jerusalem: Mossad HaRav Kook, 1975). This last source only contains the baraita listing the seven separatists and then ends with "and these, and all who do these kinds of acts, are destroyers of the world." These parallels will be cited only when significant.

or so that people will respect him, and not to grow closer to God.[8] In other words, he is doing the right thing but for the wrong reasons. If the words *the wounds* of the separatists were meant literally, then the wound referred to here seems to be Shechem's circumcision. Shechem's circumcision, in turn, represents a metaphor for any pain suffered ostensibly in the name of religion when in truth it was suffered for personal gain.

The explanation of the *shikhmi* separatist in *P. Sotah* 5:5 (20c) differs from that found in *B. Sotah*. The *P. Sotah* passage reads, "a *shikmi* separatist—who carries his commandments on his shoulders." This can be taken literally, as it was by the Arukh, who comments, "who carries his commandments on his shoulders like wood to build a *sukkah* and other such examples,"[9] or figuratively, as someone who does the commandments in an ostentatious way. This type of person does the commandments "without principle, without heart, and with deceit";[10] he acts as if he is extremely religious only to show everybody how pious he is. The wording is different from that of the *B. Sotah*, but the meaning is similar; he does the commandments for personal recognition, and not to deepen his relationship with God. He is using religion as a way of elevating his status among other people.[11] He is ostentatious and arrogant in his religious observance, showing everyone just how religious he is. The "separation" here is that he acts more pious than other people. The wound referred to here is unclear, unless it means the pain suffered by carrying the wood for the sukkah on one's shoulders.

There are parallels in the New Testament to the rabbinic criticism of ostentatious displays of piety. In Matthew 6:1–18, Jesus warns his disciple to avoid hypocritical behavior when giving charity, when praying, and when fasting:

---

8. Rashi, s.v. *ma'ase Shechem.*

9. The *Arukh,* s.v. *parush.*

10. R. Nissim Gaon, *Hibbur Yaffe,* p. 243. R. Yesha'yah Aharon (*Hiddushei Ri'az Sotah,* ad loc.) connects the *shikmi* separatist with the separated woman, since they are both deceitful.

11. Maimonides defines "the wounds of the separatists" as a person who acts piously to gain in this world; he wishes to gain, for example, the respect of other people, or hopes that God will not take away his money (Maimonides, *Commentary on the Mishnah,* ad loc.).

Be careful not to parade your religion before others; if you do, no
reward awaits you with your Father in heaven. So when you give
alms, do not announce it with a flourish of trumpets, as the
hypocrites do in synagogues and in the streets to win the praise
of others. . . . But when you give alms . . . your good deed
must be secret. . . . Again, when you pray, do not be like the
hypocrites; they love to say their prayers standing up in synagogues
and at street corners for everyone to see them. . . . So too when
you fast, do not look gloomy like the hypocrites: they make their
faces unsightly so that everybody may see that they are fasting.[12]

Matthew often uses the term *hypocritis* as a synonym for the
Pharisees,[13] but in this context it seems to be meant literally (although
it could still be a synonym for the Pharisees even here, since they were
supposedly the people behaving in this hypocritical manner).[14]

*The Anchor Bible* translates the word *hupokritai* as "the overscru-
pulous" rather than "the hypocrites." The editors write, "It was not
that these people were consciously acting a part which did not
correspond to their inner convictions, but that they were parading
their own scrupulousness in public."[15] Either one of these translations fits in with the *shikmi* separatist described in the Talmud. This

---

12. Translations from the New Testament in this study follow the *The
Revised English Bible* (Oxford: Oxford University Press, 1989).

13. See, for example, Matthew 23:23: "Woe to you, scribes and
Pharisees, hypocrites!" The word *Pharisee* became a synonym for the word
*hypocrite,* and even today, the second definition for the word Pharisee in the
*Random House Dictionary* (New York: Random House, 1981) is, in fact,
"hypocrite."

14. These claims regarding the ostentatious behavior of "the hypocrites" have a polemic ring to them. The same criticism is, in fact, directed
toward "the nations of idolators" who "only give alms in order to be
exalted" in *B. Baba Batra* 10b, and praise for giving alms in secret is found
in *B. Baba Batra* 9b: "He who gives alms in secret is greater than Moses
our teacher." These sources are cited by Willoughby C. Allen, *The International Critical Commentary; Matthew,* (Edinburgh: Clark, 1912), pp. 56–57. See
also E. P. Sanders, *Jesus and Judaism* (Philadelphia: Fortress, 1985), pp.
338–339.

15. W. F. Albright and C. S. Mann, *The Anchor Bible,* appendix to pt. IX
of the introduction (New York: Doubleday, 1971), p. cxxi. For a compre-
hensive discussion of this term, see James Barr, "The Hebrew/Aramaic
Background of 'Hypocrisy' in the Gospels," *A Tribute to Geza Vermes,* ed.

theme is repeated again, in Matthew 23:5–7,[16] where he criticizes the scribes and Pharisees who

> do all their deeds to be seen by men; for they make their phylacteries broad and their fringes long, and they love the place of honor at feasts and the best seats in the synagogues and salutations in the market places, and being called rabbi by men.

This is similar to rabbinic criticism of men who wore their tefillin all day but were not truly pious. *Pesikta Rabbati* 22:5,[17] on the verse "Do not take the Lord's name in vain" (Exodus 20:7), states:

I.    That you are not to put on tefillin and wrap yourself in your prayer shawl, and then, disregarding the name of the Lord, go forth and commit transgressions.

II.    R. Yannai taught: Because tefillin require [that the person wearing them have] a clean body.[18]

---

Philip P. Davies and Richard T. White (Sheffield: Sheffield Academic Press, 1990), pp. 307–326.

16. Cf. Luke 18:9–14, where the Pharisee boasts about his supererogatory fasts. In Colossians 2:16–23, Paul describes self-mortification as the behavior of people who are "bursting with the futile conceit of worldly minds" (verse 18) and as "forced piety" (verse 23). And in a later period (the earliest possible dating being fourth century), Abba Isidore the Priest is quoted as saying, "If you fast regularly, do not be inflated with pride, but if you think highly of yourself because of it, then you had better eat meat. It is better for a man to eat meat than to be inflated with pride and to glorify himself"; See *The Sayings of the Desert Fathers: Apophthegmata Patrum,* trans. Benedicta Ward (London: Mowbray, 1980), pp. 106–107.

17. An abridged version of this story is found in *P. Berakhot* 2:3. Other parallels are found in *Midrash HaGadol,* Exodus 20:7, and *Sefer HaMa'asiyot,* ed. Moses Gaster (Leipzig: Asia, 1924), no. 123, p. 83. In *Leviticus Rabbati* 6:3 and later in *Pesikta Rabbati* 22, a similar story is found but without mention of the tallit and tefillin. The man in this similar story is given the name of Bar (or Ger, i.e., proselyte) Telamion (Margaliot, though, leaves it out in his edition, suggesting that it is copied from *Pesikta Rabbati*—see pp. 132–133).

18. This is a literal translation based on *Pesikta Rabbati,* ed. Meir Ish-Shalom (reprint; Tel-Aviv: 1963). See William Braude's translation and notes for alternate translations: *Pesikta Rabbati* (New Haven, CT: Yale

III. The reason that the Jews avoided wearing tefillin[19] was that hypocrites were wont to mask themselves with them, as is evident from the experience of a certain man who was carrying his money on a Friday. Toward sunset he went to a synagogue where he found someone praying, with tefillin still on his head. Some say this person was a proselyte.[20] The man carrying the money said to himself: Should I not feel free to leave my money with this person who [even at this late hour in the day] wears upon himself the proof of his fear of God?

IV. Thereupon he left his money in trust with the person wearing the tefillin. But at the end of the Sabbath, when he came for his money, the other denied the transaction. The first man said: "It was not you that I believed, but the holy Name that was on your head."

In section I, Jewish men are warned against wearing tallit and tefillin, outward signs of piety, and then going and commiting sins. The story in section III tells of a case of a person (or prototype) who uses his tefillin to deceive people into thinking he is especially pious, and then steals their money. This is similar to the Geonic interpretation of the ascetic woman discussed in Chapter 3. While she used praying or fasting to cover up her sinful behavior, the man in this

University Press, 1968) 22, note 16, p. 459; and Menahem Kasher's discussion of whether this phrase meant literally "a clean body" or "a body which is free of transgression": *Torah Shlemah,* vol. 12, Jerusalem: Makhon Torah Shelemah, 1969 app. 41, pp. 254–259. The rest of the translation here follows Braude.

19. This may refer to a period when observance of the commandment of wearing tefillin was weak, possibly as a result of a Roman decree; see *B. Shabbat* 130a and 49a. The text in the Rome manuscript actually has "the reason that [the Jews] avoided wearing them *in the land of Israel* was because of bloodshed *(damim)*" (*Talmud Yerushalmi,* Codex Vatican [Jerusalem: Makor, 1971]). Alternately, some commentaries instead explain that it means, "the reason that Jews wearing tefillin were not trusted" (Tosafot *Shabbat* 49a, s.v. *ke-Elisha;* see also Braude, ibid., and Kasher, ibid., app. 42, pp. 259–63).

20. There may, once again, be a Christian-Jewish polemic reflected here, which focused on the wearing of tefillin. Matthew 23:5–7 denounces people who wear their phylacteries and fringes, and the midrash here suggest that the hypocrite who wore tefillin all day was a convert.

case used his tefillin for the same purpose. In addition to using tefillin to trick people, someone wearing tefillin but committing transgressions could easily influence other people to follow in his sinful ways, since he would be viewed as a role model and respected for his special piety.[21] People would automatically respect such a person and try especially hard to follow his teachings. Wearing tefillin all day can, thus, give someone the power to trick others and corrupt others and is, therefore, criticized by the rabbis.[22] This type of person, who wears tefillin all day for his own self-serving goals is, then, a perfect example of a *shikmi* separatist.

## 2. THE *NIKPI* SEPARATIST

"The *nikpi* separatist—is one who bangs his feet." Various explanations have been offered for this passage:

1. He claims to have walked so much in order to do so many commandments that he hurt his feet; he says that he bought a lulav, and wood for his sukkah, and then walked a great distance to a circumcision and to a bride's blessing (*birkhat kallah*),[23] but in fact, he is a hypocritical liar.[24]

---

21. Menahem Kasher, *Torah Shlemah*, vol. 12, app. 42, p. 263.

22. A Geonic responsa, probably authored by R. Natrunai Gaon, describes this type of hypocritical leader and quotes the above *Pesikta Rabbati* source. He describes a priest who "adorns himself with the tallit of scholars," yet is cruel and unscrupulous (*Teshuvot Geonei Mizrah uMa'arav*, ed. Joel Muller [Berlin: Deutsch, 1888], p. 132, and note 1). Muller suggests that this hypocritical person was a priest who converted (ibid., note 2).

23. This is, in all likelihood, a reference to the "virginity blessing" (*birkat betulim*) that was recited by a bridegroom after seeing his wife's blood (thus confirming that she was in fact a virgin) upon consummation of their marriage. This blessing was recited over wine, and family and friends were invited to celebrate. While this blessing was regarded as an obligation by various Geonim, Maimonides held that it was a blessing in vain and a despicable custom (*Otzar HaGeonim Ketubot.*, pp. 14–15; Maimonides, *Teshuvot HaRambam* 129, ed. David Yosef (Jerusalem: Makhon Or Ha-Mizrah, Makhon Yerushalayim, 1980).

24. R. Nissim Gaon, *Hibbur Yaffe*, p. 243, *Midrash haGadol* Genesis 34:24.

2. He tries to avoid pushing other people in the street, and thereby bangs into rocks.[25]
3. He walks bent over, as if he is very humble, does not watch where he is going and hurts his feet, but is evil at heart.[26]
4. He shuffles his feet along the ground and does not lift them as he walks, and because of this bruises his toes on the stones on the ground.[27]

According to explanation 1, the *nikpi* separatist tries to make himself appear very pious by bragging about the many good deeds he did that day, when in fact he is lying or, at the very least, exaggerating. He is pretending to be religious so as to gain people's respect. Once again, the rabbis are criticizing someone who has insincere internal motivations for acting in a pious manner.

According to explanation 2, this separatist is being so careful not to accidentally hurt others that he hurts himself. In explanations 3 and 4, the person is trying to act extremely humble (by appearing bent over before God), but the rabbis are condemning his excess either because he is being hypocritical (3) or because he hurts himself (4).

*P. Sotah's* explanation of "a nikpi separatist" again differs from the explanation in *B. Sotah,* stating "a nikpi separatist—"I will go around and I will do a mitzvah." *Akif* would then come from the root N.K.F, meaning to go around.[28] This could refer to someone who says "Lend me money so that I can do a mitzvah" and is only doing so to impress his neighbor with his religious dedication.[29]

The *nikpi* separatist is, thus, similar to the *shikmi* separatist discussed previously in that both represent people who separate from others by acting especially pious (according to explanations 1 and 3 and *P. Sotah*). They do not separate from others owing to any fervent desire to serve God. Instead, they do so for their own

---

25. *Arukh,* s.v. *parush.*
26. *Arukh,* ibid.
27. Rashi, s.v. *hamankif raglav.*
28. *Arukh,* s.v. *kaf, nakaf.*
29. The Arukh gives a few different definitions for the word *nakaf.* One is hitting, or banging, another is "going around," and still a third is lending money. *B. Sotah* (and Rashi, ad loc.) use the first definition, and *P. Sotah* uses either the second or the third definition.

personal gain; they are insincere and are using religion to gain the respect of others. According to B. *Sotah,* they may even go to the extent of hurting themselves, whereas according to the P. *Sotah,* their problem is limited to their attitude.

## 3.THE *KIZAI* SEPARATIST

"The kizai separatist: R. Nahman b. Isaac said: He is the one who makes his blood flow against the walls." One explanation focuses on his hypocrisy. To avoid touching other people, he scrapes his skin against the walls of the street, since he feels that he is purer than all other people.[30] In the textual version found in the *Midrash HaGadol* (Genesis 34:24), the words "when in fact he himself is the impure one" are added, followed by a quote from Isaiah 65:5: "just as it says, 'Do not come near to me, for I am holier than thou.'" In this verse, Isaiah is condemning people who are really sinners but act as if they are holier than anyone else.

Two other explanations do not assume that he is hypocritical but focus simply on the external effects of his behavior. Even if his motivations are sincere, the fact that he wounds himself invalidates the religious value of his behavior. The first is that to avoid hurting other people in the street, he scrapes himself against the walls.[31] The second is that to avoid looking at women, this separatist walks in the street as if his eyes are closed and hits his head against the walls on the side of the street, making himself bleed.[32]

The "wound" here is obvious. In this case, someone actually hurts himself to avoid "sinning" (touching others, bumping into others, or looking at women in the street). His extreme need to "separate" himself (in this case, interestingly, this word is meant both figuratively and literally) from possible sin leads to self-inflicted wounds. The rabbis are then criticizing this type of separatist for two possible reasons. One is that they assume him to be a hypocrite and a pretender. The second is that even if he is genuinely worried about hurting others or looking at women, he is nevertheless deserving of harsh criticism because of the external effects of his behavior, namely, that he makes himself bleed. The idea of someone

---

30. R. Nissim Gaon, *Hibbur Yaffe,* p. 243.
31. *Arukh,* s.v. *parush.*
32. Rashi, s.v. *mekiz dam laketalim.*

physically harming himself in an attempt to avoid what he considered to be a sin was, according to this source, considered to be behavior that "destroys the world."

*P. Sotah's* explanation of the *kizai* separatist once again differs from that of the *B. Sotah. P. Sotah* has "I will do one negative commandment (*hova*) and one positive commandment (*mitzva*) and balance one against the other (like a bookkeeper[33])." His motivations in doing the mitzvah are not for the sake of heaven, but so that he can balance out the sin he committed. He performs a premeditated balancing act, where he calculates exactly how many sins he can do and then how many *mitzvot* he can do in order to end up with an "even score." What is "separatist," though, about this behavior, is not clear.

The root of the word *kizai* is found in another passage in the Palestinian Talmud, in the form of the word *umakza* in the apocalyptic dream found in *Hagigah* 2:2 which was discussed in Chapter 3. This woman (who could be an example of an ascetic woman), may also be an example of a *kizai* separatist.[34] For the woman who was found hanging in Gehenna had apparently kept a bookkeeping system of her "merits and demerits," so to speak, in which she was dishonest. Although she fasted only one day, she counted it as two. In other words, she gave herself two points, instead of the one she deserved, to feel and/or appear more pious than she really was. The rabbis in this case are focusing on the internal motivation of the separatist. This woman did not fast to serve God. She had a need to even out the score, so to speak, presumably to avoid punishment by having an even score of merits to counterbalance the demerits.

## 4. THE *MEDUKHYA* SEPARATIST

"The *medukhya* separatist: Rabbah b. Shila said: [His head] is bowed like [a pestle in] a mortar." He walks totally bent over.[35] He does this in a hypocritical manner, to show how humble he is—as if to say, "I am so humble, I could never even lift my head in public."[36] He is, according to this explanation, a person who is showing off how

---

33. Lieberman, "Sins," p. 29.
34. Lieberman, "Tikunei HaYerushalmi," p. 101.
35. Rashi, ad loc.
36. R. Nissim Gaon, *Hibbur Yaffe,* p. 243.

religious he is to gain the respect of others. And even if his motives had, in fact, been sincere, he should have been aware that his bizarre appearance would call attention to himself and make people mock or scorn him.[37] He is being criticized, then, for ostentatiously displaying his piety to others and/or for causing a mockery of religious people by his public display. The former involves his own internal motivations, whereas the latter involves how he is affecting those around him, a recurring theme in the many cases discussed earlier. This appears to be an example of a foolish pietist (to be discussed in Chapter 5), whose religious excesses cause people to scorn and mock him.

A second explanation for the *medukhya* separatist is that he gathers all of his clothes in his hand and shows that he tries not to touch another person, lest he become impure.[38] This is similar to the explanation given for the *kizai* separatist who scrapes his skin against the walls of the street to avoid touching other people, since he feels that he is more pure than everyone else.[39]

A third description of the *medukhya* separatist is that he walks bent over, like a hunchback, and wears a large, triangular-shaped garment with which he covers himself. He does this to demonstrate that he is very modest and does not want to look at other people.[40]

The type of hyperreligious behavior described here clearly separates the person from the general public. All three definitions of the *medukhya* separatist describe a person walking in the street, engaging in strange contortions in the name of piety; this extreme "separationist" behavior is being condemned.

The fourth separatist listed in *P. Sotah* sugya, the *ma han-khei* or *ma nakhei*[41] separatist, substitutes for the *medukhya* separatist of the *B. Sotah* sugya. This term is explained by the *P. Sotah* sugya as someone who says, "Whatever I have, I leave it for doing a commandment,"[42] or "What social or utilitarian gain will I get out of doing this command-

---

37. See Maimonides, *Commentary to the Mishnah, Sotah,* 3:3, ed. J. Kapah (Jerusalem: Mossad HaRav Kook, 1965), s.v. *hasid shoteh.*
38. *Arukh,* s.v. *parush.*
39. R. Nissim Gaon, *Hibbur Yaffe,* p. 243.
40. *Midrash haGadol,* Genesis 34:24 and *Arukh,* s.v. *parush.*
41. Rome manuscript.
42. *P'nei Moshe,* ad loc.

ment?"[43] According to the first explanation, this man separates himself from others by pretending to be exceptionally pious by boasting about how he spends all his money on performing religious commandments. This is obviously untrue, since he has to provide for his physical needs, and so he is boasting about his extreme piety to gain people's admiration. According to the second explanation, he thinks about the utilitarian benefit and/or enhanced social reputation that he will get out of performing a commandment before doing it; he is not motivated by the love of God. According to both explanations, then, his internal motivations are corrupt. He is not sincerely religious and uses the commandments for his own personal gain.[44]

According to *B. Sotah,* the *medukhya* separatist isolates himself from others by acting in a bizarre manner, presumably for insincere motives. Similarly, according to *P. Sotah,* his separation involves a boastful and/or insincere attitude.

## 5. THE "WHAT IS MY DUTY THAT I MAY PERFORM IT?" SEPARATIST[45]

The *B. Sotah* sugya first exclaims that this is a positive trait, for someone who does not know the commandments and is asking what religious duties he has, in order to perform them, should be praised. The sugya then modifies the baraita's words slightly by adding the word *more:* "What *more* is my duty that I may perform it?" The word *more* implies that this person thinks that he has, in fact, already fulfilled all of his religious duties and says, "What more could possibly be left for me to do; I have already fulfilled all my obligations."[46] This separatist is arrogant—not merely insincere. Other examples of when the rabbis criticized people for appearing arrogant when they imposed stringencies upon themselves will be discussed in Chapter 7.

The *P. Sotah's* fifth separatist, the "I will know my duty and I will do it" separatist, sounds identical to *B. Sotah's* fifth category, but

---

43. *Perush miBa'al Sefer Haredim,* ad loc.

44. As is apparent, there is a great similarity between this separatist and the *shikmi* separatist (i.e., hypocrite).

45. This category is not found in R. Nissim Gaon's list.

46. Rashi, ad loc.

the sugya in *P. Sotah* explains it differently, stating, "What duties (sins) have I committed and I will do a positive commandment (*mitzvah*) [to compensate] for them." *P. Sotah*, then, understands the word *duties* (*hovot*) as sins, while in *B. Sotah* it means positive commandments (*mitzvot*). What he is saying, in other words, is "When have I ever sinned—show me that I have sinned and then I will do a positive commandment, but since I never sin, I don't have to do any commandments to counteract my sins." He speaks arrogantly, and thinks that he is extremely saintly.[47] This type of separatist is similar to the *P. Sotah*'s *kizai* separatist who keeps a bookkeeping account of his transgressions and positive commandments.

The "separatism" here, in both *B. Sotah* and *P. Sotah*, does not take the form of any specific behavior but rather of an attitude. He believes he is better than other people, since he is so exceptionally pious.

## 6-7. THE SEPARATIST ON ACCOUNT OF LOVE AND THE SEPARATIST ON ACCOUNT OF FEAR

The *B. Sotah* Talmudic sugya clearly views the baraita as including these two categories in its list of "destroyers of the world." This is demonstrated by the fact that Abbaye and Rabbah ask the tanna to separate these two categories from the negative list, since they quote Rav as saying that doing the commandments not for their own sake (the separatist on account of love and the separatist on account of fear) will lead to doing the commandments for their own sake. Doing the commandments "for their own sake" means doing them to fulfill God's commands, as opposed to doing the commandments due to anticipation of reward or fear of punishment.[48] "A separatist on account of love" is not motivated by the love of God but instead does the commandments for the sake of gaining people's love—(i.e., a good reputation) or so that God will reward him by taking away

---

47. *P'nei Moshe* and *Toldot Yizhak,* ad loc.

48. Pseudo-Rashi *B. Ta'anit* 7a s.v. *lishmah;* Tosafot *Sotah* 22b, s.v. *le-olam.* The widow in *B. Sotah* 22a who walked all the way to R. Yohanan's synagogue every morning and is praised by him for teaching confidence in the bestowal of a reward, though, does not fit into this negative description. For her confidence that God would reward her for her extra steps is viewed as model behavior.

his poverty and illness.[49] Similarly, the separatist on account of fear does the commandments because he is afraid of the punishment that he will receive if he transgresses. These separatists do not separate because of a true desire to serve God; instead, they separate for self-serving purposes.[50] Being a separatist on account of love or fear, though, according to Abbaye and Rabbah, should not be criticized, since it will ultimately lead to true religious worship.[51]

The *P. Sota* sugya, in contrast to the *B. Sotah* sugya, clearly views the separatist on account of love as favorable. Consequently "the separatist on account of love" is listed after "the separatist on account of fear" (and hence is no longer part of the preceeding negative list of separatists):

I.    The separatist on account of fear: like Job.
II.   The separatist on account of love: like Abraham.
III.  None of the above are beloved except for the separatist on account of love like Abraham.

*P. Sotah's* addition of the phrase "none of the above are beloved except for the separatist on account of love like Abraham" notes explicitly that this is a desirable category. "Love" in *P. Sotah* must, then, be understood as love of God Himself.

After describing the seven separatists (sections I–III), the *B. Sotah*

---

49. R. Nissim Gaon, *Hibbur Yaffe,* p. 243. The *Midrash HaGadol* Genesis 34:24, which is consistently very similar to R. Nissim Gaon's text here, writes that he does the mitzvot so that people will love him and call him "Rabbi."

50. The idea that there are different levels of worship of God is similar to Lawrence Kohlberg's stages of moral development. The person who does the commandments to receive a reward or avoid punishment (i.e., the separatist from love [in *B. Sotah*] and from fear) corresponds to Kohlberg's lowest level of moral thinking. People on this level interpret the labels of good and bad behavior "in terms of their physical consequences (punishment, reward, exchange of favors)"; See L. Kohlberg, "The Child as a Moral Philosopher," *Psychology Today* 2(4) (September 1968), p. 26. When asked for a motive for rule obedience or moral action, they would say that they obey rules to avoid punishment or obtain rewards (ibid., p. 28).

51. The topic of doing the commandments (and studying the Torah) "for their own sake" versus "not for their own sake" is discussed at length by Leo Levi, *Sha'arei Talmud Torah* (Jerusalem: Feldheim 1981), pp. 13–20.

sugya quotes R. Nahman b. Isaac's statement (section IV). His statement is an elaboration of the theme repeatedly expressed in the amoraic descriptions of the seven separatists, namely, that religious practices motivated by ulterior motives "bring destruction upon the world":

I.    R. Nahman b. Isaac said: What is hidden is hidden, and what is revealed is revealed;

II.   the Great court will exact punishment from those who rub themselves against the walls (*dehafu gundei*).[52]

The meaning of R. Nahman's statement is that though internal motivations are hidden from human beings, God will ultimately know who worships Him sincerely and who is insincere and hypocritical. "Those who rub themselves against the walls" are hypocritical people "whose insides are not like their outsides."[53] R. Nahman is then expanding on and rewording his earlier comments defining the *kizai* separatist as one who makes his blood flow against the walls. Although he describes this behavior using different terms, he would mean the same thing.[54]

Assuming that both of the attributions to R. Nahman are accurate,

---

52. This translation of the words *dehafu gundei* is one of two possible translations in the Arukh, and I have chosen it because of its similarity to R. Nahman's earlier statement (see s.v. *H.F.* V and *gud—guda* I). The other translation in the Arukh is "those who cover themselves with a dark cloak" (see s.v. *H.F–II* and *G.N.D.* I). Rashi's explanation is the same as the latter. He explains *dehafu gundei* as "those who wear their tallit and hypocritically pretend to be separatists." This sounds like the *medukhya* separatist discussed previously who covers himself up with a big cloak to avoid looking at other people, since he feels himself to be so humble. It also corresponds with *Pesikta Rabbati* 22:5 discussed ealier, which warns people not to put on a tallit and tefillin and then commit sins.

53. R. Nissim Gaon, *Hibbur Yaffe*, p. 243, and *Arukh*, s.v. *H.F.* V. B. M. Levin, the editor of *Otzar HaGeonim*, remarks here that this is an allusion to the Karaites but gives no source for his comment (*Otzar HaGeonim*, p. 243, note 11).

54. This explanation is supported by the version in the *Midrash HaGadol* Genesis 34:24 that contains the same verse as a source for the concept of *dehafu gundei* as it had for the *kizai* separatist; "Do not come near me, for I am holier than thou" (Isaiah 65:5). The Arukh also quotes this

then R. Nahman may have been elaborating on his earlier statement regarding the *kizai* separatist by formulating a general principle condemning this type of behavior. The Talmudic sugya may have separated the two statements since at first R. Nahman defined a specific separatist behavior, and then made a general statement that effectively summarized the entire passage.[55] He condemned the hypocrisy, insincerity, and arrogance of all the separatists listed in the baraita, and affirmed that "the Great Court," namely, God Himself, knows whose motivations are insincere and will judge accordingly.

## CHAPTER SUMMARY

As discussed above, "the wounds of the separatists" cannot be explained based on the Mishnah alone. According to *P. Sotah* 3:4, the term referred to legally means to trick people financially and is thus not relevant to this study. According, though, to *B. Sotah* 22b, "the wounds of the separatists" is directly related to this study, since it referred to separatists who behaved as if they were on a higher religious level than everybody else. They separated from other people by acting extremely pious but did so either with improper motivations or in a bizarre manner.

The fact that *B. Sotah* and *P. Sotah* have totally different explanations of the term suggests that they did not have a clear tradition explaining "the wounds of the separatists." The Palestinian Talmud quotes the baraita regarding the seven separatists in *P. Sotah* 5:5 and in *P. Berakhot* 9:5, but it does not quote it as an explanation to this Mishnah. This may indicate that in Palestine, the tradition may actually have been that this baraita was not associated with the Mishnah's "wounds of the separatists."

According, though, to *B. Sotah* 22b, the baraita in fact defines

---

verse but quotes it when he explains *dehafu gundei* as wearing black clothing and not when he explains it as rubbing against the walls.

55. It is possible that R. Nahman b. Isaac was responding directly to the previous remarks of Abbaye and Rabbah (section III); while they stated that improper motivation can lead to proper motivation, R. Nahman pointed out that only God can know people's true inner feelings. Alternately, this remark may have been made independently by R. Nahman and then juxtaposed to Abbaye and Rabbah's statements by the Talmudic sugya, since it was connected in theme.

the Mishnah's "the wounds of the separatists" and should actually be read as "There are seven types of separatists [who bring destruction upon the world]." As mentioned, the words in brackets are actually inserted into the baraita in some Geonic texts. The amoraim then explain why these separatists destroy the world.

The *shikmi* separatist, according to both the Babylonian and the Palestinian passages, behaves especially pious for his own personal gain. He is insincere and ostentatious in his religious observance and uses religion as a way of elevating his status among other people. There are New Testament parallels to the rabbinic criticism of ostentatious displays of piety, such as Matthew 6:1–18, which enjoin Christians, "Beware of practicing your piety before men in order to be seen by them." Someone who wears tefillin and then commits sins, or who wears tefillin all day for self-serving purposes, is a good example of a *shikmi* separatist.

Both the *nikpi* and the *kizai* separatists may be similar to the *shikmi* separatist in that they may all represent people who act especially pious for their own personal gain. According to the *B. Sotah*, though, they are unique in that they go to the extent of hurting themselves for "religious" goals. The rabbis censure this type of person for two possible reasons: they see him as a hypocrite and a pretender, or they object to the external effects of his behavior, namely, his self-inflicted wounds. The *kizai* separatist in *P. Sotah* differs from that of the *B. Sotah* passage. He tries to avoid God's punishment by doing the exact amount of good deeds that he needs to counterbalance his bad deeds.

The *medukhya* separatist is a person who, while walking in the street, engages in strange bodily contortions in the name of piety. This separatist is assumed to be showing off his piety to gain a better reputation; he may have the same motivation as the *shikmi* separatist but tries different means to achieve them. With this separatist, an added factor is that he may arouse feelings of scorn toward religion, since people will view him as being extremely bizarre. *P. Sotah* substitues the *ma hankhei* separatist for the *B. Sotah*'s *medukhya* separatist. This separatist either boasts about how pious he is or performs the commandments based on the amount of social or utilitarian gain that will result.

The "What is my duty that I may perform it?" separatist is arrogant rather than merely insincere. In *B. Sotah*, he thinks that he has already fulfilled all of his religious obligations and could not possibly need to do any more. According to *P. Sotah*, he thinks that he never sins and therefore does not need to do any positive commandments. According to both texts, he speaks arrogantly and presents himself as being extremely saintly; he is a separatist in that he views himself as better than others.

The common denominator between these first five categories, in both the Babylonian and Palestinian passages, is that they represent people who separate from others by acting as if they are exceptionally pious. Whereas the second, third, and fourth separatists in the *B. Sotah* also separate from society by hurting themselves or by looking strange in public, the parallel categories in *P. Sotah* are separatist only in their attitude.

The separatists on account of love and fear, according to *B. Sotah*, do the commandments for the sake of gaining a reward or people's respect or because of fear of the punishment that they will receive. These separatists do not separate because of a true desire to serve God; instead, they separate for self-serving purposes. R. Nahman then summarizes the entire baraita in *B. Sotah* by saying that God will ultimately know who worships Him sincerely and who is insincere and hypocritical. In the *P. Sotah* Talmudic sugya, though, the separatist on account of love is positive. "Love" in *P. Sotah* means love of God Himself.

Two significant differences have been noted between the Babylonian and Palestinian explanations of this baraita. The first is that in *B. Sotah*, piety that is so all-consuming that it results in self-inflicted wounds and/or in people's scorn is also condemned in this passage; this type of piety is not mentioned in the Palestinian parallels. The second difference is that in *B. Sotah*, the "separatist on account of love" is condemned, whereas in *P. Sotah*, he is praised.

According, though, to both the Babylonian and Palestinian passages, the highest level of religious observance was doing the commandments for their own sake (*lishmah*). This practice was considered the ideal goal for the Jewish people to strive for (see Aboth 6:1). The criticism of the supererogatory piety of the seven separatists in this context was, thus, due to various types of flawed motivations. The improper motivations included self-gain (in the form of reputation, respect, money, or power), insincerity, boastfulness, arrogance, and the desire for reward or fear of punishment.

# 5

# The Foolish Pietist
# (Hasid Shoteh)

The foolish pietist of the Mishnah is described in B. *Sotah* 21b:

I.   What is a foolish pietist like?

II.  for example, a woman is drowning in the river, and he says, "It is not the way of the world (*lav orah ar'a*) for me to look upon her and rescue her."

The example given by the Talmudic sugya is of a man who lets a woman drown because he thinks it is improper for him to look at her in the process of saving her life.[1] The expression "the way of the world" (*orah ar'a*), as in the Hebrew translation "*derekh eretz*," means "a proper way to behave." The usage of this term rather than

---

1. Sefer Hasidim cites this example (ed. Margaliot, #126). In the Wistinetzki edition, it discusses fear of touching the drowning woman rather than fear of looking at her: "And there is a piety which is bad, such as someone whose hands are impure and sees a book which has fallen into the fire and says, 'It is better that the book burn than that I touch it,' and likewise they said, someone saw a woman drowning in the river and said, 'It is better that she drown and I will not *touch* her'" (*Sefer Hasidim,* ed. Wistinetzki, p. 466).

"forbidden" demonstrates that what is being described here is this individual's personal idea of propriety, and not his notion (albeit grossly mistaken) of the law.[2] He feels that it is improper, or "not nice," to look at a woman, even in order to save her.

While he is aware on some level that technically, the law permits him to look at her in order to save her,[3] he nevertheless feels that it is improper to do so. He wants to be especially stringent here and not look at her even under these circumstances. By allowing his own mistaken idea of piety to replace that defined by the halakhah, he thereby "destroys the world" by letting an innocent person die.

This idea is found in *M. Sanhedrin* 4:5, which states, "He who destroys one life in Israel . . . it is as if he has destroyed the entire world." What the foolish pietist does not understand is that the obligation to save a human life overrides his reluctance to look at the woman.[4] The term "foolish pietist" would then correspond with the term "commoner" (*hedyot*), which is found in *P. Berakhot* 2:9 and discussed in Chapter 6.[5]

The parallel passage in *P. Sotah* 3:4 (19a) contains three different examples of foolish pietism:

> Who is a foolish pietiest?
>
> I.     One who sees a child drowning in the river and says to himself, "After I remove my tefillin I will save him," and by the time he removes his tefillin, the child is already dead.

---

2. The expression "not the way of the world" throughout the Babylonian Talmud means "improper" or "not nice" rather than "forbidden."

3. The general prohibition for men to look at women (to whom they are not married) in a sexual manner is mentioned in *B. Shabbat* 64b.

4. The obligation to save a person's life is derived from the verse, "Do not stand upon your brother's blood" (*B. Sanhedrin* 73a). The general principle that the saving of a human life takes precedence over all commandments of the Torah (except for three) is discussed in *B. Yevamot* 110a, *B. Yoma* 83a, 86b, and many other sources.

5. Maimonides, in fact, understands these terms as synonymous. He writes, "A foolish pietist: They said in the Talmud that it involves the exaggeration of carefulness and punctiliousness to the point of being scorned in the eyes of other people, and doing deeds that are not obligatory, as if to say "foolish in his piety." And it says in the Palestinian Talmud in Shabbat (*Berakhot* 2:9), "whoever is exempt from something and still observes it is called a commoner (*hedyot*)." See *Commentary on the Mishnah, Sotah*, 3:3, ed. J. Kapah (Jerusalem: Mossad Harav Kook, 1965).

II.   One who sees a 'first fig' [the first fruits were brought to the Temple as an offering (*bikurim*) and were eaten only by the priests] and says, "I will give this to whomever I meet first."

III.  One who sees a betrothed maiden [with a man][6] running after her [to rape her and does not save her]. This is what we have learned in the Mishnah (*Sanhedrin* 8:7), "He who pursues after his neighbour to slay him, after a male [or] after a betrothed maiden [to rape them, must be stopped by the observer, even if he must kill the pursuer]."

The first example given in *P. Sotah* is similar to the one example of *B. Sotah*: in both instances the foolish pietiest lets someone drown because of to his "religious" concerns and thus is "destroying the world" by causing someone's death. In the example in *P. Sotah*, a child is drowning (rather than a woman), and the "religious" concern of the foolish pietist is his concern lest his tefillin become wet. The expression "not the way of the world" is not used here, and there are two ways of understanding his concerns. This pietist may simply be ignorant and unaware of the law. Although he obviously knows that he is not allowed to wet his tefillin, he does not know that saving another person's life takes precedence over the other commandments,[7] including caring for tefillin.[8]

On the other hand, he might actually be aware that he is permitted to jump into the water to save the child even with his

---

6. The exact wording is "One who sees a betrothed maiden and was running after her (*ra-ah na'ara hameorasa vehaya ratz ahareha*)."

7. The Radbaz uses the term *foolish pietist* to describe a man who was told that he was sick enough for others to be allowed to transgress the laws of the Sabbath to care for him but did not want the Sabbath to be transgressed on his account (R. David ibn Abi Zimra, Responsa, section IV, responsa 1,139).

8. *B. Yomah* 84b uses this very example, of a child drowning in the ocean (in *B. Sotah* 21b it is a river), to teach how saving a person's life takes precedence over the laws of the Sabbath (this same principle would apply, a fortiori, to the fear of wetting tefillin): "Our Rabbis taught: One must remove debris to save a life on the Sabbath . . . How so? *If one saw a child falling into the sea,* he spreads a net and brings it up—the faster the better, and he need not obtain permission from the Rabbinic Court (even though he thereby catches fish [in his net])."

tefillin but feels the need to be especially careful with his tefillin. Unlike the pietist of the *B. Sotah*, this man does plan to save the child but delays doing so to first remove the tefillin and thus causes the child's death. Perhaps he simply miscalculated the time; he may have thought that he had enough time to first remove his tefillin and then save the child, but his calculations were wrong and the child drowned. This type of piety, which results in the loss of life, is condemned by the rabbis. The pietist's desire to be especially stringent in the care of his tefillin resulted in his being tragically "lenient" in the commandment to preserve human life. Likewise, the foolish pietist of the *B. Sotah* was especially stringent in his observance of the laws of proper sexual conduct, but he totally neglected to observe the overriding commandment to save the woman's life.[9]

It is not clear whether the examples discussed here involved real people and real incidents or were only theoretical caricatures of people invented by the amoraim in order to demonstrate a point. Evidence from an earlier time period, from two Qumran documents, suggests that the Qumran sect placed limitations on the permission to violate the laws of the Sabbath to save the life of someone who is drowning.[10] These are the Damascus Document (CDC 11:16), and Halakhah A-4Q251.[11] While the examples of the foolish pietist quoted here do not involve violating the Sabbath laws, they do involve the same principle (i.e., of violating the commandments to save someone's life). Assuming that the tannaim and later the

---

9. The Meiri's explanation of a foolish pietist is that he is "someone who becomes too pious, so that his piety causes harm to himself or others, such as someone who fasts every day, or someone who sees a woman drowning in a river." He then lists the example found in *B. Sotah* and only the first example found in *P. Sotah*. The Meiri adds the example of someone who fasts every day either on his own or on the basis of a text, to illustrate how a foolish pietist could harm himself. See *Beit HaBehirah, Sotah*, ed. A. Sofer (Jerusalem: 1968), note 75a, p. 46. Maimonides, as explained above, equates the foolish pietist (*hasid shoteh*) with the commoner (*hedyot*). The Meiri, though, makes no such equation.

10. See Schiffman, *The Halakha At Qumran* (Leiden: Brill, 1975), pp. 124–128, updated to include discussion of Halakha A in *Halakhah, Halikhah uMeshihiyut beKat Midbar Yehudah* (Israel: Merkaz Zalman Shazar LeToledot Yisrael, 1993), pp. 129–130.

11. Published in Robert Eisenman and Michael Wise, *The Dead Sea Scrolls Uncovered* (Shaftesbury, Dorset: MA: Element, 1992), p. 202.

amoraim knew of this type of practice, then perhaps the examples of the foolish pietist refusing to violate a commandment to save someone's life are references to earlier sectarian laws,[12] which did not accord human life the high priority that it was granted by rabbinic law.

Even if this theory is incorrect and there was, in fact, no connection between the Talmud's examples and ancient sectarian practice, the fact that both the Mishnah and the Gemara spoke out against this type of behavior, giving very specific examples, suggests that this type of behavior actually occurred. The discussion in *B. Shabbat* 121b (discussed in Chapter 2) regarding the hasidim who refused to kill snakes and scorpions on the Sabbath is a specific Talmudic example of this type of behavior. For "the spirit of the Sages was not pleased with [these hasidim]," because they endangered their lives by acting excessively stringent with regard to the Sabbath laws.[13]

---

12. A. Z. Aescoly suggests that according to Ethiopian Jewish law, it was prohibited to violate the Sabbath to save a sick person, which corresponds to ancient sectarian practices; See A. Z. Aescoly, *Sefer Ha-Falashim* (Jerusalem: Reuven Mas, 1943, reprint 1973), pp. 36–37. This prohibition is not found, however, in Michael Corinaldi's detailed study of the Ethiopian Jew's Sabbath laws: *Yahadut Etiyopiyah* (Jerusalem: Reuven Mas, 1980), pp. 64–73. Cf. Maimonides, *Yad,* Shabbat 2:3, where he refutes the *minim* who hold that the Sabbath may not be violated to save a life (ed. Frankel; Jerusalem: 1975; the word *apikorsim* is found in the printed edition).

13. The medieval *Midrash HaGadol,* compiled in thirteenth-century Yemen by R. David b. Amram Ha-Adani, has an interesting compilation of sources in its passage on the foolish pietist (Numbers: Naso 5:27). It first cites the *B. Sotah*'s first example, the woman drowning in the river. It then cites the *P. Sotah*'s first example, the child drowning in the river, and concludes by saying, "From this our Rabbis said: Whoever is exempt from doing something and still observes it is called a commoner (*hedyot*)" (*P. Berakhot* 2:9). The compiler of this passage, in all likelihood, quoted the first example from *B. Sotah,* the second from *P. Sotah,* and then connected the third statement, regarding the commoner, either because Maimonides did so in his *Commentary to the Mishnah,* ad loc., or on his own initiative. The compiler of the *Midrash HaGadol* may, though, have had an ancient Midrash combining these three sources. This passage would then be an early source equating the terms *foolish pietist* and *commoner.* This is unlikely, however, since the *Midrash HaGadol* was compiled at such a late date.

Returning to the passage regarding the foolish pietist in P. Sotah 3:4, the second example found in this passage involves a first fig. In this case, the fig would have been brought as a first fruit offering (*bikurim*) to the priests in the Temple. Once, however, the Temple was destroyed, this obligation no longer existed, and anyone was allowed to eat the first fruit. The foolish pietist, though, does not eat the fig, either because he thinks he is still not allowed to (even though the Temple was destroyed) or because he wants to remember the Temple practice. Nonetheless, he then says that he will give it to the first person he sees.

This constitutes foolish behavior, for if (according to his reasoning), the fruit is prohibited to him, then he should have realized that it would also be prohibited to the first man he sees. For only priests were allowed to eat the first fruits in Temple times, and the first man he sees would probably not be a priest. If the person had wanted to remember the practice in the times of the Temple, then he should have buried the fig, so that nobody could eat it.[14]

This example seems to demonstrate a case of extremely confused thinking, not merely ignorance of a particular law. In this case, the foolish pietist's role in "destroying the world" may have been meant figuratively, since he does not seem to be hurting anyone but simply confusing the law.[15] This example is clearly different from the cases of the drowning woman and the drowning boy, since in those cases, the foolish pietist actually hurts another person, whereas here he confuses the law but does not hurt anyone in a physical sense.

The third example given in the P. Sotah passage is quoted most cryptically, with a key phrase missing from the Mishnah.[16] The wording of the third example (quoted above) is as follows:

---

14. R. David Frankel, *Korban Ha'Edah,* ad loc.

15. R. David Frankel, though, feels that this is a case of hypocritical behavior, similar to the "wounds of the separatists" and the "deceitful villain" (which will be discussed later). He states that this man is not eating the first fruit and is giving it away to trick people into saying that he is very pious (*Korban HaEdah,* s.v. *amar*).

16. This is an example of what S. Lieberman writes regarding mistakes found in the Palestinian Talmud. He discusses how the Palestinian Talmud often leaves out part of the sugya when it transfers from another source, thus making it difficult to understand. See *Al HaYerushalmi* (Jerusalem: Darom, 1929), p. 13.

One who sees a betrothed maiden [with a man] running after her. This is what we have learned in the Mishnah, "He who pursues after his neighbor to slay him, after a male, after a betrothed maiden."

The Mishnah referred to here is found in *Sanhedrin* 8:7, and the section in italicized letters is the phrase missing in our example:

*The following must be saved even at the cost of their lives:* He who pursues after his neighbor to slay him, after a male [to rape him] and after a betrothed maiden [to rape her].

Once the full text of the Mishnah is seen, the meaning of the example cited in *P. Sotah* 3:4 (19a) becomes clear. The text of the *P. Sotah* passage is reconstructed here:

One who sees a betrothed maiden with a man running after her [to rape her, but does not kill the man, since he thinks he is not allowed to kill him].
This is what he have learned in the Mishnah:

[The following must be saved even at the cost of their lives:]

He who pursues after his neighbor to slay him, after a male [to rape him], [or] after a betrothed maiden [to rape her].

In this case, the foolish pietist seems to be ignorant of the law. He does not kill the pursuing rapist because he thinks he is not allowed to spill his blood, when in fact he is obligated to kill him to save the girl from being raped and/or to save him from sinning.[17]

---

17. Rashi (*B. Sanhedrin* 73a, s.v. *ve'elu* and *lepogmah*). Tosafot also discusses these two possible meanings of the term "must be saved." It can refer to the person being chased, who must be saved from being killed or raped even at the cost of killing the pursuer, or it can refer to the sinner, who must be saved from sinning even at the cost of losing his life (s.v. *lehatzilo benafsho*). Evidence for this latter suggestion can be found in the baraita cited in the *B. Sanhedrin* 73a Talmudic sugya, which states that one may kill the pursuer only if the crime that he is trying to commit is punishable by death. If the Mishnah were concerned with saving only the girl being chased, the punishment that the pursuer deserves would be irrelevant.

It is also possible that he is aware of the law but feels that by not killing he is being more pious than the law—perhaps he sees himself as going beyond the letter of the law, since he is not spilling blood. His foolishness lies in his failure to recognize that in this case, killing is actually a religious obligation, and the most pious act that he can perform is, ironically, to kill the pursuer.

This case is a bit more complicated and less clear cut than the other examples found in both the Babylonian and Palestinian Talmud. For the pursuer, in this case, may be killed only if the woman he is attempting to rape is forbidden to him in marriage (such as a betrothed or married woman); if he rapes her, then his punishment would be death. If he rapes a single woman, however (whom he is permitted to marry), then his punishment is not death; consequently, it is forbidden to kill him to protect the single woman.

This difference in the law leaves more room for mistakes and confusion,[18] since a simple person may confuse the laws of single and betrothed women or may not be sure, in the tense few minutes during which he has to decide how to act, whether the woman is single, betrothed, or married. The "foolishness," therefore, of the foolish pietist in this case is less obvious because the law is more complex. The *P. Sotah* sugya, however, seems to be assuming that the man knew that the woman was betrothed and yet failed to kill the pursuer because of his pious concerns.

The "destruction of the world" caused by this foolish pietist lies in the profound evil that can result from his purported piety. He had the ability and, therefore, the obligation to prevent the rape from occurring, but he failed to fulfill that obligation because of his foolishness. Ironically, this pietist is destroying the world by his failure to kill someone (the pursuing rapist), whereas in the *B. Sotah* example (and the *P. Sotah*'s first example), his "destruction of the world" involved letting someone die.[19]

---

18. See B. *Sanhedrin* 73a.

19. The medieval commentaries add various examples to those cited in the Talmud itself as to what constitutes a foolish pietist. Such examples cited above included the *Sefer Hasidim*'s cases, which describes the man who allows a book to burn rather than touch it with impure hands and who allows the woman to drown rather than touch her. The Radbaz added a dangerously ill man who refuses medical care on Shabbat.

In summary, the foolish pietist is criticized by the rabbis for two reasons: he is ignorant or grossly mistaken in his notions of what constitutes true piety, and his behavior causes emotional and/or physical harm to others. This idea logically extends to include someone who causes emotional and/or physical harm to himself as well.[20]

The emotional and physical harm caused to others by the foolish pietist is best illustrated by the case of the betrothed maiden in which he fails to kill the rapist. In addition to the emotional and physical suffering of the rape itself, the woman lives with the painful knowledge that the rape could have been prevented; that a witness stood by and did nothing, even though he was not only permitted but obligated by Jewish law to kill the rapist.[21] The physical harm to the drowning victims described in the Talmud is obvious; his foolish pietism led to the loss of their lives.

Still a third category of harm to others caused by the foolish pietist lies in the sphere of social-ethical behavior; by acting so strangely, he causes others to mock and scorn him, thus leading them to sin against him. The piety of the foolish pietist is thus not merely foolish but also harmful and potentially life threatening.

---

Maimonides applies the term *foolish pietist* to yet another category. *M. Arakhin* 8:3 states that a person is not allowed to devote *all* of his possessions to the Temple. When Maimonides summarizes this law *(Yad,* "Laws of Arakhin veHaramin," 8:13) he adds that someone who does this is not pious but is foolish, since he will have no more money and will need charity. He then quotes our Mishnah's statement that "a foolish pietiest is among those who destroy the world." Maimonides is, thus, applying the concept of a foolish pietist to a new category—someone who feels that he wants to devote all of his money and possessions "to God" and, in doing so, leaves no provisions for himself and his family to live in this world.

20. The medieval commentators expand the definition of the foolish pietist in this manner. The Meiri, *Sotah* ad loc. (quoted earlier), calls someone who fasts every day (and thus physically weakens his body) a foolish pietist. The emotional harm to himself, according to Maimonides, is that his "exaggeration of carefulness and punctiliousness" leads others to scorn and ridicule him (*Commentary to the Mishnah, Sotah* 3:4).

21. According to the position discussed in Tosafot that one is obligated to kill the rapist to prevent him from sinning and not to save the victim, the harm resulting to the rapist, then, would be that he now is deserving of the very severe punishment of death by stoning (*Deuteronomy* 22:23–24).

## CHAPTER SUMMARY

The foolish pietist is criticized by the Rabbis for two reasons: his internal motivation is flawed, and the external effects of his behavior are negative. The flaw in his internal motivations is that while he may truly wish to worship God, he is grossly mistaken, or perhaps ignorant, in his notions of what constitutes true piety. The negative effect of his behavior is that he hurts other people (or himself), physically and/or emotionally.

*M. Sotah* 3:4 and the sources related to it have been the focus of Chapters 3, 4, and 5. What is evident from this analysis is that one of the reasons for the severe condemnation of the four categories of people in the Mishnah was the negative effects that their behavior would have on themselves or on others. The ascetic woman (according to the simplest reading of the tannaitic sources), some of the seven separatists, and the foolish pietist, were all criticized by the rabbis because their self-imposed stringency could harm themselves, other people, or the Jewish community as a whole.

The theme, though, that surfaces most prominently from this discussion is the tremendous concern that the rabbis had that proper intentions motivate religious behavior. The categories of people who were criticized by R. Joshua in the Mishnah for their self-imposed stringencies were, for the most part, criticized for their improper motivations. The ascetic woman (according to the medieval commentators on *B. Sotah* and *P. Sotah*) was viewed as a deceitful fraud, using self-imposed piety as a camouflage for her sins. Many of the seven types of separatists were insincere, hypocritical, and arrogant; they used religion for their own personal gain, be it money, respect, power, or avoidance of punishment. If one's intentions in behaving stringently were not to serve God, then their behavior could be totally invalidated. The superogatory behavior discussed above was not even considered merely worthless but instead was actually condemned as bringing destruction on the world.

# 6

# *The Commoner (Hedyot)*

*P.* Berakhot 2:9 (5d), discussed in Chapter 1, quotes the tanna Hizkiyah's statement: "Anyone who does something from which he is exempt is called a commoner (*kol hapatur midavar ve'osehu nikra hedyot*)." The term *commoner* was used in this passage in criticism of R. Samuel b. R. Isaac, who stopped eating with his colleague to pray *minhah*. The relevant sections are repeated here:

XVI. It occurred that R. Miyasha and R. Samuel b. R. Isaac were sitting and eating . . .

XVII. The time for prayer arrived, and R. Samuel b. R. Isaac got up and prayed.

XVIII. R. Miyasha said to him: "But didn't Rebbe teach us, 'If one already started (eating), one is not required to stop (in order to pray)'?"

XIX. And Hizkiyah has stated: "whoever does something from which he is exempt is called a commoner (*hedyot*)."

Hizkiya's baraita (section XIX) will be the focus of this chapter; the meaning of the term, the type of supererogatory behavior that "merited" this label, and the reasons for this criticism will be examined.

175

## DEFINITIONS OF THE TERM *COMMONER* (*HEDYOT*)

The word *hedyot* stems from the Greek word *idiotes*,[1] meaning (in both Hebrew and Greek) "a private person (as opposed to one holding public office), a common man, plebian, one who has no professional knowledge, 'layman,' unpracticed, unskilled, generally, a raw hand, an ignoramus. It is also used as a term of abuse."[2] In Greek then, the word has two usages. One is uneducated and simple, and the other is as an insult, meaning an ignoramus and a fool.

The statement that "whoever does something from which he is exempt is called a commoner" appears only once in the Palestinian Talmud and does not appear at all in the Babylonian Talmud.[3] The word *hedyot* does not appear in any other Talmudic sources as part of criticism of supererogatory behavior. Exactly what the term meant, though, needs further clarification; what exactly did Hizkiyah mean when he called someone a *hedyot*?

*Hedyot* has been translated in this study as "a commoner," meaning "a common person, as distinguished from one with rank, status, etc."[4] The term, however, has many different nuances of meaning, since it is used in contrast to many different ranks or statuses within the Talmudic literature,[5] but what Hizkiyah referred

---

1. Samuel Krauss, *Griechisch und lateinische Lehnworter im Talmud, Midrasch und Targum* vol. II (Berlin: 1898; reprint, Hildesheim: Georg Olms Verlagsbuchhandlung, 1964), p. 220; Michael Sokoloff, *A Dictionary of Jewish Palestinian Aramaic* (Ramat Gan: Bar Ilan University Press, 1990).

2. Henry George Liddel and Robert Scott, *A Greek English Lexicon*, ed. Henry Stuart Jones, vol. I (Oxford: Clarendon, 1948), p. 819.

3. In fact, at least one halakhist suggests that the Babylonian Talmud actually disagreed with this statement: R. Jacob Reisha, *Shevut Ya'akov* [reprint, Jerusalem: 1972], p. II, 30.

4. *The Random House Dictionary* (New York: Random House, 1981).

5. Other ranks and statuses that are contrasted to *hedyot* are commoner versus king, president, priest, prophet, judge; common priest versus chief priest; common versus holy (to be used in the Temple); common or unskilled laborer versus skilled laborer; and common person versus *haver*— trusted on tithes. See Krauss, *Greek and Latin Words*, pp. 220–221; Kassowski, *Otzar Leshon HaMishnah*, vol. III, p. 514. *Hedyot* is also used to mean Samaritans in *B. Sanhedrin* 21b and non-Jewish in *P. Sanhedrin* 7:12.

to here was a common, uneducated person as opposed to a learned person.

The term is sometimes used in the Talmud to describe an uneducated person without passing judgment, but it is also used as an insult, meaning not only uneducated but also stupid, foolish, lowly, and sometimes even evil. This parallels the usage of the term in Greek, for as was quoted earlier, the word *idiotes* meant common and simple but is also used as a term of abuse. What first needs to be explored is whether Hizkiyah meant that the person is merely uneducated or that the person is stupid and foolish. Examples of different usages of the term will be given, to demonstrate the meaning of the term in Hizkiyah's baraita in a more precise manner.

## "COMMONER" AS UNEDUCATED

Talmudic sources use the word *hedyot* to mean simply "uneducated people," but not in a derogatory or insulting manner. They describe a certain type of person: simple, uneducated, and, hence, easily misled. In *P. Berakhot* 1:5 (3c), R. Aha objected to reading the Shema publicly after the third hour on the morning of a public fast because of the confusion it would cause to uneducated people (*hahedyotot*) who would not know that they should have already recited the Shema before the third hour. *T. Ta'anit* 3:12[6] teaches that though greeting friends on the Ninth of Ab is prohibited, one is, nevertheless, permitted to answer the greetings of uneducated people (*hahedyotot*) in a weak voice, presumably to avoid hurting their feelings. Once again, *hedyot* is used to describe uneducated people who do not know the law.[7] The usage of the expression "because of the commoners" (*mipnei hahedyotot*) as a reason for extra care in Halakhic

---

6. A parallel to this passage is found in *P. Ta'anit* 1:9. Other examples of the same exact usage of this term can be found in *P. Meggilah* 2:4, *P. Hagigah* 3:3, and *P. Sotah* 7:1.

7. *Hedyot* is understood in this context as a synonym for "the ignorant masses (*amei ha'aretz*)" by various medieval commentators such as R. Samson b. Zaddok, *Sefer Tashbetz* (Lemberg: 1858), 441, and the Magen Abraham (*Orah Hayim* 554:20), who substitute the word *hahedyotot* here with the word *amei ha'aretz* when quoting this Talmudic statement (S. Lieberman, *Tosefiah KiPeshutah Ta'anit,* p. 341). See also *Midrash Mishlei* 6:13 and *B. Sanhedrin* 91a.

ruling lest the uneducated be misled is limited to the Palestinian Talmud and is not found in the Babylonian Talmud.

There are many references scattered throughout the Talmud to courts of commoners, or lay courts (*beit din shel hedyot*). These references are found in the Mishnah,[8] the Palestinian Talmud,[9] and especially in the Babylonian Talmud.[10] The judges on these courts were not learned judges who were authorized by the rabbis. Instead, they were unskilled, basically uneducated common people who were nevertheless allowed to carry out certain legal functions.[11] "A common court" is used to describe this type of non-Rabbinic court but is not used as a term of reprobation.

## "COMMONER" AS AN INSULT

In the above examples, the term *hedyot* is descriptive rather than necessarily disapproving.[12] In other sources, however, *hedyot* is used in a disparaging, insulting manner. It is used to describe someone common and lowly—an insignificant person.[13] In another passage, it means unworthy and improper,[14] and in yet another, it is used synonymously with light-headed (*hahedyotot vekalei hada'at*).[15] In other sources, it means poor and contemptible,[16] stupid and arrogant,[17] and even foolish and evil.[18]

---

8. *M. Yebamot* 12:1.

9. *P. Yebamot* 12:1.

10. See, for example, *B. Shabbat* 46b; *B. Yebamot* 101a, *B. Nedarim* 77a, 78b, *B. Baba Kama* 14b, and *B. Baba Metzia* 32a.

11. The exact qualifications of the members of the lay court are discussed at length by the medieval commentaries. Some require that they must know the laws (*gamir*), even if they have no rabbinic ordination or ability to reason logically (*savir*). Others require that only one of them know the laws—see *Encyclopedia Talmudit*, vol. III, p. 156, s.v. *beit din*.

12. Cf. *B. Shabbat* 12b, where *hedyot* is used in contrast to important.

13. *P. Sanhedrin* 7:12, *B. Sanhedrin* 84a.

14. *B. Ta'anit* 18b.

15. *Siphre debei Rab*, 103, ed. H. S. Horowitz (Leipzig: Libraria Gustav Fock, 1917), p. 102.

16. Targum to Samuel I 18:23; the *Arukh*, s.v. *hedyot*.

17. *B. Meggilah* 12b.

18. *B. Sanhedrin* 67a. The word is extremely derisive in this source—it describes someone whose crime is so despicable that he is sentenced to

It is not at all surprising to find the word for "uneducated" being used as a term of disparagement. While ignorance is generally frowned on in many societies, it is seen as a nearly tragic state of affairs in Jewish society, where such paramount importance is accorded to Torah learning. The transition, then, from a descriptive to an abusive use of the term is very natural. No clear historical or geographic pattern to this transition can be traced here, since both usages of the term (descriptive and disparaging) are found in tannaitic sources as well as in both the Babylonian and the Palestinian Talmud.

Of all the Talmudic sources using the term *commoner* as an insult, the one most similar to Hizkiya's usage is found in *P. Baba Batra* 8:1 (16a). In this source, there is a debate regarding whether a daughter and son are treated equally when it comes to inheriting property from the mother. The Talmudic sugya quotes R. Malokh in the name of R. Joshua b. Levi who says that the law is in accord with R. Zechariah, who stated that the son and daughter have an equal claim of inheritance on the estate of the mother (and that the son does not have a superior claim). The Talmud then records that R. Yannai of Cappodocia had a case involving a son and a daughter who were to inherit from their mother's estate. The judges of the case were Palestinian amoraim: R. Huna, a Palestinian amora who came from Babylonia,[19] R. Judah b. Pazzi, and R. Aha (both of whom lived in Lod).[20] R. Aha said to his fellow Palestinian judges:

> Our brethren who live outside the land of Israel are commoners (*hedyot*), for they do not know the correct law. Further, they rely upon the statement of R. Malokh in the name of R. Joshua b. Levi, but that statement is false.

The Talmud passage then goes on to mention names of many tannaim and amoraim stating that the law goes against R. Zechariah (i.e., against R. Malokh).

The term here does not mean simply "uneducated," since the people referred to here were the judges and scholars of their

---

death without even being given a warning (Rashi ad loc., s.v. *velo zo af zo katanei*).

19. Hyman, vol. I, pp. 344–345.
20. Hyman, vol. II, p. 573; vol. I, p. 119.

generation who lived in Babylonia and who relied upon the statement of R. Melokh but did not know that it was false. "Our brethren" did not mean the common people; it meant the Babylonian peers of these Palestinian amoraim. The term was clearly meant as an insult to the judges of Babylon who were ignorant of the correct law; in other words, "our brethren who live outside of Israel are just like a court of commoners. They [are stupid and ignorant], and they do not know Torah as well as we do."

The information gathered above regarding the usage of the term *hedyot* as an insult can now be applied to the case of R. Samuel b. R. Isaac in *P. Berakhot* 2:9 (5d). *Hedyot* in Hizkiyah's baraita appears not merely to be a descriptive term, describing the educational status of someone who does something from which he is exempt. Instead, Hizkiyah appears to be using the term in an insulting manner, similar to R. Aha's statement that "our brethren outside of Israel are commoners." Assuming, on the one hand, that he really did not know that he was exempt, then the label would mean ignorant—an insult to anyone, but especially to a scholar. If, on the other hand, he knew that he was exempt yet still chose to fulfill the obligation, then the insult has a different nuance. Rather than ignorant, it then would connote foolish judgement.

Assuming that Hizkiyah's criticism was leveled at someone who knew he was exempt yet chose to fulfill the religious duty anyway, then *hedyot* and "the foolish pietist" of the previous chapter appear to merge in meaning.[21] The foolish pietist substitutes his own idea of exceptional piety for the behavior required by the law. Similarly, someone who is exempt from a religious duty yet chooses to do it anyway is also substituting his own idea of piety for the behavior required by the law. Because he decided to follow his own subjective ideas of proper religious behavior rather than following the objective law, he is called foolish by Hizkiyah.

The major difference, though, between the foolish pietist and the "commoner" is that the foolish pietist may actually be dangerous. Through his piety, he hurts other people (by allowing them to

---

21. Maimonides (as noted earlier) indeed equates the two terms. After defining a foolish pietist, Maimonides then quotes Hizkiya's baraita as a supporting text (*Commentary to the Mishnah, Sotah* 3:3).

drown or be raped, for example).[22] The person being called a commoner, though, is not physically dangerous.[23]

## THE TYPE OF BEHAVIOR THAT ELICITED THE LABEL "COMMONER" AND THE REASONS FOR THIS LABEL

To understand why Hizkiyah viewed self-imposed stringency as foolish behavior, what first must be clarified is which behaviors he actually had in mind. On the one hand, Hizkiyah's statement, "Anyone who does something from which he is exempt is called a commoner" may have been meant literally— that is, as a general condemnation of all supererogatory behavior. On the other hand, it is quite conceivable that his statement was not meant literally; he may have spoken in an overly exaggerated, hyperbolic manner and may, in actuality, have referred to only certain types of stringency.

While one can only speculate regarding which types of stringencies Hizkiyah himself had in mind, R. Miyasha (or the Talmudic sugya) applied his statement to the case of R. Samuel b. R. Isaac in *P. Berakhot* 2:9 (5d). This case is the only case in either Talmud in which Hizkiyah's baraita is explicitly invoked. It is, therefore, necessary to examine the case of R. Samuel b. Isaac carefully, since it may serve as the paradigm of the type of stringency to which Hizkiyah's baraita was applied.

When R. Samuel b. R. Isaac went to pray *minhah,* he was exempt from doing so because he had already started eating. This exemption had already been taught explicitly by R. Judah the Prince in a Mishnah (*Shabbat* 1:2) that states that one who started eating before the time of *minhah* began is not required to stop to pray. Hizkiyah's baraita was then quoted as a reprimand to R. Samuel b. R. Isaac for praying even when exempt.

The sugya does not state explicitly why R. Samuel b. R. Isaac's actions were considered foolish by R. Miyasha. At least three possible reasons, however, can be suggested. First, R. Miyasha may

---

22. The example given in *P. Sotah* 3:4 of the first figs, however, simply reflects confusion rather than dangerous thinking.

23. The Meiri explains that the foolish pietist causes harm to himself and to others (*Beit HaBehirah Sotah* 3:3), while the "commmoner" is doing something that yields no positive results but does not hurt anyone (*Beit HaBehirah Baba Kama* 86a).

have been accusing R. Samuel b. R. Isaac of ignorance—he simply
did not know the relevant halakhah. Second, people might have
become confused regarding what the law actually required, when
they saw R. Samuel b. R. Isaac publicly deviating from an explicit
Mishnah. In an effort to standardize Jewish law, subjective deviation
from the already established law was discouraged by Hizkiyah (as
understood by R. Miyasha).

The third possible reason for R. Miyasha's application of
Hizkiyah's baraita to criticize R. Samuel b. R. Isaac when he went to
pray was that by separating from his colleague R. Miyasha (who
continued to eat), he appeared to be acting as if he were more pious
than his colleague. The problem with this behavior is in the "holier
than thou" attitude that it reflects. For by doing something that he is
exempt from doing, the individual separates himself from his peers
in what appears to be a haughty fashion.[24] This superior, presumptuous presentation, in addition to being a weakness in his own
personality profile, also hurts the feelings of those around him.
*Hedyot* in this baraita would, then, be closely related to the Babylonian term *arrogance* (*yohara*), which is the subject of Chapter 7.
Hizkiyah, in other words, may have held that self-imposed stringency was foolish behavior precisely because it was motivated by
and/or appeared arrogant to others.[25]

It should be noted that there is another passage (*P. Berakhot* 3:1

---

24. The *Orhot Hayim* writes, "And there are those who explain that he
is called a *hedyot* when there is no one else acting like him—as here (in the
case of R. Samuel b. Isaac) where no one else stopped eating except for him,
and therefore he was called *hedyot* because it appears arrogant (*gasut ruah*),
as if to say, 'look at me, I am a hasid.' But if there are others acting like him,
of course he is not called *hedyot* even if he is exempt from the mitzvah."
Therefore, someone who goes around on hills and forests, to find bird nests
and observe the commandment of *shiluach haken*, gets a reward and is not
called a *hedyot* even though he is exempt from looking for them (the nests).
The *Orhot Hayim* thus derives a general principle from the case of R. Samuel
b. R. Isaac; when someone does something that makes him stand out from
the others and appear arrogant, then he is called *hedyot*, but if he does
something different that other people also do, then he is not called common
because he does not appear arrogant (R. Aharon HaKohen of Lunel, *Sefer
Orhot Hayim,* Laws of Shabbat, Laws of *Kiddush haYom*, 63b, 20).

25. *Ra'avyah, Meggilah* 597, p. 339, ibid.; R. Isaac b. Moses, *Or Zaru'ah,*
vol. I, "Laws of Tefillin," 543; R. Aharon HaKohen of Lunel, *Sefer Orhot*

[6a]'s discussion of the next Mishnah) in which someone who fulfilled a religious duty from which he was exempt is criticized. While Hizkiyah's baraita is not explicitly quoted there, the same idea may be expressed in this source.[26] The issue discussed in this passage is whether a priest may become impure to study Torah:[27]

I.      May a priest render himself impure in order to honor [i.e., to study] the Torah?

II.     R. Yose was sitting and teaching, and a corpse was brought up [to the study hall for a eulogy]. To [all those priests studying there] who went out, so as not to become impure, he did not say anything. And to all those who remained seated, he did not say anything. [For he was in doubt about this matter.]

III.    R. Nehemiah, son of R. Hiyya bar Abba said, "My father would not pass under the arch at Caesarea."

IV.     R. Ammi, R. Hizkiyah, R. Kohen and R. Jacob bar Aha were walking in the plazas of Sepphoris. When they reached the arch [an impure area], R. Kohen separated from them. And when they reached a pure area, he rejoined them.

V.      He [R. Kohen] said to them, "What were you discussing [in my absence]?"

VI.     R. Hizkiyah said to R. Jacob bar Aha, "Do not tell him anything."[28]

VII.    [And this story does not prove anything because] we do not know whether [he instructed R. Jacob bar Aha to remain silent] because he was angry that he [R. Kohen] had left, because [a priest] is permitted to become impure in order to study Torah,

---

*Hayim*, Laws of Shabbat, Laws of *Kiddush haYom*, 63b, 20; R. Isaac Krasilchikov, *P. Berakhot* 2:9, s.v. *vetanei Hizkiyah*.

26. Leiberman, *Hilkhot HaYerushalmi LeHaRambam*, p. 26, note 30.

27. Translation here based on J. Neusner, *The Talmud of the Land of Israel, Berakhot* (Chicago: University of Chicago Press, 1983).

28. The similarity between the names of Hizkiyah and R. Hizkiyah is purely coincidental. Hizkiyah of the baraita was a tanna, while R. Hizkiyah was a fourth-generation Palestinian amora who lived in Ceasarea (Hyman, vol. II, pp. 421–422).

VIII.  or whether [R. Hizkiyah told him to be silent] because he
        [R. Kohen] was a *taysan* [impetuous].[29]

This Talmudic discussion tries, initially, to prove that a priest
may allow himself to become impure for the sake of studying Torah
by citing the exchange between R. Hizkiyah and R. Kohen in
sections IV through VII. The assumption was that R. Hizkiyah
refused to allow R. Kohen to be informed of the part of the
discussion that he had missed, because he was angry (*baish*) that he
had left, when in fact he had been permitted to stay.

The Talmudic sugya, however, is not sure of how to interpret R.
Hizkiya's reaction to R. Kohen's request and suggests this only as
one possible explanation. The other possible explanation that it
gives is that he (R. Kohen) was a *taysan,* meaning impatient or
impetuous (from the root *tas,* meaning to fly).[30] R. Hizkiyah, then,
just did not want to repeat the discussion for R. Kohen, simply because
he did not want to be bothered with his annoying questions.[31] The

---

29. The parallel text in *P. Nazir* 7:1 (56a) has "*saysan*" rather than
"*taysan.*" Leiberman emends this word to read *goysan* and translates it as
arrogant (*yahir*) and impetuous (*vepaziz*). He bases this suggested change on
the Rome and Leiden manuscripts, which have *noysan,* and on Nahmanides'
*Torat HaAdam,* "Hotza'ah," 34b (Chavel's edition of this text, though, has
*taysan* [*Kitvei R. Moshe b. Nahman,* ed. Haim D. Chavel (Jerusalem: Mossad
HaRav Kook, 1964), p. 105]). See Leiberman, *Hilkhot HaYerushalmi Le-
HaRambam,* p. 26, notes 48–49; Leiberman, "Tikunei Yerushalmi," *Tarbiz* II
(1931), p. 106; Leiberman, "Review of S. Krauss, *Tosafot HeArukh HaShalem,*"
*Kiryat Sefer* XIV (1937–38), p. 224; the *Arukh,* s.v. *gas* II; Ginzberg, *Perushim
VeHidushim BaYerushalmi,* vol. II, p. 86.

30. M. Kassowski, *Otzar Leshon Talmud Yerushalmi,* s.v. *taysan.* Kassowski lists *taysan, saysan,* and *maysan* together under the same listing. He,
like Leiberman, suggests that these are all the same word. They both quote
*P. Gittin* 1:1, where the word *maysan* appears in a description of a man who
(impetuously) threw a writ of divorce to his wife, and then took it back
when she began screaming ("like that Hinena son of R. Asi who was
*maysan*"). R. Moses Margaliot (followed by Neusner), ad loc., however,
explains that he came from a place called "*Maysan,*" and no character
description was intended.

31. The *P'nei Moshe, P. Nazir* 7:1, s.v. *dehava saysan;* R. Isaac Krasilchikov,
*Toledot Yitzhak,* ad loc., s.v. *i mishum.* Another explanation is that the word
means long-winded and thus refers to the lesson and not to the person. The

story, according to this second option, would not prove anything regarding a priest becoming impure to learn Torah and would, consequently, be irrelevant to this study.

According to the first suggestion, though, made by the sugya, R. Hizkiyah was angry with R. Kohen for having separated from the group when he was exempt from doing so. Any, or all of the three reasons, in turn, presented earlier as the rationale behind Hizkiyah (the tanna's) dictum could now be invoked. First, R. Hizkiyah (the amora) may have been angry at R. Kohen because he thought that R. Kohen was ignorant of the law.[32] Second, R. Hizkiyah may have been angry at R. Kohen for having substituted his own subjective idea of piety for the established halakhic society's norm—thereby weakening the standardization of halakhah within society.

The third possible reason for R. Hizkiya's displeasure was that R. Hizkiyah may have felt that R. Kohen was arrogant for having separated from his colleagues when he was exempt from doing so. For although it is not known whether R. Hizkiyah or R. Jacob bar Aha were priests, R. Ammi was a priest.[33] This means that R. Kohen was separating himself, in the very least, from R. Ammi, who was also a priest, in what might have been a "holier than thou" manner. R. Kohen's foolishness, then, was to impose a stringency on himself without considering how his behavior would appear to his friends. This could, then, be an amoraic application of Hizkiyah (the tanna's) baraita stating that "whoever does something from which he is exempt is called a commoner."[34] The specific behaviors to which Hizkiyah (the tanna's) label of *hedyot* was applied were, thus, praying when prayer was not required and, possibly, separating from impurity when it was not required.

As was discussed at length in Chapter 1, R. Simeon b. Gamaliel

part of the discussion that R. Kohen had missed was long and difficult to explain, and R. Hizkiyah did not want to repeat what had already been taught (*Ba'al Sefer Haredim,* s.v. *taysan*).

32. In this particular case, his ignorance of the law actually led him to stop learning Torah unnecessarily—*bitul Torah.*

33. *B. Sotah* 28b, Hyman, *Toledot,* vol. I, p. 220.

34. Lieberman connects this incident with Hizkiyah's baraita via the word *goysan* (his emendation of *taysan*), which he translates as arrogant (*yahir*) and impetuous (*vepaziz*). See *Hilkhot HaYerushalmi LeHaRambam,* p. 26, notes 48–49.

(in *T. Ta'anit* 1:7, quoted in *P. Berakhot* 2:9, a few lines before Hizkiyah's baraita is quoted) permitted supererogatory behavior for scholars if it involved "matters of praise" and allowed the imposition of supererogatory practices that involved "matters of anguish" to everyone. The first behavior discussed here, namely, extra prayers, is considered "a matter of praise." Since R. Samuel b. R. Isaac was a scholar, accepting this stringency on himself should have been permitted according to R. Simeon b. Gamaliel, yet it is still criticized by R. Miyasha. The second behavior, which involved supererogatory separation from impurity, fits into the category of matters of anguish (separation from impurity is a typically ascetic type of behavior). This certainly should have been permitted according to R. Simeon b. Gamaliel (who permitted such super-erogatory behavior for everyone—scholar and common person alike).

Hizkiyah's baraita may, thus, have been applied to both "matters of praise" (even in the case of a scholar) and "matters of anguish." His position would then be in opposition to R. Simeon b. Gamaliel's position in the Tosefta passage (quoted earlier in *P. Berakhot* 2:9). The sugya itself (in *P. Berakhot* 2:9) does not attempt to harmonize Rabban Simeon b. Gamaliel and R. Miyasha, but the contradiction is significant, since the two statements appear in the exact same passage.

If Hizkiyah intended to criticize self-imposed stringencies only in cases that were parallel to the paradigmatic case of R. Samuel b. Isaac, three limiting principles would emerge insofar as when Hizkiyah's censure of super-erogatory behavior was applied. To simplify the following discussion, the assumption being made here is that the person was aware of the objective law and, nonetheless, wished to act above and beyond the standardized, objective demands of the halakhah. Consequently, only the problems of arrogance and subjective deviation from the norm remain to be further developed.

The first limiting principle is that Hizkiyah's criticism was applied to public situations rather than private. R. Samuel's supererogatory prayer, for example, took place in public, in front of his colleague. Had he stopped his own private meal to pray *minhah*, then he may not have been criticized. The label of "commoner," then, was applied specifically to public supererogatory acts and may not have been applied to stringencies imposed in the privacy of one's home.[35]

Supererogatory behavior in private limits the problems of arrogance and subjective deviation from standardized Halakhah as follows. First, the private nature of the practice would, by definition, insure that the individual practicing the supererogatory behavior would not be trying to impress anyone. Additionally, since no one would feel that he was acting presumptuously or arrogantly, he would not be hurting anyone's feelings. Second, the private nature of the supererogation would ensure that others would not try to follow in his ways and thereby distort or confuse the Halakhah. While he would be going against the accepted practice of his time, nobody would see him doing so and no arguments would be caused by his actions.

The second limiting principle is that Hizkiyah's criticism was applied to an individual fulfilling a rabbinic religious duty from which he is only temporarily exempt. (R. Samuel b. R. Isaac was only temporarily exempt from praying *minhah*.) His criticism was not applied by the Talmud to groups of people who are permanently exempt from commandments yet wish to observe them nonetheless, such as women who want to observe time-bound positive commandments from which they are exempt.[36]

The third limiting principle hinges on the Torah's dividing the commandments into two categories—those between man and God, and those between man and his fellow man. R. Samuel b. R. Isaac was criticized for his supererogatory prayer, a commandment be-

---

35. R. Jacob Reisha, *Shevut Ya'akov,* pt. II, 44. A great deal of literature has been written on this topic, some of it by medieval commentators but most of it by modern commentators. These views are summarized and discussed by R. Haim Medini, *Sefer Sdei Hemed HaShalem* (New York: Friedman, 1967), vol. III, 20:16, pp. 80–93; and Leo Levi, *Sha'arei Talmud Torah* (Feldheim: Jerusalem: 1981), pp. 114–138.

36. While women are exempt from these commandments even on a rabbinic level, many authorities hold that a blind man is exempt on a Pentateuchal level but nevertheless has a rabbinic obligation to observe these commandments. Hizkiyah's baraita, then, according to that position, would not apply to blind men. See *B. Baba Kama* 87a and Tosafot, ad loc., s.v. *vekhen haya;* R. Yom Tov Alashvili, *Hiddushei HaRitva Kiddushin* 30a (New York: Merkaz HaSefarim, 1975), pp. 58–59.

tween humans and God, rather than between man and his fellow man. This third principle, then, is that Hizkiyah's baraita was applied to supererogatory observance of a positive commandment between man and God. It was not applied to someone who fulfilled a religious duty that involved another person even though he was not obligated to do so.

If Hizkiyah's criticism was actually limited only to this type of observance, it may have been because positive commandments that involve interpersonal relations (but do not involve money) have the general commandment to "love thy neighbor as thyself" as an overriding principle. This commandment is an ongoing, limitless commitment, and the more kindness one shows to other human beings, the better one fulfills that commandment.[37] For example, if someone visits the sick, he does not then become exempt from visiting the sick (unless he is involved in fulfilling another religious duty). Instead, someone who visits the sick very frequently is held in very high regard.[38]

For positive commandments between humans and God, however, there are specific exemptions given to individuals in specific circumstances. Although there is an overall commandment to love God, this would not apply as an overriding principle when an individual is explicitly told that he is temporarily exempt from doing a certain commandment. Examples of these exemptions from commandments between humans and God include exemptions from the following obligations: prayer at certain times, separating from impurity (both of which have already been discussed), as well as eating in a *sukkah* in the rain[39] or putting on *tefillin* when one is physically ill. When a person insists on performing these man-God religious duties even when one is exempt, he shows a certain

---

37. Maimonides classifies these types of "limitless" commandments as positive commandments that are done via a person's body, as opposed to "positive commandments that are done via a person's money." The latter category does have limits imposed on it, such as not being allowed to give away too much money to charity (*Commentary to the Mishnah, Peah* 1:1).

38. R. Hayim Yosef David Azoulay, *Petah Eynayim, B.M.* 30, reprint, p. 16b, s.v. *veki ze*. See also R. Haim David HaLevi, *Aseh Lekhah Rav,* vol. VIII (Tel Aviv: 1988), Responsa 21, pp. 49–52.

39. See, for example, *Hagahot Maimoniyot*, "Laws of Sukkah," 6:3, note 3, in the name of R. Simhah.

disregard, or disrespect, for the law. He assumes that the reasons behind these exemptions do not apply to him, thus placing himself above the law.[40] There will likely be a certain arrogant quality to this kind of attitude. Only very unique individuals, with an extremely close relationship with God, can fulfill a commandment from which they are exempt temporarily, owing to extenuating circumstances, and retain only sincere motivations. Such an individual would be R. Gamaliel, in *M. Berakhot* 2:5, who recited the Shema even as a bridegroom because he refused to remove from himself "the yoke of heaven even for a moment."

From the context of *P. Berakhot* 2:9, one can, thus, see that the label of "commoner" may have been applied by R. Miyasha (or the Talmudic sugya) to an individual who accepted a super-erogatory observance but only in the following circumstances:

1. Publicly (rather than in private), demonstrating actual or perceived arrogance, and potentially causing confusion regarding the law's requirements
2. While under temporary exemption from a rabbinic commandment because of extenuating circumstances
3. Behavior involving a commandment between humans and God rather than interpersonal relationships.

The case of R. Samuel b. R. Isaac may thus serve to limit the application of Hizkiyah's baraita to this particular case and its parallels.[41]

---

40. The verse in Kohelet 7:16, "Do not be overly righteous" (*al tehi tzaddik harbeh*) is understood in this manner by the rabbis. It is applied to the actions of Saul, who did not kill all of the tribe of Amalek, because he felt that the commandment was unjust, thus placing himself above God's commandments (*B. Yoma* 22b, *Numbers Rabbah* 25:5, *Kohelet Rabbah* 7:16).

41. The Meiri severely limits the application of Hizkiyah's baraita, as follows. After stating that "a person who is exempt from a religious obligation yet still wishes to perform it, is permitted to do so," he explains that Hizkiyah's baraita (which appears to contradict this statement) applies only "when one is also exempt from any other similar religious duties— when one imposes on oneself something that yields no intellectual or moral growth, no exalted feelings (*silsul*), humility of the spirit, or any other noble results" (*Beit HaBehira Baba Kama* 86b). The Meiri, in this case, appears to

Hizkiyah's statement, alternately (as mentioned earlier), may very well have been intended to be a general rule with no exceptions. Support for this interpretation can be seen from the wording of "*Anyone* (kol) who does something from which he is exempt is called a commoner." This, according to the simplest meaning of the words (*pe-shat*), constitutes a universal condemnation of self-imposed stringency.

Hizkiyah may have made this very strong, all inclusive statement because he felt that the Halakhic system had to be respected as is, not added to and not subtracted to, since the licensing of supererogatory behavior could, ultimately, lead to religious excess and extremism. Perhaps he felt that permitting self-imposed stringency would lead to an erosion of Halakhic authority. People would not take the law too seriously, since the option of creating their own private rituals would always be open.

Super-erogation, then, would be frowned on by Hizkiyah even when done with sincere motivation, even when it involved in private and/or involved commandments between fellow human beings. It would also extend to other situations as well.[42] It would apply to cases of supererogation for which no obligation exists whatsoever and to an individual who fulfills a commandment from which he personally is always exempt, but other individuals or groups of Jews are obligated to perform. Women fulfilling the time-dependent positive commandments from which they are ex-

---

reflect a general tendency among both the medieval and modern commentators to limit the application of Hizkiyah's baraita—see sources in Medini, *Sefer Sdei Hemed HaShalem*, vol. III, 20:16, pp. 80–93; and Levi, *Sha'arei Talmud Torah*, pp. 114–138.

42. Hizkiyah's baraita is, in fact, extended by some early medieval commentaries and applied to various areas of Jewish law. Among these are mentioning the New Moon on New Year's Day (*Sefer Hefetz LeTalmud* in *Sefer HaMetivot*, ed. B. Lewin [Jerusalem: Merkaz, 1934], p. 121), standing to recite the Shema rather than sitting (*Seder Rav Amram HaShalem*, ed. Frumkin [Jerusalem: Zuckerman, 1912], p. 209, par. 27:33), making lines on tefillin before writing in the letters (quoted in the name of R. Ya'akov by the *Sefer HaTerumah*, "Laws of Sefer Torah," 196, and attributed to R. Tam in Tosafot in *Git.* 6b, s.v. *amar rav yizhak* and *Menahot* 32b, Tosafot s.v. *ha'*), and staying in the Sukkah even when one is exempt (*Hagahot Maimoniyot*, "Laws of Sukkah," 6:3, note 3).

empt then would be regarded as commoners.[43] The severity of his censure (i.e., whether he spoke in a derisive and disdainful manner[44] or merely with a mildly critical intonation) must, however, remain speculative. For the Talmudic text does not convey the facial expression and intonation with which he spoke.[45]

## CHAPTER SUMMARY

The statement "Whoever does something from which he is exempt is called a commoner" is found only once in the Palestinian Talmud and is not found in the Babylonian Talmud. The term *commoner* was used by Hizkiyah as an insult, meaning "ignorant" or "foolish." The categories of "commoner" and "foolish pietist" are similar, in that both are people who do foolish things in the name of piety. The foolish pietist, though, based on the examples provided in the Babylonian Talmud and the Palestinian Talmud (Chapter 5), actually poses a threat to himself or to others, while the "commoner" is not viewed as being physically dangerous.

Hizkiyah's baraita was applied explicitly in *P. Berakhot* 2:9 to the case of R. Samuel b. R. Isaac. This case involved:

---

43. The medieval commentators discuss whether women are permitted to observe commandments from which they are exempt, or if they are considered a *hedyot* if they do so. Nahmanides writes that "commoner" applies only when one observes something that is not in the Torah at all, for then he is adding to the Torah; when an individual does a commandment that is already in the Torah but that he just was not obligated to observe (like women observing time-bound positive commandments), then that person deserves a reward for this observance. Nahmanides' explanation does not, prima facie, explain why R. Samuel b. R. Isaac was labeled a commoner when he prayed *minhah*, which is a religious duty that was already in the Torah (*Hiddushei haRamban*, reprint, Jerusalem: 1928, *Kiddushin* 31a). The *Ra'avya* also discusses this issue at length (*Sefer Ra'avya* Laws of Megillah, 597, p. 339); his position will be presented in Chapter 7, since he links "commoner" to "arrogance."

44. *Hedyot* in this sense—to use a later and more colloquial usage—would mean "idiotic."

45. S. Leiberman, "Kach haya veKach yihiyeh—Yehudei Eretz Yisrael veYahadut haOlam biTekufat haMishnah veHaTalmud," *Cathedra* 17 (October 1980), p. 3.

1. an individual fulfilling a rabbinic religious duty from which
   he was temporarily exempt, and not a religious duty from
   which he personally was always exempt, but which other
   individuals or groups of Jews are obligated to perform;[46]
2. a positive commandment (*mitzvat aseh*) involving man and
   God (*bein adam laMakom*); and
3. a stringency that was performed in public and that may have
   made him appear arrogant, since he separated from those
   around him and acted as if he were more pious than those in
   his company. The public nature of his stringency may,
   additionally, have led to confusion regarding the law's requirements.

While the Talmud applies Hizkiyah's baraita explicitly to the
specific context of R. Samuel b. R. Isaac, it may not necessarily mean
to limit the application of the baraita *only* to cases parallel to that
particular incident. The case of R. Samuel b. R. Isaac may, in fact,
have been only one example of many possible situations to which
Hizkiyah's baraita could apply. This suggestion is supported by the
fact that when taken literally, as an independent statement, Hizkiyah's baraita constitutes a general condemnation of supererogatory
behavior. It could apply to an individual who fulfills a positive
commandment from which he is temporarily exempt or to an
individual who fulfills a religious duty from which he personally is
permanently exempt but that other individuals or groups of Jews are
obligated to perform. Both matters of praise and anguish would be
included in the criticism, as would commandments between man
and God as well as commandments between man and his fellow
man. The label "commoner" would apply even to people whose
motivations are totally sincere—even to people who limit their
supererogatory behavior to the very privacy of their own homes.

---

46. If Hizkiyah meant to limit his criticism only to this type of
stringency, then women who choose to perform positive commandments
from which they are exempt would not be labeled as "commoners."

# 7

# The Issue of Arrogance (Yohara)

An important theme that emerged in the previous chapters is the issue of arrogance. *T. Ta'anit* 1:7, discussed in Chapter 1, addressed the question of "who may declare himself an individual" and differentiated between matters of anguish (ascetic behaviors) and matters of praise. Matters of praise involved adding to one's religious observance in a manner that would elicit the respect of other people. Scholars were allowed these practices, such as dressing in a certain way; both R. Simeon b. Eleazar and Rabban Simeon b. Gamaliel, however, agreed that "not every person who wishes to declare himself an individual may do so" when it involves matters of praise. The reason for this prohibition was, presumably, that when common people attempt to stand out as being particularly pious, then they appear arrogant and presumptuous. This concern for appearing arrogant seems, in fact, to have been why Rabban Simeon b. Gamaliel held that not every bridegroom "who desires to take the name [of a scholar and recite the Shema] on his wedding night may do so" in *M. Berakhot* 2:6.

In *P. Berakhot* 2:9 (5d) (compare also *B. Baba Kama* 81b: both sugyot were discussed in Chapter 1), R. Judah b. Papus was criticized by R. Gamaliel for "pointing a finger at himself" by walking in the middle of the pitted road even though he was permitted to walk on the private sidewalks. R. Gamaliel accepted the validity of R. Judah b. Papus's stringency only when R. Joshua explained that R. Judah b. Papus's motivations were sincere and not presumptuous or arrogant, since "all his deeds are done in the name of heaven." According to that sugya, supererogatory behavior is permissible only when one's motivations are of a religious nature, namely, to serve God. If the individual is arrogant and engages in supererogatory behavior to display his exceptional piety, then his actions are condemned.

The emphasis in this particular passage is on internal motivation rather than on the reactions of other people. The sugya continues, though, with R. Zera's statement, "As long as he does not shame others," thus raising the issue of how public stringency could cause other people to react negatively. If someone engages in supererogatory acts of praise or anguish in public, acting more pious than those around him, then the people who see him may feel hurt or embarrassed. They may feel that he is putting them down by acting as if he is superior to them.

Thus, the sugya in *P. Berakhot* 2:9 (5d), while it does not use the word *yohara* (a Babylonian term meaning arrogance not found in the Palestinian Talmud), deals with this same issue. It may refer to the issue of arrogance again in its later discussion of R. Samuel b. R. Isaac (discussed in the previous chapter) who separated from R. Miyasha to pray *minhah* even though he was exempt, and of R. Kohen who separated from his colleagues to avoid impurity even though he did not have to do so (*P. Berakhot* 3:1 [6a]). R. Samuel b. R. Isaac may have been called a commoner by R. Miyasha, and R. Kohen may have been rebuked by R. Hizkiyah (the amora), precisely because their stringent behavior occurred in public and therefore appeared arrogant to their colleagues.[1] Following the context of *P. Berakhot* 2:9 (5d), then, whether behavior is considered "common" (*hedyot*) may depend on whether it reflects arrogance.

The theme of arrogance is also found in the discussion of the ascetic woman in Chapter 3, according to *P. Sotah* 3:4 (19a), which explains that the separated woman is someone who mocks the words of the Torah. This woman is called a destroyer of the world, then, because she acts as if she is more modest than the Torah itself; her behavior is arrogant and haughty. In *P. Sotah* 5:5 (20c)'s discus-

---

1. Leiberman, *Hilkhot HaYerushalmi LeHaRambam*, p. 26, note 30.

sion of the separatists who "bring destruction upon the world," the issue of arrogance surfaces again (see Chapter 4). The first separatist, the *shikmi* separatist who "carries his commandments on his shoulders," is ostentatious and arrogant in his performance of his religious duties. The fifth separatist, the "what is my duty and I will perform it" separatist in *B. Sotah* 22b, who acts as if he is so exceptionally pious that he has already fulfilled any commandment that he could possibly be expected to perform, is condemned for his presumptuous demeanor. Similarly, the parallel "I will know my duty and I will do it" separatist in *P. Sotah* 5:5 (20c), who speaks as if he commits no sins, is likewise overly impressed with himself.

The problem of arrogant behavior was also a concern of the early Christians, as was seen in the New Testament passages discussed in the discussion of the *shikmi* separatists in Chapter 4. Arrogant behavior within the context of religious observances (such as praying, giving alms, and fasting) is criticized in passages such as Matthew 6.

The issue of arrogance will be further developed in this chapter, since it is discussed explicitly in various sources in the Babylonian Talmud in which the rabbis criticize people who take on self-imposed stringencies. The term *arrogance* (*yohara*) is used in the Babylonian Talmud in reference to three different Halakhic issues involving individuals who accept supererogatory practices.[2] The three Halakhic issues are whether a bridegroom may recite the Shema on his wedding night, working on the fast day of the Ninth of Ab, and eating snacks and drinking in the sukkah. These sources will be analyzed to determine what type of self-imposed stringencies were labeled as arrogant by the tannaim and amoraim and why they were thus labeled.

## DEFINITION OF THE TERM *ARROGANCE (YOHARA)*

The earliest tannaitic source utilizing the root of the word *arrogant* (Y.H.R.) is found in *T. Sotah* 14:8:

---

2. In *B. Hullin* 111a–b, the term is used to criticize a young scholar who behaved in the opposite manner; he followed a self-imposed leniency regarding the preparation of liver and meat at the same time. He was labeled arrogant because he allowed himself to do something that the rabbis had ruled was actually forbidden ab initio; he thus went against the ruling of his elders.

I.   When they who draw out their spittle multiplied, disciples
     diminished and the Torah lost its honor.
II.  When the arrogant (*yehirim*) increased, the daughters of
     Israel began to marry arrogant men, because our generation
     looks only to the outward appearances (*lapanim*).

This selection is part of a much longer passage that lists
numerous problems that arose as the spiritual level of the Jewish
community apparently diminished at some point in tannaitic or
pre-tannaitic times.[3] *B. Sotah* 47b quotes a parallel baraita:

I.   When they who draw out their spittle multiplied, *the
     arrogant increased,* disciples diminished, and Torah went
     about [looking] for those who would study it.
II.  When the arrogant increased, the daughters of Israel began
     to marry arrogant men, because our generations looks only
     to outward appearances (*lapanim*).

The addition of the phrase "the arrogant increased" in section I
adds further clarification to the baraita, explaining that "drawing out
spittle" was a sign of arrogance.[4]

Various other amoraic sources in the Babylonian Talmud use the
word *yahir* (arrogant—singular), *yehirim* (arrogant—plural), or *yohara* (arrogance) to describe arrogant behavior.[5] In this study, however, only those sources in the Babylonian Talmud that apply the

---

3. Some of the names mentioned in *M. Sotah* 47b (which precede the
Talmudic sugya's quote of this Tosefta found below) are Yose b. Yoezer of
Zeredah, Yose b. Judah of Jerusalem, and Johanan the High Priest, all of
whom lived in the second century B.C.E. Although the baraita may have
been written much later, the names in the parallel Mishnah may indicate
that it was refering to an earlier time period.

4. See Rashi, ad loc., and Leiberman, *Tosefta Kifeshutah Sotah,* pp.
754–755, lines 41–42. The Amoraic sugya that immediately follows this
Tosefta quotes a verse in *Habakuk* 2:5 supporting this definition of *yohara* as
arrogance. This term is used in one other biblical source, namely, Proverbs
21:24.

5. See, for example *B. Baba Batra* 10b: "all the charity and kindness that
the heathen do is counted as sin to them, because they only do it to display
arrogance," and *B. Meggilah* 14b: "R. Nahman said: Arrogance does not befit
women. There were two haughty women, and their names are hateful."

term *yohara* specifically to religious observance, and not simply to personality descriptions, will be discussed.[6]

## THE RECITAL OF THE SHEMA BY A BRIDEGROOM AND WORKING ON THE NINTH OF AB

The primary Talmudic sugya that discusses arrogance (*yohara*) as a factor to be considered in evaluating supererogatory practices is *B. Berakhot* 17b.[7] This passage compares the views of the anonymous Mishnah and Rabban Simeon b. Gamaliel (*Berakhot* 2:8) vis-à-vis two different issues, namely, a bridegroom's reciting of the *Shema* on his wedding night, and working on the Ninth of Ab. (This Mishnah was quoted and discussed in Chapter 1, but it will be quoted again here to facilitate understanding of the Talmudic sugya):

I.      *Mishnah:* If a bridegroom desires to recite the *Shema* on the first night, he may do so.

---

6. Within the Dead Sea Scrolls, there is one passage that may be dealing with arrogant behavior. In the *Manual of Discipline* (1QS 7:5), the word *bemarim* or *bemarom* is translated by Weinfeld as "arrogance": "The one who speaks to his neighbor with arrogance (*bemarom*) or plays false (*remiyah*) with his comrade, shall be fined for six months." Licht and Wernberg-Moller, however, both connect *bemarim* with the following *remiyah* and explain it as a form of trickery (Licht uses the word *mirmah,* and Wernberg-Moller translates it as "deceit"). This latter explanation seems to be correct, since then the same root with the same definition would be used twice in the same sentence; the first phrase refers to one who speaks deceitfully, while the second refers to one who acts deceitfully. Even if Weinfeld would be correct in his understanding that *bemarim* (or *bemarom*) and *remiyah* have different meanings—the first meaning "arrogantly" and the second meaning "deceitfully"—this source would still not be directly relevant here, because it deals with arrogance solely as a personality trait and not as motivation for religious behavior. What it would show, though, is that arrogant behavior in general was a concern for leaders of the Qumram community, as it was for the tannaim and amoraim. (See Moshe Weinfeld, *The Organizational Pattern and the Penal Code of the Qumram Sect* [NTOA] (Schweiz: Universitäts-verlag Freiburg Schweiz, 1986), pp. 35–37; *Megillat HaSerakhim,* ed. Jacob Licht (Jerusalem: Mossad Bialik, 1965), p. 161, line 5; and *The Manual of Discipline,* ed. P. Wernberg-Moller (Leiden: Brill, 1957), pp. 14–15).

7. This exact same passage is found in *B. Pesahim* 55a. (Compare also Munich manuscript *B. Brakhot* 176.)

II.     Rabban Simeon b. Gamaliel says, "Not everyone who desires to take the name [i.e., to call himself a scholar] may do so."

III.    *Talmud:* May we conclude from this that R. Simeon b. Gamaliel is concerned about arrogance while the rabbis do not share this concern?

IV.     But do we not understand them to hold the opposite views, as we have learned:

V.      "Where it is the custom to do work on the Ninth of Ab, one may do it; where it is the custom not to do work, one may not do it. And in all places scholars cease [from work on that day]. Rabban Simeon b. Gamaliel said: Every man (*kol adam*)[8] should act as a scholar."

VI.     We have here a contradiction between two sayings of the rabbis, and between two sayings of Rabban Simeon b. Gamaliel!

VII.    R. Johanan said: "The opinions are reversed."

VIII.   R. Shesha the son of R. Idi said, "There is no need to reverse. There is no contradiction between the two sayings of the rabbis. In the case of the recital of the *Shema,* since everybody else recites, and he also recites, he will not appear arrogant (*lo mehzei keyohara*) [but in the case of the month of Ab], since everybody else does work and he does no work, he will appear arrogant.

IX.     Nor is there a contradiction between the two sayings of R. Simeon [b. Gamaliel]. In the case of the *Shema,* the validity of the act depends on the mental concentration and we are witnesses that he is unable to concentrate. Here, however, anyone who sees will say, 'He has no work; go and see how many unemployed there are in the market place.'"

The assumption of the text quoted here is that the debate between the anonymous Mishnah (permitting the bridegroom to say the Shema) and Rabban Simeon b. Gamaliel (prohibiting him)

---

8. In the Kaufmann manuscript on *M. Pesahim 4:5,* the word here is "the whole nation" (*kol ha'am*) instead of "every man"; this all-inclusive term further strengthens R. Simeon b. Gamaliel's point (*Mishnah,* Codex Kaufmann [Jerusalem: 1968]).

centers around the issue of arrogance. It therefore asks whether we should conclude that Rabban Simeon b. Gamaliel, who states, "Not everyone who wishes to take the name [of a scholar] may do so" is concerned about arrogance, while the rabbis (i.e., the anonymous Mishnah), who state that any bridegroom who wishes to say the Shema may do so, do not share this concern. It then questions this assumption by quoting *M. Pesahim* 4:5 (cited in section V) regarding working on the ninth of Ab, wherein the two positions appear to be reversed.

In this Mishnah, it is Rabban Simeon b. Gamaliel who states that "all men should consider themselves scholars," thus apparently contradicting his position with regard to the Shema and exhibiting no concern regarding arrogance. The rabbis here also appear to contradict themselves, since in *M. Pesahim* 4:5 they state that only (true) scholars refrain from working in all places, thus, apparently, showing that they are, in fact, concerned about arrogance.

Two responses are offered to this question. The first is that of R. Johanan, who states, "The opinions are reversed (*muhlefet hashitah*)."[9] He held that either the rabbis or Rabban Simeon b. Gamaliel were concerned about arrogance, while the other party did not share that concern.

The second response, that of R. Shesha son of R. Idi, maintains that the positions should not be reversed. He, instead, explains that both the rabbis and Rabban Simeon b. Gamaliel were, in fact, concerned about arrogance. They disagreed, however, about whether people would attribute arrogance to the individuals involved in these two situations.

It is important to note that the Talmudic sugya seems to be focusing on whether other people will view the individual's actions as being arrogant; it is not necessarily discussing the feelings of the individual performing the action. This differs from *P. Berakhot* 2:9 and its parallel, *B. Baba Kama* 81b, in which R. Judah b. Papus's (or R. Judah b. Nekosa's) ostensibly arrogant actions were justified by R. Joshua (or R. Hiyya) because his motivations were totally sincere

---

9. This phrase—"R. Johanan said: 'Reverse the positions'"—is used frequently in the Babylonian Talmud in order to explain contradictions between mishnayot. See, for example, *B. Berakhot* 49b; *B. Eruvin* 99a; *B. Bezah* 3a and 9b; and Hyman, *Toldot,* vol. II, p. 667.

despite appearances to the contrary. The concern about arrogance attributed to the tannaim in *B. Berakhot* 17b is, however, a concern about appearing arrogant (*mehzei keyohara*), and not about the individual's feelings.

According to the rabbis of the *B. Berakhot* sugya, in the case of the Shema, the groom reciting the Shema will not appear arrogant since he is reciting it along with everyone else (and hence will not stand out). In the case of working on the Ninth of Ab, though, an individual who abstains from working will appear to be arrogant since every other common person will be working (and hence will, in fact, stand out). According to Rabban Simeon b. Gamaliel, on the other hand, in the case of the Shema, he will appear arrogant since everyone knows that he is acting as if he can indeed concentrate when he is really unable to do so.[10] In the case, though, of the Ninth of Ab, people will attribute his refraining from working to unemployment, and not view him as an arrogant individual pretending to be a scholar.

What determines, then, whether something constitutes an act of arrogance is the social context—if he is the only person behaving in this way and stands out, then his behavior may be perceived as arrogant.[11] If, however, other people are also doing the same thing and his supererogation would not be noticed, then arrogance would not be a problem.[12] *Yohara,* then, is integrally related to the time,

---

10. Rashi, ad loc. Ironically, this concern for the appearance of arrogance, which led Rabban Simeon b. Gamaliel to prevent bridegrooms from reciting the Shema, is later cited by Tosafot as a reason for instructing all bridegrooms to recite the Shema. Tosafot ruled that since people no longer have proper intention in their daily prayers, then someone who refrains from reciting the Shema on his wedding night would appear arrogant. For he would then be implying that he (as opposed to everyone else) normally has proper intentions (*Tosafot, B. Berakhot* 17b, s.v. R. Shesha).

11. R. Jacob Reisha in fact writes that any self-imposed stringency that is done in public and is not accepted as standard practice by most or all of the public is considered *yohara*. He writes this in condemnation of a group of approximately thirty men who would gather in the synagogue in the middle of the night to mourn the destruction of the Temple. This type of behavior, though, if done by an individual in private, would be praiseworthy (Jacob Reisha, *Shevut Ya'akov* (reprint, Jerusalem: 1972), pt. II, Responsum 44.

12. The Ra'avyah explains that it is permitted for women to fulfill commandments from which they are exempt, such as Sukkah, Shofar, and lulav, for "regarding women who observe positive commandments, every-

place, and social-religious mores of the community in which one lives.[13] The same principle may apply to the label of "commoner," which might, according to P. *Berakhot* 2:9, be integrally related to the

---

one agrees that there is no issue of arrogance, since everybody (*kulei alma*) sits in the sukkah and blows the shofar and holds the lulav." "Everybody" here must refer to the men and not to "all women," for he is discussing women who choose to observe these laws; this, by necessity, means that only some women made this choice while others did not—"everyone" then must refer to the men. (This is expressed most explicitly by his statement "everybody sounds the shofar"—this is clearly a reference to men, since women do not sound the shofar—they listen to it when it is sounded by a man.) This implies that an individual woman who wishes to voluntarily observe a positive command-ment from which she is normally exempt would not be considered arrogant, even if women as a group did not observe this commandment. As long as the commandment she volunteers to observe is observed by men, then she does not appear arrogant, since "everybody" (*kulei alma*) is already observing the commandment. The Ra'avyah's position is not limited to those command-ments that women voluntarily observe as a unified group, such as shofar, which became a commandment that Jewish women as a group accepted on themselves. For in addition to shofar, he also lists sitting in the sukkah and making a blessing on the lulav, two commandments that women as a group never accepted universally. See *Sefer Ra'avyah, Meggilah* 597, vol. II, p. 339, *Berakhot* 56, vol. I, p. 33.

13.   Observance of the commandment to wear tefillin was weak in the land of Israel in Geonic times, possibly as a result of earlier Roman decrees (see Chapter 4). This phenomenon involved a laxity in the actual fulfillment of the commandment of wearing tefillin altogether (it was not simply that people were not wearing tefillin all day); see explanations for this phenom-ena above in Chapter 4. As a result, the Geonim discuss whether someone who wears them needs to be concerned about appearing arrogant (*Otzar HaGeonim Rosh Hashanah,* Teshuvot, 18–20, pp. 28–29; Kasher, *Torah Shelemah,* vol. 12, app. 42, pp. 260–261). Another example of how the appearance of arrogance is dependent on time and place is found in a responsum of R. Israel of Bruna, the fifteenth-century Halakhist. He is asked whether students can wear their fringed garment (*tzizit*) on top of their outer garments. He responds by saying that now, in his times, that is the way in which the rabbis dress, not students, and that it would, therefore, be arrogant for students to dress in that way. In another place or time, then, the law could be different. See Responsum 96, quoted in H. Medini, *S'dei Hemed HaShalem,* vol. III (New York: Friedman, 1967), p. 87. Likewise, see *Tosafot* (quoted earlier) in *B. Berakhot* 17b, s.v. R. Shesha.

issue of arrogance. For, as already suggested, one may be labeled a commoner if he engages in supererogatory behavior that appears arrogant and presumptuous, as might have been the case with R. Samuel b. R. Isaac who stopped eating to pray when R. Miyasha did not (see Chapter 6).

The Talmudic sugya in *P. Berakhot* 2:9 (5d) following this Mishnah (regarding the bridegroom saying the Shema despite his exemption) contains no parallels to the discussion in *B. Berakhot*. It does, however, quote *T. Ta'anit* 1:7, a source that could very simply solve the contradiction in the *B. Berakhot* sugya. This source (which is also found in *B. Ta'anit* 10b) states that, according to Rabban Simeon b. Gamaliel, anyone who wishes to observe supererogatory anguish may do so, while only a scholar may "declare himself an individual" in a matter involving praise. With regard to working on the Ninth of Ab, then, which is a matter involving anguish since a day's work will be lost,[14] Rabban Simeon b. Gamaliel permitted (in this case, encouraged) the average person to "call himself a scholar" (i.e., "declare himself an individual") and refrain from working.[15] With regard to the Shema, however, which is a matter involving praise, since he will gain a better reputation by reciting the Shema, Rabban Simeon b. Gamaliel held that common people should not call themselves scholars (and therefore, should not recite the Shema).[16]

While *P. Berakhot* 2:9 (5d) does not compare the case of the

---

14. R. Eleazar Azkiri, *Perush miBa'al Sefer Haredim,* ad loc.

15. R. Moses Margaliot, in his *Mareh Happanim, Berakhot,* ad loc. While not working on the Ninth of Ab was described above as a matter of anguish since a day's wages would be lost, it can, alternatively, be viewed as a matter of praise. For refraining from working allows one to better concentrate on fasting, thus enhancing one's religious observance. Other people would see that he is not working so that he can have a more meaningful fast and would praise his piety. Rabban Simeon b. Gamaliel, then, who limited supererogatory matters of praise to scholars (*T. Ta'anit* 1:7; see Chapter 1) would be making an exception in this case and encouraging all people to behave as scholars. This explanation, though, would not solve the contradiction between his position against reciting the Shema versus his position in favor of refraining from work on the Ninth of Ab. For both would be matters of praise, yet one would be discouraged and the other encouraged.

16. Y. N. Epstein assumes that *P. Berakhot* 2:9 is quoting *T. Ta'anit* 1:7 precisely in order to solve this contradiction. See *Mavo LeNusah HaMishnah* (Jerusalem: Magnes, 1964), pp. 252–253.

Shema to working on the ninth of Ab and does not specifically mention arrogance, it is an underlying theme of the sugya (as was discussed earlier). This is not, however, the case in *P. Pesahim* 4:5 (30d). This sugya, which deals with working on the Ninth of Ab, does not appear to be discussing the issue of arrogance, even implicitly.[17]

---

17. This sugya is difficult; while two different explanations have been proposed, each is problematic. According to the first explanation, Rabban Simeon b. Gamaliel's statement that "every man should act as a scholar" and refrain from working on the ninth of Ab was said in astonishment. The word *kematmihah* is used, which has the root *T.M.H.*, indicating amazement, or astonishment. See Benjamin Z. Bacher, *Erkhei Midrash,* trans. A. Z. Rabinowitz (Tel-Aviv: Ahdut, 1923), s.v. *T.M.H.*; and Michael Sokoloff, *A Dictionary of Jewish-Palestinian Aramaic of Byzantine Period* (Ramat Gan: Bar Ilan University Press, 1990). The anonymous Mishnah stated, "And in all places scholars cease (from work on that day)," and Rabban Simeon b. Gamaliel protested against this idea, stating, "Every man should act as a scholar?!" He felt that if scholars were advised not to work regardless of the local custom, then "every man" would "become a scholar" on the Ninth of Ab to avoid working. The Ninth of Ab would then become a day of idleness in all locations, whereas the rabbis had instructed people not to work only if that was their local custom. Rabban Simeon b. Gamaliel, therefore, felt that scholars had to follow the local custom and were not allowed to cease from work on the Ninth of Ab unless that was the local custom. See R. David Frankel, *Korban HaEdah,* s.v. *kematmiah;* R. Moses Margaliot, *Penei Moshe,* s.v. *R. Simeon b. Gamaliel omer;* L. Ginzberg, *Perushim VeHidushim,* vol. I, p. 400. According to this explanation, arrogance was not, in fact, the concern of the Mishnah. Instead, the debate between the anonymous Mishnah and Rabban Simeon b. Gamaliel would be about the nature of people's reaction to seeing scholars refrain from working on the Ninth of Ab. This interpretation thus contrasts strongly with the *B. Sotah* sugya's understanding of the Mishnah. If it is correct, then the problem raised by the *B. Sotah* would not exist. For if arrogance was not the concern of this Mishnah, then there is no contradiction between Rabban Simeon b. Gamaliel's position on working on the Ninth of Ab versus his position regarding a bridegroom reciting the Shema. His position, then, that scholars should work on the Ninth of Ab so that all people will not remain idle by declaring themselves to be scholars is, in a sense, in agreement with his position on the Shema. For in both cases he limits the individual's rights to take on extra obligations. Although the reason behind his limitation differs in each case, the same desire to limit subjective self-imposed stringencies is

## EATING IN THE SUKKAH

The term *arrogance* (*yohara*) is also used in the Talmudic discussion of whether casual food (snacks) must be eaten in the *sukkah* (*B. Sukkah*

---

found. This explanation, however, is problematic. First, there is no indication in the Mishnah that Rabban Simeon b. Gamaliel was speaking "in astonishment." Second, this interpretation contradicts another baraita, attributed to Rabban Simeon b. Gamaliel. In *B. Ta'anit* 30b, R. Simeon b. Gamaliel states that on the Ninth of Ab, "every man should act as a scholar *so that he may fast."* The addition of the phrase "so that he may fast" indicates that Rabban Simeon b. Gamaliel was not speaking in an astonished tone of voice but rather was seriously stating his position. He held that ideally, no one should work on the Ninth of Ab (i.e., every man should consider himself a scholar on that day) so that he would not need to eat due to the strain of working and/or so that the fast would simply be more meaningful. (Some medieval commentators actually have the words "so that he may fast" in their quote of Rabban Simeon b. Gamaliel's statement in *M. Pesahim* 4:5 itself [H. Malter, *Ta'anit* 30b, p. 143, note 18.]) While the text in the Munich manuscript is somewhat different, the same position is attributed to Rabban Simeon b. Gamaliel there as well (Codex Munich, ad loc., ed. M. Rabinowicz, *Dikdukei Soferim, Ta'anit* 30b note 30 (New York: M. P. Press, 1977); L. Ginzberg, *Perushim VeHidushim,* pp. 400–401). Perhaps for this reason, a different explanation of this passage is suggested by R. Eleazar Azkiri (found in R. Solomon HaAdani's *Melekhet Shlomo* on *M. Pesahim.* 4:5, and quoted by Lieberman in *HaYerushalmi Kifeshuto* [Jerusalem: Darom, 1934], p. 441. He suggests that the word "in astonishment" (*kematmihah*) is really the word *bematmihah,* meaning "in the case of an astonisher"—someone who constantly works and is never idle and would, therefore, astonish others by not working. Rabban Simeon b. Gamaliel, according to R. Azkiri, was not speaking in astonishment but instead was seriously stating his position. While various modern scholars accept this explanation of the word *bematmihah,* R. Azkiri's explanation of the rest of the passage is problematic, since it has no textual basis (see Lieberman, *HaYerushalmi Kifeshuto,* p. 441; Ze'ev Wolf Rabinovitz, *Sha'are Torat Eretz Yisrael* (Jerusalem: 1940), p. 222; Epstein, *Mavoh,* p. 252; HaLivni, David Weiss, *Meqorot U-Mesorot: Be'urim Ba-Talmud Le-Seder Mo'ed, Masekhet Pesahim* (New York: Jewish Theological Seminary, 1982); and *The Talmud of the Land of Israel: A Preliminary Translation and Explanation. Vol. 13, Yerushalmi Pesahim,* trans. Baruch M. Bokser, completed and ed. Lawrence H. Schiffman (Chicago: University of Chicago Press, 1994).

26b).[18] *M. Sukkah* 2:4 states, "Casual (*arai*) eating and drinking are permitted outside the Sukkah." It then proceeds to relate the following incidents in 2:5:

I.   It once happened that they brought cooked food to R. Yohanan b. Zakkai to taste, and two dates and a pitcher of water to R. Gamaliel and they said, "Bring them up to the *sukkah*."

II.  But when they gave R. Zadok food less than the bulk of an egg, he took it in a cloth,[19] ate it outside the *sukkah*, and did not say the benediction after it.

The Talmud, in *B. Sukkah* 26b, then comments:

III. Does not the incident contradict? [for R. Yohanan b. Zakkai and R. Gamaliel ate casual food in the *sukkah*, even though the preceding Mishnah had stated that this was unnecessary.]

IV.  There is a lacuna, and it should be taught thus [*hisurei mehsera vehakhi katanei*]:

V.   But if he wishes to be strict with himself, he may do so, and it does not constitute arrogance,

VI.  and so it also happened that "They brought cooked food to R. Yohanan b. Zakkai."

Without the Talmudic sugya, it would be conceivable to interpret that these tannaim actually disagreed about whether small amounts of food may be eaten outside of the *sukkah*. The sugya, however, clearly assumes otherwise. It states that R. Yohanan b. Zakkai and R. Gamaliel would both have agreed with the prior Mishnah's ruling that casual eating was permitted outside the *sukkah*, yet they wished to act in a more stringent manner for themselves. The Talmudic sugya then, based on their actions,

---

18. The exact determination of what is considered a snack is debated on *B. Sukkah* 26a.

19. He held that less than the bulk of an egg did not require the ritual washing of hands, sitting in the *sukkah,* or reciting the Grace after meals and wrapped it in a cloth for cleanliness purposes only (Rashi, ad loc., s.v. *natlo*). According, though, to Tosafot, he wrapped it in a cloth for purity purposes, since he was a priest (Tosafot, ibid.).

concludes that one who wishes to eat even casual food in the *Sukkah* does not have to worry lest he appear arrogant.

The rewording of the Mishnah (sections III–IV) is not based on an alternative Mishnaic text but rather is the anonymous sugya's reformulation of what the Mishnah should have stated.[20] Evidence for this is the fact that the restoration contains a great deal of aramaic and is not simple Mishnaic Hebrew. The parallel to this Talmudic sugya in *B. Yoma* 79a quotes what seems to be an abbreviation of this amoraic reformulation:

I.    Once they brought R. Yohanan b. Zakkai . . . "Take them up to the sukkah."

II.   In connection therewith it was taught [*uteni alah*]

III.  [They ordered so] not because that was the law, but because they wished to be more stringent for themselves.

It is possible, though, that a separate baraita is being quoted here. For the phrase "in connection therewith it was taught" (*uteni alah*—section II) is used to introduce a baraita.[21] The sugya, then, may have based its reformulation of the Mishnah on this baraita. Some manuscripts,[22] however, do not have section II at all; the Talmudic sugya of *B. Yoma* 79a would then simply be quoting the Talmudic reformulation of the Mishnah as if it really were the original text of the Mishnah.[23]

Following these explanations of the Mishnah, the similarities and/or differences between the case of the sukkah and the cases of the Shema and working on the ninth of Ab can be analyzed. According to *B. Sukkah* 26b, one need not worry lest he appears arrogant if he eats even casual food in the *sukkah*, even though eating such food outside the sukkah is permissible. In the case of the

---

20. Epstein, *Mavo,* ibid., p. 595 quotes the *Seder Tannaim veAmoraim,* which explains "there is a lacuna and it should be taught thus" in this manner (*Seder Tannaim veAmoraim*; R. Yosef Tov-Ellem, 1857), par. 64.

21. Y. N. Epstein, *Mavo LeNusah HaMishnah* (Jerusalem: Magnes, 1964), vol. II, p. 605.

22. The Oxford and London manuscripts do not have the words *uteni alah* (*Dikdukei Soferim,* ad. loc., note 8), and R. Joshua Boaz in *Masoret haShas,* ad. loc., suggests that Tosafot's text did not have these words.

23. Tosafot *Yoma* 79b, s.v. *lo mipnei;* and Epstein, *Mavo,* vol. II, p. 605.

bridegroom, he also did not have to worry lest he appear arrogant if he recited the Shema (according to the rabbis), and a person who wanted to remain idle on the ninth of Ab was permitted to do so, even in a place where the custom was to work (according to Rabban Simeon b. Gamaliel). In each of these three cases, the assumption is that people would not view the individual's supererogatory behavior as being arrogant.

In the case of eating casual food in the *sukkah*, one could argue, though, that if the accepted common practice was to eat only full meals in the *sukkah*, then someone who would go to the *sukkah* to eat even casual food might in fact be seen as arrogant. The sugya in *B. Sukkah* 26b, though, did not hold this to be a problem, stating, "But if he wishes to be strict with himself, he may do so, and it does not constitute arrogance" (see section V). The reason for this may be that the very nature of the commandment of *sukkah* eliminates the possibility of the appearance of arrogance. The Mishnah in *Sukkah* 2:9 states:

I.   All seven days [of the festival] a man must make the sukkah his permanent abode and his house his temporary abode.

The Talmud (*B. Sukkah* 28b) then asks, "In what manner?" and then answers:

I.   If he had beautiful vessels, he should bring them up into the sukkah, beautiful divans, he should bring them up into the sukkah;

II.  he should eat and drink and stroll in the sukkah.

What is clear from this source is that the more time one spends in the *sukkah* and the more activities that one does within it, the greater the reward. For this reason, a person eating only casual food and not a full meal would not, then, stand out as arrogant, since people would view him as trying to fulfill the commandment of dwelling in the *sukkah* as completely as possible. This idea is similar to the explanation given in Chapter 6 for why the label of "commoner" applied only to people who performed commandments between man and God even when they were exempt, not to people who performed commandments between people even when they were exempt. The overriding concern of "Love thy neighbor as thyself" was the reason that the label "commoner" would not apply to someone imposing stringencies on himself within the realm of commandments between people. Even though *sukkah* is a commandment between man and God, there is also an overriding concern here that prevents the label of "arrogance" from being applied to someone who eats all of his food in the *sukkah*. That overriding concern is the commandment to make the *sukkah* into a permanent abode as much as possible.[24]

This clearly positive attitude about doing as much as possible in the *sukkah* is not the case, though, with regard to the Shema and working on the Ninth of Ab. In these two cases, it is certainly possible for people to indeed view the individual's supererogatory behavior as being arrogant. For this reason, there is a controversy between Rabban Simeon b. Gamaliel and the anonymous Mishnah regarding the reaction of the public to these two cases. A common thread, though, linking all three cases discussed here is that the main focus of the amoraic discussion may be other people's perceptions of arrogance, not on the individual's internal feeling or motivation.

## CHAPTER SUMMARY

The issue of appearing arrogant when performing supererogatory commandments was certainly a concern of the tannaim. It is mentioned explicitly in *P. Berakhot* 2:9, in the incident in which R. Gamaliel asks R. Joshua, "Who is that pointing a finger at himself?" in reaction to seeing R. Papus b. Judah walking in the road pegs. The tannaim associated with this incident in *B. Baba Kama* 81b are R. Judah the Prince and R. Hiyya, who ask, "Who is that showing his greatness in our presence?"

Various other tannaitic sources address this concern implicitly.

---

24. According, however, to R. Simhah, someone who does not leave the *sukkah* even though he is exempt would not receive a reward and would be labeled a commoner (R. M. Padua, *Hagahot Maimoniyot,* "Laws of Sukkah," 6:3, note 3, in the name of R. Simhah). To what extent R. Simhah applied this concept is not clear. He may, on the one hand, have meant people who were exempt for specific reasons, such as being sick, or being unable to sleep in the *sukkah* because of the wind or to insects. On the other hand, he many have meant to include anyone who was exempt from the *sukkah*, including women.

Rabban Simeon b. Gamaliel, who discouraged "just any" bridegroom from reciting the Shema (in *M. Berakhot* 2:6) was concerned with the appearance of arrogance, according to the Talmudic sugya. Similarly, he (and R. Simeon b. Eleazar in *T. Ta'anit* 1:7) did not allow common people to declare themselves individuals with regard to matters of praise, presumably because such behavior would appear arrogant.

The issue of arrogance is not addressed explicitly in the amoraic sources in the Palestinian Talmud. It may, though, have been the reason for R. Miyasha's criticism of R. Samuel for praying when he was exempt from doing so, and for R. Hizkiyah's reprimanding of R. Kohen for separating from his colleagues unnecessarily. R. Zera speaks out against shaming other people.

It is only in the Babylonian Talmud, in the sources discussed in this chapter, that the actual wording of "the appearance of arrogance" (*mehezei keyohara*) appears. The concept of the appearance of arrogance, while found in the tannaitic incident of R. Judah b. Papus, is discussed and developed most fully in the Babylonian Talmud, in the sources examined in this chapter.

Any (or all) of the following reasons may have motivated the amoraim (and the tannaim mentioned earlier) to criticize behavior that could appear arrogant:

1. They wished to promote a feeling of religious unity; they wanted to avoid arguments and splitting into groups within the community.
2. They wanted people to be aware of how their behavior affects others. They wanted religious people to be positive role models and therefore demanded that they avoid doing things that made them appear pompous and superior.
3. They assumed that the public's perception probably corresponded to the individual's internal reality. If someone separates from other people by acting as if he is more pious than those around him, then the rabbis suspected that his actions were motivated by an internal feeling of arrogance. Otherwise, he would have practiced his self-imposed stringencies in private.[25]

---

25. *Otzar HaGeonim Rosh Hashanah,* Teshuvot, 20, p. 29.

Another important factor to be considered is that whether a religious observance is considered arrogant (and, therefore, "common") often depends on time and place. When evaluating whether supererogatory behavior appears arrogant, therefore, the norms of the particular society in which one lives are of crucial importance.

As was mentioned in Chapter 6, the categories "foolish pietist" (*hasid shoteh*) and "commoner" (*hedyot*) are closely related, in that both describe people who do foolish things in the name of religion. The category of "commoner," in turn, may additionally be linked to the category of "the appearance of arrogance." This is because Hizkiyah's baraita, "Whoever does something from which he is exempt is called a commoner," within the context of *P. Berakhot* 2:9, was applied to a situation in which R. Samuel b. R. Isaac may have appeared arrogant. Supererogatory behavior, then, may have been called "common" by Hizkiyah because it can appear to be arrogant behavior, if done in front of other people.[26] By attempting so very hard to please God (by doing extra commandments), the individual in fact hurts other people's feelings. His actions may cause other people to feel that he is showing disdain for them, as if he is saying that their observance of the law is not sufficient for him—he needs to do more, because he is so exceptionally pious.[27] The sources discussed here thus demonstrate that within Talmudic literature, both one's own intentions as well as the reactions of other people to self-imposed stringency were considered to be of crucial importance.

---

26. The *Ra'avyah*, discussed above, explicitly links these two terms. In his discussion of women who wish to observe commandments from which they are exempt, he explains that as long as one does not appear arrogant, then one is not considered a commoner (Meggilah 597, p. 339).

27. An example of this would be the *Halakhah* that if one takes more than three steps backward at the end of the *amidah*, then he is considered arrogant, for he acts as if he needs to give more respect to God than everybody else (*Shulhan Arukh Orah Hayim* 123:4.

# Conclusion

S everal major religious issues related to the topic of supererogatory behavior were discussed in the Introduction to this study. One
question raised was when religious stringency, which is often
viewed as a positive expression of religious passion, or piety was
instead viewed by the rabbis as fanatical or elitist behavior that had
to be curtailed. Another question was to what extent did the rabbis
try to limit supererogatory behavior, which was, ostensibly, a
personal, subjective expression of religious zeal?

Asceticism was yet another religious issue discussed. What
types of self-denial were practiced by Jews in Talmudic times, and
when and why were such practices criticized by the rabbis? The
final issue discussed in the Introduction was that of intention. To
what extent does the individual's intention impact on the religious
value accorded to the stringency? Were insincere motivations alone
enough to invalidate the stringency, and, alternatively, were sincere
motivations sufficient to validate the stringency? An overall conceptual summary of the information gathered in this study will be
presented here, to generate answers to these questions.

## CRITICISM OF STRINGENCY: EIGHT POSITIONS

From the voices raised in Talmudic literature to criticize self-imposed religious stringency, different degrees and types of condemnation have been heard and explained. The factors considered by the rabbis in their evaluation of self-imposed stringency include the type of stringency and circumstances involved, as well as the type of person imposing the stringency and his or her motivation. How others will react and whether the self-imposed stringency will hurt the person or others—be it physically, emotionally, or financially—are further factors considered.

Eight conceptual positions are summarized below:

### The "All-Inclusive" Approach

Hizkiyah's baraita, "Whoever does something from which he is exempt is called a commoner," can be understood as a general rule without exceptions. His all-inclusive wording of *"whoever* (i.e., anyone—*kol*) does something . . . commoner," when taken literally, would mean that he intended to universally condemn self-imposed stringency of all types. His statement would then constitute the most extreme condemnation of supererogation that exists in any of the Talmudic sources.

This interpretation of Hizkiyah's position would extend to all types of supererogatory behavior. It would include both matters of anguish (ascetic stringencies) and matters of praise (non-ascetic stringencies that involve adding to or extending one's religious observances in a manner that would elicit the praise of other people). Scholars and commoners would be included. Stringencies involving man and his fellow man, man and God, and even stringencies performed in private would all be included in his reprobation.

Hizkiyah's position would extend to cases of supererogation for which no obligation exists whatsoever for any Jew. It would also apply to an individual who fulfills a commandment from which he personally is exempt but that other individuals or groups of Jews are obligated to perform. Women fulfilling the time-dependent positive commandments from which they are exempt (and perhaps even studying aspects of Torah that they are exempted from studying) would then be regarded as commoners. This all-inclusive criticism

would apply even when the self-imposed stringency were undertaken with totally sincere motivation.

### The Antiascetic Approach

A second type of criticism censuring self-imposed stringency limits
itself to stringencies involving self-denial (matters of anguish). This
position is attributed, most notably, to R. Eleazar HaKappar and/or
R. Eliezer HaKappar Beribi, who hold that a nazirite is a sinner.
Though this criticism is less global than Hizkiyah's (as interpreted
earlier), applying as it does only to self-denial, it utilizes stronger
language. For Hizkiyah uses the term *commoner*, which means
uneducated and foolish, whereas R. Eleazar HaKappar uses the term
*sinner*, a far more serious condemnation.

R. Eleazar HaKappar's reasoning, as stated in *B. Ta'anit* 11a, is
that the nazirite is a sinner because he denies himself pleasures that
the Torah permits. Ascetic behavior (when it extends beyond the
restrictions of the Torah), according to this position, is "sinful"—
presumably even if motivated by pious concerns. The notion lying at
the very root of ascetic behavior,[1] that an oppressive or unfriendly
physical world was considered to be a stumbling block to the pursuit
of more heroic (religious) goals, was thus considered false by R.
Eleazar HaKappar and those who agree with his position. Ironically,
according to this viewpoint, it would seem that ascetic behavior
(above and beyond the restrictions of the Torah) rather than physical
pleasure permitted by the Torah would constitute a stumbling block
to the pursuit of higher spiritual goals. This could be because
engaging in such ascetic behavior would involve going against the
Torah's ideals, which are considered to be the blueprint for attaining
spiritual perfection.

The condemnation of the nazirite appears to reject the view of
Rabban Simeon b. Gamaliel. For Rabban Simeon b. Gamaliel held
that anyone may "become an individual" with regard to self-
imposed matters of anguish. R. Eleazar HaKappar, however, regards
the nazirite, who imposes matters of anguish on himself, as an actual
sinner.

The theme of the "nazirite as sinner" is, at times, used in the

---

1. Wimbush, *Ascetic Behavior*, p. 2.

Talmud as a paradigm to condemn other, nonnazirite forms of self-denial as well. Such self-denial includes frequent fasting (according to R. Yose, in tannaitic times, and Samuel in amoraic times), vowing not to eat bread (which, in actuality, was a severe hardship, since bread was the staple food), or injuring oneself.

At other times, Talmudic references criticize self-denial and/or affirm the need to preserve life but do not use the nazirite as a paradigm. Three such examples include (1) the passage discussing how a father or husband can annul a daughter or wife's vows of self-denial, (2) Rav's statement that a person is held responsible for the welfare of his body, and (3) R. Hanina's statement "A person who should take [charity from others because he has no food] but does not take is considered to be a killer."

## The "Pro-Pleasure" Approach

A more extreme version of the anti-ascetic viewpoint would maintain that not only is it wrong to deny oneself pleasure, but it is virtually a religious obligation to pursue those pleasures of this world that are permitted by Jewish law. This idea is expressed most cogently in *P. Kiddushin* 4:12 by R. Hizkiyah (the amora—not to be confused with Hizkiyah the tanna discussed earlier) in the name of Rav, when he says, "In the future, a person will be asked to give a justification for everything which his eye saw but which he did not eat." A person must actively pursue the experiences of pleasure that his eye beheld. He is, thus, held accountable if he abstains from any such experience of permitted pleasure.

This position is explained by Urbach as a way of shielding people from other sins: if certain physical pleasures were permitted, then people would be able to avoid those that were forbidden.[2] Rav's viewpoint, however, need not be viewed merely as a means of preventing sins. For Rav's wording suggests that God expects people to experience the wonders and pleasures of His creation; such experiences, presumably, have independent religious value. As such, according to Rav, whenever one fails to experience God's world, he will have to justify himself in the world to come.

Another statement attributed to Rav contains a similar theme.

---

2. Urbach, *Hazal,* p. 422.

In *B. Ta'anit* 22b, he states that God holds people responsible for keeping their "living spirit" (i.e., their body) alive. This statement explains why R. Yose held that people should not afflict themselves with fasting. While this source does not discuss pleasure per se, it does reflect a positive attitude toward the human body and the idea that taking good care of one's body is a religious obligation.[3]

Historically speaking, Rav's position encouraging the active pursuit of pleasure appears to find a precursor in Hillel. Hillel (in opposition to Shammai) held that one should eat good food every day and not save it just for the Sabbath. As "God is blessed every day," earthly pleasure should be enjoyed on a daily basis, as long as it is done "in the name of heaven."[4]

## The "Scholarly Elite" Approach

R. Simeon b. Eleazar and R. Meir condemn all self-imposed stringencies for common people (i.e., both in "matters of praise" as well as "matters of anguish") but permit such stringency for scholars. Thus, they were not against ascetic self-denial, per se, or against accepting extra religious duties (as was Hizkiyah in the "all-inclusive" approach). They were against such flexibility only for a specific population group, namely, common people.

As discussed in the introduction to this study, an important question raised by Steven Fraade was to what extent the "rabbinic elite should adopt an abstinent course of conduct more demanding than what could be expected of the people under its authority."[5] R. Simeon b. Eleazar and R. Meir thus represent tannaim who permitted the rabbinic elite to adopt ascetic behaviors that exceeded the

---

3. A third statement attributed to Rav (and to R. Nahman as well) suggests that this positive attitude toward the physical expressed itself in the realm of sexuality as well. Thus, we find in *B. Yevamot* 37b and *B. Yoma* 18b, "Rav, whenever he happened to visit Dardeshir, used to announce, 'Who would be mine for the day'"; he would, then, marry a woman for a short time period. These statements would, obviously, represent a consistent, unified approach on the part of Rav only if the attributions are correct.

4. Taking a bath and even using the bathroom were then also considered to be religious activities (*mitzvot*), in a source attributed to Hillel (*Aboth deRabbi Nathan* Version B, chap. 30).

5. Fraade, "Ascetical Aspects," p. 272.

norms of the general population. The Halakhah, according to these tannaim, did not determine "both the norms and *limits* of abstinence" for scholars. Instead, the individual scholar was left "free to abstain from what was otherwise permitted."[6] More flexibility was, thus, allowed for these scholars in the expression of their own spiritual yearnings, above and beyond the demands of the law.

### The Moderate "Scholarly Elite" Approach

A fifth approach—that of Rabban Simeon b. Gamaliel and R. Yose—also differentiates between scholars and common people. This differentiation is limited, though, only to supererogatory behavior involving matters of praise. For common people, it is prohibited; for the scholar, it is allowed. With regard to supererogatory matters of anguish, however, both common people as well as scholars are permitted to impose stringencies on themselves. This approach was the one accepted by the *P. Sotah*, for it is the only position cited in *P. Berakhot* 2:9; R. Simeon b. Eleazar's position (the fourth approach described) is not mentioned.

The category of "matters of praise," which involves adding to or extending one's religious observances in a manner that would elicit the praise of other people, is applicable, by definition, only to public behavior. Private self-imposed stringencies, such as private supererogatory prayer (and perhaps even the private recital of the Shema for a bridegroom on his wedding night), though, would then be permissible to all individuals. Occurring as it does in private, this behavior does not elicit the praise of others and is, therefore, not a "matter of praise." Rabban Simeon b. Gamaliel's curtailment of self-imposed stringencies would, then, be limited to the common person who publicly imposes such stringencies on himself.

Rabban Simeon b. Gamaliel (as well as R. Simeon b. Eleazar) thus allowed the scholar a certain leeway in his religious expression that the common person was not allowed. Women, with a few scholarly exceptions, would be subsumed under the Halakhic status of "commoner," since they were not scholars.[7] Consequently, they would not be allowed to impose stringencies upon themselves in

---

6. Ibid.

7. The wives of scholars, though, may have been considered scholars,

"matters of praise." They would, however, still be allowed to impose stringencies upon themselves when it came to "matters of anguish." The condemnation of the ascetic woman in *M. Sotah* 3:4, and the praying and fasting virgin in the baraitot, then, may be in dispute with Rabban Simeon b. Gamaliel's general permission for commoners (including, presumably, women) to impose matters of anguish, such as fasting, upon themselves.

## The "Motivation" Approach

The sixth approach focuses explicitly on motivation as the criterion used to judge the worthiness or unacceptability of supererogatory behavior. Various positions regarding internal motivations were discussed. Among the tannaim, one position is expressed by R. Joshua in *P. Berakhot* 2:9 in his defense of R. Judah b. Papus who walked on the road pegs. His position appears to be that an individual is permitted to impose matters of anguish on himself, even in public, as long as his motivations are sincerely religious. Even if they appear arrogant to others, their actions are still acceptable, because of their sincere motivations. R. Hiyya (or R. Judah the Prince),[8] though, in the parallel to this story in *B. Baba Kama* 81b, holds that behaving stringently in public, even if one's motivations are sincere, still deserves criticism.

Several amoraim deal explicitly with the concern for other people's reactions as a limiting factor in permitting people to act stringently. R. Zera's statement in *P. Berakhot* 2:9 stating, "As long as he does not shame others," teaches that supererogatory behavior, even when done "in the name of heaven" is wrong if it will hurt other people's feelings. Sincere motivation, then, would not in and of itself justify supererogatory behavior; the reactions of other members of the community must be considered.

According to this position, then, R. Judah b. Papus should not have walked on the road pegs, since it was in public and he may have shamed others. Interestingly, R. Gamaliel may not have been ashamed at all; instead, he may simply have been angry at R. Judah

---

following the principle that "the wife of a scholar is like a scholar" (*B. Shebuot* 30b, *B. Abodah Zarah* 39a).

8. It is not clear which of these tannaim spoke to R. Judah b. Nekosa, who was walking on the road pegs.

b. Papus's arrogance. This can be inferred from his exclamation, "Who is that who is pointing a finger at himself?" This same feeling of annoyance or anger at the individual's arrogance is reflected in the Babylonian Talmud parallel "Who is that man who wants to show off his greatness in front of us?" Perhaps these tannaim did not feel ashamed when they saw someone behaving stringently precisely because they were scholars—they were secure in their own knowledge of the law and therefore had the self-confidence to know that they themselves were behaving halakhically. They may have been angry at his arrogance rather than being ashamed at their own "shortcomings." Had common people, and not scholars, though, observed R. Judah b. Papus's stringency, then they might have felt ashamed at their implied imperfection. They might have felt that they were not sufficiently pious, because they would not have known that what he was doing was actually unnecessary.

In the *P. Berakhot* sugyot, R. Miyasha and R. Hizkiyah (respectively) may have criticized R. Samuel b. R. Isaac and R. Kohen for separating from their colleagues and, thereby, appearing arrogant. The issue of arrogance is thus implicit in the Palestinian Talmud but is discussed explicitly only in the Babylonian Talmud. The Babylonian Talmud focuses on the appearance of arrogance rather than the internal feeling of arrogance. The two do not automatically go together, as can be seen from the case of R. Judah b. Papus (and R. Judah b. Nekosa in the parallel *B. Baba Kama* 81b passage), who appeared arrogant but had sincere feelings.

The amoraim thus focus on the effects of supererogation on the community, rather than on the individual himself. A behavior was, apparently, deemed worthy or not worthy based on whether other people would perceive it as arrogant. In the case of the Shema, the Talmudic sugya in *B. Berakhot* focuses on how other people in the synagogue would react, and not on the individual's feelings. Likewise, in the case of the Ninth of Ab, what matters is whether the community will think the individual is arrogant. This focus on the reactions of other people, rather than the individual's internal motivation, may also be true of the issue of arrogance as presented in *B. Sukkah* 26b: one may eat a snack in the *sukkah* since people will not assume one is arrogant. The primary concern of the Babylonian amoraim thus appears to have been the public perception of arrogance. The individual's internal feelings may actually, at times, have been irrelevant.

An important factor to be remembered here is that whether a religious observance is considered arrogant (and, therefore, "common") is time- and place-dependent. For what is considered arrogant depends, to a large extent, on the societal context in which one lives.

The issue of motivation surfaces again in the amoraic discussion of the ascetic woman. While the Mishnah and the baraitot regarding the fasting and praying virgin appear, prima facie, to express a general condemnation of the ascetic woman, the *B. Sotah* 22a Talmudic sugya concludes that only a certain type of ascetic woman was condemned by the tannaim, namely, women like Johani bat Retibi. The Talmud itself does not explain what type of woman she was; the Talmudic commentators explain that she was a fraudulent pretender who used her piety in order to conceal her witchcraft.

Similarly, the ascetic woman criticized in *P. Sotah* 3:4 is arrogant and haughty, acting as if she were more modest than the Torah itself. The message conveyed by this passage and by the Talmudic commentators on *B. Sotah* 22b is, thus, that self-imposed stringency, if motivated by hypocrisy, arrogance or haughtiness, is contemptible behavior. A sincerely religious ascetic woman, though, would be allowed to follow her chosen spiritual path without being criticized or condemned as a "destroyer of the world." Flawed motivation for self-imposed stringency is, likewise, the underlying theme of the amoraic discussion regarding the wounds of the separatists in the *B. Sotah* 22b. These flawed motivations include: self-gain (in the form of reputation, respect, money, or power), insincerity, boastfulness, arrogance, and the desire for reward or fear of punishment.

Along the same lines, rabbinic suspicion of ascetic behavior can be seen in the case of the slaughterer who sold unkosher meat (*B. Sanhedrin* 25a) and then let his hair and nails grow long as a sign of repentance. He was not trusted by Raba, who suspected that he was hypocritical and was using ascetic behavior to pretend that he had repented. He was thus suspected of feigning "piety" to gain back his business.

In summary, this sixth position posits that one of the fundamental, overriding values employed by Judaism to evaluate religious stringency was the requirement that a sincere love of God guide the internal motivation for the stringent behavior. While piety is, ideally, motivated by the love of God, human nature is such that many other factors influence one's behavior. Ulterior motives (and even the perception of ulterior motives)—such as the desire for personal gain in the form of power, respect, money, reward or avoidance of punishment—may negate the value of the stringent behavior.

## The "Prevention of Hurtful Behavior" Approach

A seventh approach to supererogatory behavior was to condemn self-imposed stringencies that involved hurting other people or the individual himself—physically, emotionally, or financially. As with the ulterior motives just discussed, hurtful behavior may, likewise, negate the value of the stringent behavior.

This theme can be found in both tannaitic and amoraic stat-ments. *T. Ta'anit* 2:12 states that a person in a dangerous situation may not fast, lest he become weak and thereby lessen his chances of survival. R. Yosi holds that a person should not afflict himself with fasting, lest he become a burden on a community reluctant to provide him with support. *T. Baba Metzia* 8:2 states that an individual should not starve himself and then go to work, because he will be stealing labor from his employer. Shammai was not permit-ted to force his child to fast on the Day of Atonement, for this endangered the child. The baraita quoted in *P. Peah* 8:8 states that a person who needs charity but does not take it is considered a killer, since he does not take care of his own life.

Among the amoraim, Samuel echoes R. Yose's position, stating that a person should not afflict himself with fasting. R. Yohanan in *P. Demai* 7:3, expanding on *T. Baba Metzia* 8:2, states that a teacher of Torah is especially obligated to avoid excessive fasting, since his employer is God himself. R. Jeremiah b. Abba in the name of Reish Lakish, and R. Sheshet in *B. Ta'anit* 11b, criticize scholars who fast excessively, since they will not be able to study properly. Rabba bar R. Huna states that "the spirit of the Sages is not pleased" with hasidim who refuse to kill snakes and scorpions on the Sabbath, thus endangering their lives (*B. Shabbat* 121b).

The theme that self-imposed stringency is condemned when it results in hurting specifically other people is most prominent in the case of the foolish pietist (who failed to save the woman or child; see the beginning of Chapter 5). His internal motivations are sincere—he is, after all, called a foolish *pietist*, not simply a fool. His gross ignorance or mistaken notions of what constitutes true piety, however, actually cause death or fail to prevent a rape.

His behavior, which causes irreparable harm to other people, thus qualifies as fanaticism, as defined in the introduction of this study. For the foolish pietist allows his own obsession with his idiosyncratic version of "piety" to outweigh the more fundamental values of his own religion. The result is the tragic and unwarranted suffering and even death of another innocent human being, owing to his purported "piety."

The concern lest religious stringency hurt the individual or others may also be relevant vis-à-vis the ascetic woman, criticized in *M. Sotah* 3:4 by R. Joshua as bringing destruction on the world. For the ascetic woman would not have children, thus harming the Jewish people by decreasing the Jewish birthrate. Additionally, R. Joshua may have been concerned lest her excessive piety lead herself to sin, since the ascetic measures she adopted would be too difficult to uphold.[9]

The condemnation of self-imposed stringency when it hurts the individual himself is also found in the discussion of two of the seven separatists in *B. Sotah* 22b (it is not found, however, in the parallel Palestinian passage). The *nikpi* and *kizai* separatists, according to *B. Sotah* 22b, represent people who go to the extent of physically hurting themselves for "religious" goals (at least according to some of the interpretations presented in Chapter 4). These cases, in which individuals are criticized for doing something in the name of religion that hurts themselves or others, are further examples of unchecked religious zeal resulting in fanaticism.

In all these Talmudic examples, a number of religious values are "overvalued" by the individuals. Some of these are the importance of fasting, respect for the Sabbath, avoidance of sexual temptation, and the desire to treat tefillin with respect, thereby avoiding erasing God's name from the parchment. Other values assigned exaggerated importance include the desire to avoid killing another person, even though they are about to commit a heinous crime, and the yearning to devote one's life to spirituality by praying and fasting. The "overvaluing" of these concerns can lead to the neglect of other extremely important religious values. These latter values include not hurting someone else's feelings, establishing Jewish families and having many Jewish children, caring for one's body properly, preventing rape, and, ultimately, the transcendent concern of pre-

---

9. *Arukh,* s.v. SH.V. 8.

serving human life. Self-imposed religious stringency that resulted in a distortion of more fundamental Jewish values was thus condemned by both the tannaim and the amoraim.

## The "Narrowly Limiting" Approach

An eighth approach to self-imposed stringency is to criticize it only under certain very specific, limited circumstances. Hizkiyah's statement "Whoever does something from which he is exempt is called a commoner," which was explained earlier as a universal condemnation of supererogatory behavior under any circumstances, can also, ironically, be understood as being extremely limited in scope. It would, in fact, be more limited than any of the other approaches presented so far.

This explanation is based on the assumption that his baraita applies only to situations which were exactly parallel to the context of *P. Berakhot* 2:9. This context involved the case in which R. Samuel b. R. Isaac interrupted his meal in order to pray minha when he was exempt from doing so. He was, therefore, called "a commoner" by R. Miyasha (or by the Talmudic sugya). The label of "commoner," then, would apply only if the self-imposed stringency had all the following qualifying limitations:

1. It is performed in public and hence makes him appear arrogant.
2. It is a positive commandment that is rabbinic in nature, which involves man and God (as opposed to a commandment between man and his fellow man).
3. The individual would be fulfilling a religious duty from which he is temporarily exempt. This last limitation would not include religious duties from which he personally is always exempt but that other individuals or groups of Jews are obligated to perform. Women who choose to perform positive commandments from which they are permanently exempt would not, then, be labeled as "commoners."[10]

---

10. This issue is not raised by the Talmud itself. It is, though, raised by the medieval commentators and is of special interest in today's society.

## HISTORICAL, GEOGRAPHIC, AND TEACHER-STUDENT PATTERNS

Some of the concepts presented here appear to be limited to either the tannaitic or amoraic time periods, geographic areas (Palestine or Babylonia), or particular tannaim or amoraim. Rabban Simeon b. Gamaliel, for example, stands out as having the most permissive attitude toward self-imposed stringency (among the positions described in this book), since he permitted supererogatory matters of anguish to common people. Hizkiyah, on the other hand (as described in the first approach), who states that someone adopting self-imposed stringencies is a commoner, stands out as having the most restrictive attitude toward self-imposed stringency.

While Rabban Simeon b. Gamaliel's position is found in both the Palestinian and Babylonian Talmud, Hizkiyah's position is found only in the Palestinian Talmud. Evidence that Hizkiyah's statement is reflective of a specific trend against stringency in Palestine as opposed to Babylonia, though, is lacking. Aside from Hizkiyah's statement, no substantial evidence has has been found to support the idea that the more severe and difficult life of the Palestinian Jews influenced the Palestinian amoraim to relate either more positively or negatively to ascetic behavior than their Babylonian counterparts. Anti-ascetic views, simply criticizing self-denial or actually viewing pleasure as an actual religious obligation, are expressed by both tannaim and amoraim, in both the Palestinian and in the Babylonian Talmud. Both Hillel (a tanna) and Rav (a Babylonian amora who studied in Palestine for many years) in particular stand out for their positive views toward pleasure, demonstrating that this trend of thought was not limited to a particular time period or geographic location.

R. Joshua, in his reaction to R. Judah b. Papus's walking on the road pegs (*P. Berakhot* 2:9), seems to show that he accepts the legitimacy of pure motivation alone as sufficient validation for self-imposed stringency. R. Hiyya, though, in the parallel source in the Babylonian Talmud rejects this contention. He apparently opposed public supererogatory behavior, even if one's motivations were sincere. Interestingly, R. Hiyya was Hizkiyah's father. Hizkiyah, then, who may have condemned supererogatory behavior in general, could have been expanding on an anti-stringency stance that he had already learned from his father.

R. Zera (*P. Berakhot* 2:9) expresses the concern that one should be sure not to shame others when behaving stringently, while the Babylonian Talmud expresses the concern for "the appearance of arrogance." Both of these concerns are similar in that they involve other people's reactions to stringent behavior. They are different, however, in that R. Zera focused on the individual's potential to hurt other people's feelings. The Babylonian Talmud's "concern for arrogance" is that other people will evaluate the individual behaving stringently in a negative fashion, rather than that other people's feelings will be hurt.

While the many anti-nazirite and anti-ascetic views quoted in this study clearly demonstrate that rabbinic criticism of asceticism applied to men as well as women, there are tannaitic sources in which female asceticism is singled out for censure. This idea is found in R. Joshua's condemnation of the ascetic woman in *M. Sotah* 3:4 and in the baraitot's criticizing the praying virgin and the fasting virgin. Additionally, women's vows of self-denial are singled out in *M. Nedarim* 11:1 as the only type of vow that the father/husband may annul.[11] The tannaim's criticism thus applies to both single or married women.

The amoraim in *B. Nedarim* 79b affirm the Mishnah's stance, by explaining that a husband's annulment of his wife's vows of self-denial lasts even when they are no longer married. The amoraim in both the Babylonian and Palestinian sugyot discussing the ascetic woman, however, qualify the tannaitic censure of the female ascetic.

### Rabban Simeon b. Gamaliel and His Father, Rabban Gamaliel

Since Rabban Simeon b. Gamaliel is such an important spokesman on this topic, his views are summarized here:

1. Only some (very special) bridegrooms are permitted to say the Shema on their wedding night. In other words, concerning "matters of praise," only scholars may engage in supererogatory behavior.

---

11. *Sifrei Numbers* 144, ed. Horovitz, pp. 206–207.

2. He encourages everyone not to work on the Ninth of Ab so that they may fast. That is to say, in "matters of anguish," commoners and scholars alike may act stringently.

The views of his father, R. Gamaliel, are also of interest here. As will be recalled, he recited the Shema on his wedding night, even though he had taught his students that a groom is exempt from this commandment (*M. Berakhot* 2:5). In two other cases discussed in chapter 1, he also behaves differently from the norm. In these cases, however, he is more lenient with the law rather than more stringent. These two cases are interesting in that they appear to form a conceptual continuum with the case of reciting the Shema. In all three cases, R. Gamaliel appears to be demonstrating that the objective law allowed for flexibility in certain subjective circumstances—independent of whether a stringency or a leniency was involved.

In other words, Rabban Gamaliel deviated from the communal norm in the following three cases because he felt that the general rules did not apply to his particular situation. He bathed right after his wife died because he was very sensitive to dirt (*M. Berakhot* 2:6). Likewise, he allowed himself to observe mourning rituals for his slave Tabi, even though this was not the accepted ruling, because he held that his slave was exceptional (*M. Berakhot* 2:7). Finally, when he himself was a bridegroom, he recited the Shema because of his intense religious feelings (*M. Berakhot* 2:5): "I will not listen to you to remove from myself the yoke of heaven even for a moment." This was the reason he gave for reciting the Shema as a bridegroom— even after he himself taught his students that bridegrooms were exempt.

Rabban Simeon b. Gamaliel seems to have been following in his father's footsteps. He too allowed space within the Halakhah for individualized religious expression, even to common people, as long as they involved "matters of anguish" or were non-ascetic rituals that were observed in private. In matters of praise, though, he excluded common people from this flexible approach, presumably because of the problems of internal motivation and assumed public perception. His permitting common people to accept on themselves stringencies involving self-denial demonstrates that he had a relatively positive view of ascetic behavior.

## CHRISTIAN PARALLELS

Certain parallel ideas found in Christian sources of roughly the same time period were compared and contrasted to the ideas found within the Talmudic sources. The main similarity lies in the area of motivation for religious behavior. Numerous passages in the New Testament criticize people for observing commandments in an ostentatious manner, "so that all their deeds may be seen by men" (Matthew 6:1–18, 23:5–7, Luke 18:9–14; Colossians 2:16–23).

A strong contrast between the Talmudic sources and the Christian sources lies in the area of the ascetic woman. While many Christian sources glorify this behavior, the Talmudic sources condemn it. The tannaitic sources in particular, understood independently of the amoraic interpretation, appear prima facie quite severe and universal in their reprobation.

The amoraic sources' interpretation of the tannaitic positon, on the other hand, is more willing to accept the legitimacy of at least some ascetic women. If indeed a historical change did occur between the tannaitic and amoraic approach to the ascetic woman, it was likely due to a decline, in amoraic times, in the rabbis' concern lest "holy virginity" would become popular among Jewish women (or the fear, perhaps, that ascetic women were actually Jewish Christians). The idea that women might take on ascetic practices for sincere reasons may, therefore, have become more acceptable to the amoraim.

It is possible that the baraitot in the Babylonian and the Palestinian Talmud condemning "the praying virgin" and "the fasting virgin" were actually alluding to the early Christians. For the baraitot use the term *betula,* and the early Christians, who were often dedicated to celibacy, were simply referred to as "virgins": *betula* (masculine) and *betulta* (feminine) in some early sources.[12]

Within the area of oaths and vows of self-denial, the Biblical and Talmudic sources grant the father/husband the prerogative to annul the daughter/wife's ascetic vows. In Christian sources, this is not the case; in fact, specific Christian sources actually encourage married women to accept oaths of abstinence. Aside from these similarities and contrasts, no further correlations between the Talmudic and Christian sources have been discovered.

---

12. Voobus, *History of Asceticism,* vol. I, pp. 103–104.

## THE IMPACT OF INTENTION

Eight different approaches to supererogatory behavior were summarized here. What has been clearly established is that ulterior motives, in and of themselves, often negate the potential value of self-imposed stringency. In this area of religious behavior, when one's intentions are improper, then one's actions may have no value. This corresponds to the importance of proper intentions in many areas of Jewish law. In the sacrificial laws, for example, improper intentions can totally invalidate the sacrifice.[13] Likewise, in the area of stringency, certain improper intentions can totally negate the value of the stringency.

These findings are consistent with the scholarly literature regarding intention in Jewish law (see the introduction to this study). As Howard Eilberg-Schwartz writes, in mishnaic law, "human beings have the power to transform the character of objects around them. . . . [T]he thoughts and intentions of human beings have the effect of restructuring the very character of reality."[14] Eilberg-Schwartz points out that intention is important both in determining whether one transgressed religious law, as well as whether an individual's actions satisfy a religious obligation.[15] This study adds another dimension to previous scholarly findings, namely, that intention is a critical issue in the realm of supererogation as well. When one wishes to go beyond what is commanded or required and is, consequently, neither transgressing religious law nor attempting to satisfy a religious obligation, his intentions are often of critical import. The character of what could have been an acceptable self-imposed stringency is then restructured by the individual's ulterior motives, transforming the self-imposed stringency into unacceptable behavior.

The opposite of these ulterior motives, which would, presumably, imbue the stringency with value, would be pure and sincere motives. These pure motivations entail the desire to do more than is required to serve God and to establish a closer relationship with Him. As an expression of a sincere desire to express total devotion to God, an individual may indeed choose to do more than is halakhi-

---

13. Leviticus 19:7.
14. Howard Eilberg-Schwartz, *The Human Will* (Atlanta, Georgia: Scholars Press, 1986), pp. 182–183.
15. Ibid., p. 23.

cally required. Just as the ideal way of performing the actual commandments is "for the sake of Heaven," the ideal way of performing supererogatory religious behavior is "for the sake of Heaven," following the model of R. Gamaliel who recited the Shema even as a bridegroom.

As may be recalled, a crucial question asked at the outset of this study was whether sincere intentions, in and of themselves, legitimate self-imposed stringency. This study has demonstrated that the answer to this question is, basically, a resounding, "No!" Multiple Talmudic sources raise various different concerns that nullify the value of sincere intentions. For the first three of the positions outlined here, intentions are irrelevant. The first of these is that of Hizkiyah (when his statement is understood literally), who holds that supererogation is always prohibited, even if one's motivations are truly "for the sake of heaven" (*lishmah*). The second of these is R. Eleazar HaKappar's view of the nazirite as a sinner. The nazirite's motivations are not mentioned at all—he was called a sinner for denying himself wine, even if he did so out of a true desire to serve God. Likewise, the "pro-pleasure" position would posit that any limitation in pleasure sanctioned by God is undesirable.

The remaining five positions prohibit supererogation—even if one's intentions are sincerely "for the sake of Heaven" (*lishmah*)—as follows:[16]

1. If you are not a scholar and impose either supererogatory matters of praise or anguish on yourself (R. Simeon b. Eleazar—the "scholarly elite" approach).
2. If you are not a scholar and impose stringencies involving matters of praise on yourself (Rabban Simeon b. Gamaliel—the "moderately elite" approach). This applies only to public, nonascetic stringencies, such as reciting the Shema in public when exempt from doing so.
3. If others will perceive your actions to be arrogant (*B. Berakhot* 17b and *B. Pesahim* 559)
4. If others will be hurt physically, emotionally, or financially by your actions (positions against excessive fasting and then

---

16. In the following list, names are used to identify positions when they are provided by the sources. When the sources are anonymous, then the textual reference is provided.

working, against imposing fasts on children, against those who do not kill snakes and scorpions on the Sabbath, the foolish pietist, the ascetic woman, the wounds of the separatists, and R. Zera)

5. If you will be hurt—physically, emotionally, or financially—by your own actions (the Tosefta against excessive fasting in times of danger and R. Yose and Samuel against excessive fasting in general, the baraita censuring someone who does not take charity when he needs to do so, negative views of oaths and vows of self-denial, positions against those who do not kill snakes and scorpions on the Sabbath [*B. Shabbat* 121b], the ascetic woman, and the wounds of the separatists according to *B. Sotah* 22b).

These five positions can actually form the basis of a conceptual understanding of when individualized religious stringency—as an expressed attempt to enhance religiosity—can negate other crucially important religious values. These fundamental values, as was discussed, include avoiding the appearance of arrogance, assuring that no one is hurt by the stringent behavior, and that no compromise in other areas of halakhah will result.

## UNEQUIVOCAL PRAISE OF
## SUPEREROGATORY BEHAVIOR

One cannot help noticing that the self-imposed stringencies that were discussed throughout this study generally involved commandments between people and God; almost none of the critical voices raised against stringency spoke of commandments between man and his fellow man. The factors that delegitimized supererogatory behavior, even when performed with sincere motivation, do not, generally, apply to commandments between people. The Tosefta's "matters of anguish" and "matters of praise" are not categories that apply to interpersonal relationships.

Criticism of self-imposed stringency is applicable only to interpersonal commandments that involve spending money. For example, an individual is not permitted to spend more than a certain amount of his income on charity. When a person, though, stands out for his exceptional performance of commandments between people that do not involve spending money, such as acts of kindness or visiting the sick, he would not be perceived as arrogant. The concern lest stringency hurt the individual or others is not a concern when one engages in supererogatory acts of kindness toward others.

There are, however, two exceptions to this principle. One is Hizkiyah's baraita, which may have included all types of stringency, including commandments between people, in its critique. The second is the case of R. Judah b. Papus, who was criticized for walking in the center of the road even though he was permitted to walk on the side. He did so to avoid damaging another person's crops—a commandment that did not require him to spend any money. He was, nevertheless, criticized most vehemently (before he was identified) for imposing this stringency on himself, even though he was trying to help the owner of the field by not crushing his crops.

This commandment, however, is exceptional in that it is a commandment between people instituted as a public policy. When an individual openly goes against public policy, he appears to be undermining the authority of the public policy maker. Furthermore, R. Judah b. Papus's act may have suggested a certain degree of arrogance, for he appeared to be saying that what the rabbinic authorities had permitted was not really proper and that he, therefore, would not follow such compromising ways.

The rabbinic criticism of stringency discussed in this study, then, with these two possible exceptions, is limited to commandments between man and God and does not usually apply to commandments between man and his fellow man. In light of this conclusion, R. Judah's dictim in *B. Baba Kama* 30a is perfectly reasonable. In that passage, R. Judah suggests that if one wishes to be especially pious, he should be particularly careful to observe commandments between man and his fellow man:

I.    R. Judah said, "He who wishes to be a hasid, let him observe the laws of damages (*nezikin*) [very carefully]."
II.   Rabba[17] said, "The laws of *Aboth* (Ethics of the Fathers)."
III.  Still others said, "The laws of blessings."

The laws of damages obviously involve commandments between one human being and another and are, therefore, recommended

---

17. Some manuscripts, as well as medieval commentators here, have Ravina (Rabinowitz, *Dikdukei Soferim,* ad loc., note 10).

areas for stringency. Reworded, R. Judah's message is that if one feels a need for personal religious expression, which goes above and beyond the law, then he should express this need by being an especially kind person, concerned with the welfare of others.

As quoted here, R. Judah's statement is followed by two other recommendations for stringent behavior. While these two positions are not limited to commandments between man and his fellow man, they are still consistent with the findings of this study. Rabba's position is that one should be extremely careful with regard to the laws of *Aboth* (section II). The laws of *Aboth*, are, in the main, generalized ethical values rather than specific behaviors. Thus, when Rabba recommends being stringent with regard to the laws of *Aboth*, he is not encouraging supererogatory behavior but is, instead, suggesting that one diligently monitor his value system and try hard to develop his religious character.

The third opinion expressed in this passage is that of the anonymous "others" who hold that one who wishes to be a hasid should observe the laws of blessings with particular care (section III). While blessings do involve the individual's relationship with God and are not commandments between man and his fellow man, they are not necessarily public observances. The area of blessings is basically a private area of religious activity. Being sure always to say a blessing, to say the correct blessing, and to have the proper intent are private activities that would not shame or hurt anyone else. An individual who is especially careful in the area of blessings would certainly not be perceived as arrogant even if he were to be "discovered."

An individual, then, who feels a passionate desire to piously serve God in a manner that goes above and beyond what is halakhically required and wishes to avoid all criticism can pursue any one of the three avenues of expression recommended in *B. Baba Kama* 30a. None of the eight critical voices described earlier apply to any of these three recommendations. One, in the area of interpersonal relationships, involves heightened observance of the commandment to "Love thy neighbor as thyself" (Leviticus 19:18). The second, in the area of *Aboth*, involves developing one's religious character and one's value system, in order to better one's relationship with his fellow man as well as with God.

The third recommended avenue of expression, in the area of commandments between man and God, involves being especially scrupulous in the Halakhic area of blessings. For blessings is an area of Jewish law that is often observed in private situations. Pious stringency, then, in this area—along with the two other recommended avenues of expression—guided by the Halakhic principles developed throughout this book, will not likely result in fanaticism, elitism, or excessive asceticism. Consequently, harm will not likely occur to the individual, other people, or the Jewish nation as a whole—physically, emotionally, or financially.

# Bibliography

## PRIMARY SOURCES

Aharon Hakohen of Lunel (1950). *Sefer Orhot Hayim*. Jerusalem. (Reprint.)

Aharon, R. Y., and Trani, R. Y. (1971). *Piskei haRid, Piskei Ri'az, Ta'an*. Jerusalem: Makhon HaTalmud HaYisraeli HaShalem.

Alashvili, R. Y. T. (1975). *Hiddushei HaRitva, Kid*. New York: Merkaz HaSefarim.

——— (1980). *Hiddushei HaRitva, Ta'an*. Jerusalem: Mossad HaRav Kook.

Albeck, C., and Theodor, J., eds. (1965). *Midrash Rabbah, Bereishit*. Jerusalem.

Alfasi, R. Y. (1969). *Hilkhot Rav Alfas*, ed. R. N. Zaks. Jerusalem: Mossad HaRav Kook.

Ambrose. (1983). "Concerning Virgins." In *A Select Library of Nicene and Post-Nicene Fathers of the Christian Church*, vol. X, book I, chap. XII, p. 373. Ed. Philip Schaff. Grand Rapids, MI: Eerdmans. (Reprint.)

*The Apocalypse of the Virgin Mary. The Apocryphal New Testament*. (1975). Trans. Montague R. James. Oxford: Clarendon.

233

Amram Ha-Adani, R. D. b., ed. (1975). *Midrash HaGadol.* Jerusalem: Mossad HaRav Kook.

Assaf, S., ed. (19xx). *Teshuvot HaGeonim mitokh haGenizah.* Jerusalem: Darom, 1929.

Azoulay, H. Y. D. (1970). *Petah Einayim* (Reprint). Jerusalem: Ha-Tehiyah, 1959.

Baruch b. Isaac. (1970). *Sefer HaTerumah.* Warsaw: Jacob Unter-hander, 1897.

Buber, S., ed. (1965). *Midrash Mishlei.* Jerusalem (Reprint).

Buber, S., ed. (1967). *Yalkut HaMakhiri.* Jerusalem.

Buber, S., ed. (1968). *Pesikta deRav Kahana.* Lyck.

Chavel, H. D., ed. (1964). Moses b. Nahman. *Kitvei R. Moshe b. Nahman.* Jerusalem: Mossad HaRav Kook.

Clement of Alexandria (1991). *Stromateis,* book 3, trans. J. Ferguson. Washington, D.C.: Catholic University of America Press.

David ibn Abi Zimra (1967). *Teshuvot haRadbaz.* New York: Otzar HaSefarim.

Didache—teaching of the Twelve Apostles (1969). *The Fathers of the Church, The Apostolic Fathers,* trans. F. X. Glum, J. M. Marique, and G. G. Walsh. Washington D. C.: Catholic University of America Press.

*Didascalia Apostolorum, The Syriac Version* (1929). Trans. R. H. Connoly. Oxford: Clarendon.

Emden, Y. (1884). *She'elat Ya'avetz.* Lemberg: Uri Ze'ev Wolf Salat.

Epstein, I., ed. (1959). *The Babylonian Talmud.* London: The Soncino Press, 1936.

Finkelstein, L., ed. (1969). *Sifrei (Deuteronomy).* New York: Jewish Theological Seminary.

Frumkin, Aryeh, ed. (1912). Amram Gaon. *Seder Rav Amram HaShalem.* Jerusalem: Zuckerman.

Gaster, M., ed. (1924). *Sefer HaMa'asiyot.* Leipzig: Asia; London: M. P. Press, 1977 (reprint).

Ginzberg, L., ed. (1970). *Sridei HaYerushalmi.* New York: Jewish Theological Seminary (Reprint).

Halevi, R. Eliezer b. Joel (1983). *Sefer Ra'avyah,* Optowitzer, A., ed. New York: Mekitzei Nirdamim.

Halevi, R. H. D. H. (1988). *Aseh Lekhah Rav,* vol. VIII. Tel Aviv NP.

Higger, M., ed. (1935). *Masekhtot Derekh Eretz.* New York.

Horovitz, C., ed. (1970). *Baraita deNiddah* in *Tosefta Atikata.* Frankfurt a Mainz: Oscar Lehmann, 1889.

Horowitz, C. M., ed. (1970). *Tosefta Atikata*. Frankfurt a Mainz: Oscar Lehmann 1889.

Horowitz, H. S., ed. (1960). *Mekhilta deRabbi Ishmael*. Jerusalem: Bamberger & Wahrmann.

———— (1966). *Sifrei debei Rab (Numbers)*. Jerusalem: Wahrmann.

Irenaeus (1992). *Against the Heresies*, trans. D. J. Unger. New York: Paulist.

Isaac b. Moses. *Sefer Or Zarua*. New York: Lyon. (Reprint).

Ish-Shalom, M., ed. (1963). *Pesikta Rabbati*. Tel Aviv. Opst Esther (Reprint).

Jacob b. Asher (1929). *Tur*. (Reprint). NP Jerusalem.

Jellinek, A., ed. (1938). *Beit HaMidrash*, vol. I. Jerusalem: Bamberger & Wahrmann.

Josephus (1965). *Jewish Antiquities*, trans. L. Feldman. The Loeb Classical Library. London: Heinemann.

———— *The Jewish War* (1961). The Loeb Classical Library. London: Heinemann.

Kapah, J., ed. (1965). Moses b. Maimon. *Commentary to the Mishnah*. Jerusalem: Mossad HaRav Kook.

Karo, R. J. (1966/67). *Shulhan Arukh*. New York (Reprint).

Kasher, M., ed. (1969). *Torah Shelemah*. Jerusalem: Makhon Torah Shelemah.

Klein, M., ed. (1980). *The Fragment Targums of the Pentateuch*. Analecta Biblica 76. Rome: Biblical Institute Press.

Kohut, A., ed. (19xx). Natan b. Yehiel, *Sefer Arukh HaShalem*. Vienna: Menorah, 1926.

Krasilchikov, I., ed. (1980). *Talmud Yerushalmi*. B'nei Brak: Machon Mutzal MeEsh.

Leiberman, S., ed. (1973). *Tosefta*. New York: Jewish Theological Seminary.

Lewin, B., ed. *Sefer HaMetivot*. Jerusalem: Merkaz.

Lewin, B. M., ed. (1941). *Otzar HaGeonim*. Jerusalem: Central.

Licht, J., ed. (1965). *Megillat HaSerakhim*. Jerusalem: Mossad Bialik.

Lieberman, S., ed. (1948). *Hilkhot HeYerushalmi LeRabeinu Moshe b. Maimon*. New York: Jewish Theological Seminary.

Lis, A., ed. (1977). *Talmud Bavli im Shinuyei Nusha'ot. Masekhet Sotah*. Jerusalem: Makhon HaTalmud HaYisraeli HaShalem.

Maharal of Prague (1972). *Hiddushei Aggadot, Sotah* Jerusalem. (Reprint).

Mandelbaum, D., ed. (1987). *Pesikta deRav Kahana.* New York: Jewish Theological Seminary.

Margaliot, M., ed. (1967). *Sefer HaRazim.* Tel-Aviv: Yedi'ot Aharonot.

————— (1993). *Midrash Rabbah, Leviticus.* New York: Jewish Theological Seminary.

Margaliot, R., ed. (1957). *Sefer Hasidim.* Jerusalem: Mossad HaRav Kook.

*Midrash Rabbah.* (1961). Jerusalem (Reprint).

*Midrash Tanhuma* (1962). Commentary of H. Zundel. Jerusalem: Lewin-Epstein (Reprint).

*Mishnah* (1968). Codex Kaufmann. Jerusalem.

*Mishnah* (1973). Codex Paris. Jerusalem: Makor.

*Mishnah* (1970). Codex Parma. Jerusalem: Kedem.

Moses b. Maimon (1948). *Mishneh Torah.* Tel Aviv: Opst, Brady & Katz, 1959.

Moses b. Nahman (1928). *Hiddushei HaRamban.* Jerusalem (Reprint).

Moses of Coucy (1973). *Sefer Mitzvot HaGadol.* Jerusalem: Opst, Brody-Katz.

Muller, J., ed. (1888). *Teshuvot Geonei Mizrach Uma'arav.* Berlin: Deutsch.

*Neophyti I, Exodo* (1970). Madrid: Consejo Superior de Investigaciones Cientificas.

Nissim Gaon. *Hibbur Yaffe min HaYeshuah.* Amsterdam: 1746.

Pardo, D. (1776). *Hasdei David.* Livorno.

*Pesikta Rabbati* (1968). Trans. W. G. Braude. New Haven, CT: Yale University Press.

*Philo.* The contemplative life, vol. IX, trans. F. H. Colson. The Loeb Classical Library. Cambridge, MA: Harvard University Press.

Rabinowitz, M., ed. (1977). *Dikdukei Soferim.* New York: M. P. Press.

Rahlfs, A., ed. (1935). *Septuaginta.* Stuttgart: Privilegiert Wurttembergische Bibelanstalt.

Reisher, J. (1972). *Shevut Ya'akov.* Jerusalem.

*The Revised English Bible* (1989). Oxford: Oxford University Press.

Samson b. Zaddok (1858). *Sefer Tashbetz.* Lemberg.

*The Sayings of the Desert Fathers (Apophthegmata Patrum)* (1980). Trans. Benedicta Ward. London: Mowbray.

Schafer, P., and Becker, H.-J., eds. (1991). *Synopse zum Talmud Yerushalmi.* Tubingen: Mohr (Paul Siebeck).

Schechter, Solomon, ed. (1967). *Aboth deRabbi Nathan.* New York: Feldheim.

Schiffman, C. H., ed. (1994). *The Talmud of the Land of Israel: A Preliminary Translation and Explanation. Vol. 13. Yerushalmi Pesahim,* trans. B. M. Bokser. Chicago: University of Chicago Press.

*Seder Tannaim VeAmoraim* (1857). R. Yosef Tov-Ellem.

*The Septuagint Version: Greek and English* (1970). Trans. L. C. L. Brenton. Grand Rapids, Michigan: Regency Reference Library.

Sofer, A., ed. (1977). Meiri. *Beit HaBehirah.* Jerusalem: Kedem.

Strack, H., ed. (1912). *Talmud Bavli.* Codex Munich. Leiden: Brill.

*Talmud Bavli.* Codex Venice (Reprint). Jerusalem: Tzalmon, 1968.

*Talmud Bavli.* Jerusalem: Peninim, 1970.

*Talmud Yerushalmi* (1971). Codex Leiden. Jerusalem: Kedem.

*Talmud Yerushalmi* (1971). Codex Vatican. Jerusalem: Makor.

*Talmud Yerushalmi* (1948). Krotoschin ed. New York: Shulsinger Bros.

*Talmud Yerushalmi* (1976). New York: M. P. Press.

*Talmud Yerushalmi* (1925). Venice ed. Berlin: Sefarim (Reprint).

Tam, R. Y. (19xx). *Sefer HaYashar* Vienna (Reprint). N. Y. Shai Publications, 1959.

*The Acts of Thomas* (1962). Supplements to Novum Testamentum, pp. 108–123, trans. A. F. J. Klijn. Leiden: Brill.

Waddell, H., ed. (1936). *The Desert Fathers.* New York: Holt.

Wernberg-Moller, P., ed. (1957). The Manual of Discipline. Leiden: Brill.

Wistineski, ed. (1924). *Sefer Hasidim.* Frankfurt: Wahrmann.

Yosef, D., ed. (1980). Moses b. Maimon. *Teshuvot HaRambam.* Jerusalem: Makhon OrHaMizrah, Makhon Yerushalayim.

Zuckermandel, M. S., ed. (1963). *Tosefta.* Jerusalem.

## SECONDARY SOURCES

Aescoly, A. Z. (1943). *Sefer HaFalashim.* Jerusalem: Reuven Mas.

Albeck, H. (1946). "Midrash VaYikra Rabbah." *Jubillee Volume for Levi Ginzberg.* New York: American Academy for Jewish Research.

——— (1958). *Commentary on the Mishnah.* Jerusalem: Bialik Institute and Dvir.

——— (1969). *Mavo LaTalmudim.* Tel Aviv: Dvir.

Albert, A. R. (1988). "On Women and Hasidism: S. A. Horodecky and the Maid of Ludmir tradition." In *Jewish History: Essays in Honour of Chimen Abramsky,* pp. 495–525, ed. A. Rapaport-Albert and S. J. Zipperstein. London: Halban.

Alexander, P. (1988). Jewish Aramaic translations of the Hebrew Scriptures in *Mikra*, ed. M. J. Mulder. Compendium Rerum Iudaicarum ad Novum Testamentum. Philadelphia: Fortress.

Allen, W. C. (1912). *The International Critical Commentary: Matthew.* Edinburgh: Clark.

Alon, G. (1932). LeYishuvah shel baraita ahat. *Tarbiz* 4:285–291.

——— (1967). *Toledot HaYehudim BeErets Yisrael BiTequfat HaMishnah VeHaTalmud.* Tel-Aviv: Hakibbutz Hameuchad.

——— (1980). *The Jews in their Land in the Talmudic Age*, trans. and ed. by G. Levi. Jerusalem: Magnes.

*The Anchor Bible.* Ed. W. F. Albright and C. S. Mann. New York: Doubleday and Co., 1971.

Avi-Yonah, M. (1976). *The Jews of Palestine.* Oxford: Blackwell.

Bacher, B. Z. (1923). *Erkhei Midrash*, Trans. A. Z. Rabinowitz. Tel Aviv: Ahdut.

Baer, M. (1975). *Amoraei Bavel.* Ramat Gan: Bar Ilan University.

Baer, Y. (1955). *Yisrael Ba-Amim.* Jerusalem: Mossad Bialik.

Baron, S. (1952). *A Social and Religious History of the Jews.* New York: Columbia University Press.

Barr, J. (1990). The Hebrew/Aramaic background of "hypocrisy" in the Gospels. In *A Tribute to Geza Vermes*, pp. 307–326, ed. P. P. Davies and R. T. White. Sheffield: Sheffield Academic Press.

Baumgarten, J. (1990). The Qumran-Essene restraints on marriage. In *Archaeology and History in the Dead Sea Scrolls.* The New York University Conference in Memory of Yigael Yadin. Ed. L. H. Schiffman. Journal for the Study of the Old Testament Supplemental Series 8. Sheffield: JSOT Press, 1990.

Beall, T. S. (1988). *Josephus' Description of the Essenes Illustrated by the Dead Sea Scrolls.* Cambridge: Cambridge University Press.

Berman, S. (1977). Lifnim Mishurat HaDin. Journal of Jewish Studies (26:1–2). 1975:86–104, *Journal of Jewish Studies* 1977:(28:2)181–193.

Bokser, B. M. (1980). *Post Mishnaic Judaism in Transition.* Brown Judaic Studies 17. Chico: California Scholars Press, 1980.

——— (1983). Rabbinic responses to catastrophe: from continuity to discontinuity. *Proceedings of the American Academy for Jewish Research-PAAJR* 50:37–61.

Bonsirven, J. (1964). *Palestinian Judaism in the Time of Jesus Christ*, trans. W. Wolf. New York: Holt, Rinehart & Winston.

Boyarin, D. (1991). Internal opposition in Talmudic literature: the case of the married monk. *Representations* 36 (Fall):87–113.

—— (1993). *Carnal Israel: Reading Sex in Talmudic Literature.* Berkeley: University of California Press.

Brown, P. (1988). *The Body and Society: Men, Women and Sexual Renunciation in Early Christianity.* New York: Columbia University Press.

Buchler, A. (1922). *Types of Jewish-Palestinian Piety.* London: Jew's College.

Bynum, C. W. (1987). *Holy Feasts and Holy Fasts.* Berkeley: University of California Press.

Chadwick, H., and Oulton, J. (1964). *Alexandrian Christianity.* Philadelphia: Westminster.

Charlesworth, J. H. (1980). The origin and subsequent history of the authors of the Dead Sea Scrolls: four transitional phases among the Qumran Essences. *Revue de Qumran* 10:213–233.

—— (1987). *The New Testament Apocrypha and Pseudepigrapha.* Metuchen, NJ: American Theological Library Association and The Scarecrow Press.

Clark, E. A. (1986). *Ascetic Piety and Women's Faith.* Lewiston, NY: Mellen.

—— (1990). Early Christian women: sources and interpretation. In *That Gentle Strength: Historical Perspectives on Women and Christianity,* pp. 19–35. Ed. by Lynda L. Coon, Katherine J. Haldone and Elisabeth W. Sommer. Charlottesville: University Press of Virginia.

Clark, G. (1989). *Women in the Ancient World: Greece and Rome.* New Surveys in the Classics No. 21. Oxford: Oxford University Press.

Cohen, B. (1966). *Jewish and Roman Law.* Vol. I. New York: Jewish Theological Seminary.

Cohn, R. L. (1988). Sainthood on the periphery: the case of Judaism. In *Sainthood: Its Manifestations in World Religions,* ed. R. Kieckhefer and G. D. Bond. Berkeley: University of California Press.

*The Compact Edition of the Oxford English Dictionary.* Oxford: Oxford University Press, 1971.

Corinaldi, M. (1989). *Yahadut Etiyopiyah,* pp. 69–73. Jerusalem: Reuven Mas.

Corrington, G. P. (1992). The defense of the body and the discourse of appetite: continence and control and the Greco-Roman world. *Semeia* 57, pt. I:65–74.

De Vaux, R. (1961). *Ancient Israel,* trans. J. McHugh. London: Darton, Longman & Todd.

*The Diagnostic and Statistical Manual of Mental Disorders* (1994). 4th ed. Washington, D. C.: American Psychiatric Association.

Dinari, Y. (1980). Minhagei Tum'at Niddah—Mekoram Vehishtalshelutam. *Tarbiz* XLIX:3–4, 302–324.

—— (1984). *Holkmei Ashkenaz BeShilhi Yemei HaBeinayim.* Jerusalem: Bialik Institute.

Eisenman, R., and Wise, M. (1992). *The Dead Sea Scrolls Uncovered.* Shaftesbury, Dorset: Element.

Elon, M. (1973). *HaMishpat HaIvri.* Jerusalem: Magnes.

*Encyclopedia Judaica* (1972). Jerusalem: Keter.

*Encyclopedia Talmudit* (1951). Jerusalem: Encyclopedia Talmudit Publications.

Epstein, J. D. E. (1969). *Mitzvat HaShalom.* New York: Torat Ha'Adam.

Epstein, Y. N. (1964). *Mavo LeNusah HaMishnah.* Jerusalem: Magnes Press.

Eshel, E., Eshel, H., and Yardeni, A. (1990/91). A scroll from Qumran which includes part of Psalm 154 and a prayer for King Jonathan and his kingdom. *Tarbiz* LX:314.

Fox, F. L. (1989). *Pagans and Christians.* New York: Knopf.

Fraade, S. (1987). Ascetical aspects of ancient Judaism. In *Jewish Spirituality from the Bible to the Middle Ages,* pp. 253–288, ed. A. Green. New York: Crossroad.

—— (1990). The Nazirite in ancient Judaism (selected texts). In *Ascetic Behavior in Greco-Roman Antiquity,* pp. 213–226, ed. V. L. Wimbush. Minneapolis: Fortress.

—— (1991). *From Tradition to Commentary.* Albany: State University of New York Press.

Fraenkel, J. (1975). *Darko shel Rashi bePerusho leTalmud Bavli.* Jerusalem: Magnes.

Frankel, Z. (1870). *Mavo HaYerushalmi.* Reprint. Jerusalem: Opst HaOmanim, 1967.

Gafni, I. (1990). *Yehudei Bavel bitekufat HaTalmud.* Jerusalem: Zalman Shazar Center for Jewish History.

Gartner, J. (1974). Fasting and penitential prayers before Rosh HaShanah. *HaDarom* 38:69–77.

Geiger, A. (1857). Letter to Ig. Blumenfeld. In *Otzar Nehmad,* vol. II, pp. 99–101. Vienna: I. Blumenfeld.

Gilath, Y. D. (1967). Kavana U'Ma'aseh BaMishnah. *Annual of Bar-Ilan University* IV–V:104–116.

—— (1969). *Genizah studies I.* New York: Hermon.

—— (1971). *Peirushim VeHidushim baYerushalmi.* New York: Ktav.

—— (1982). Ta'anit BeShabbat. *Tarbiz* 52(1).

—— (1990). Ben Shelosh Esreh leMitzvot? *Mehkerei Talmud,* vol. I, ed. J. Sussman and D. Rosenthal. Jerusalem: Magnes.

Ginzberg, L. (1912). Aphraates, The Persian Sage. *The Jewish Encyclopedia,* vol. I. New York: Funk & Wagnall.

Goldberg, A. (1990). Derakhim shel Tzimtzum mahloket etzel Amoraei Bavel. In *Mehkerei Talmud,* vol. I, pp. 135–154, ed. J. Susman and D. Rosenthal. Jerusalem: Magnes. Hebrew University.

Goldenberg, R. (1987). Law and spirit in Talmudic religion. In *Jewish Spirituality from the Bible to the Middle Ages,* pp. 232–252, ed. A. Green. New York: Crossroad.

Goren, S. (1961). *HaYerushalmi Hameforash.* Jerusalem: Mossad HaRav Kook.

Greenberg, D., and Witztum, E. (1991). The treatment of obsessive-compulsive disorder in strictly religious patients. In *Current Treatments of Obsessive-Compulsive Disorder,* pp. 157–172, ed. M. Tortora Pato and J. Zohar. Washington, D.C.: American Psychiatric Press.

Haberman, A. M., ed. (1959). *Megillot Midbar Yehuda.* Tel Aviv: Mahbarot LeSifrut.

Halberstam, J. (1986). Supererogation in Jewish Halakha and Islamic Shari'a. In *Studies in Islamic and Judaic Traditions,* ed. W. M. Brinner and S. D. Ricks. Brown Judaic Studies 110. Atlanta: Scholars.

HaLivni, D. W. (1968). On the supposed anti-asceticism of Simon the Just. *Jewish Quarterly Review* 58:243–252.

—— (1982). *Meqorot U-Mesorot: Be'urim Ba-Talmud Le-Seder Mo'ed, Masekhet Pesahim.* New York: Jewish Theological Seminary.

Hall, T. C. Asceticism (Introduction). *Encyclopedia of Religion and Ethics,* pp. 63–69, vol. II, ed. J. Hastings. New York: Scribner's, 1909.

Harpham, G. G. (1987). *The Ascetic Imperative in Culture and Criticism.* Chicago: University of Chicago Press.

Harvey, S. A. (1990). *Asceticism and Society in Crisis*. Berkeley: University of California Press.

Herzog, I. (1965). *The Main Institutions of Jewish Law*, app., pp. 381–386. London: Soncino.

Heschel, A. J. (1962). *Torah min haShamayim beAspaklarya shel haDorot*, pp. 127–130. London: Socino.

Higger, M. (1971). *Studies in Jewish Jurisprudence*, pp. 235–293, vol. I, ed. Edward M. Gershfield. New York: Hermon.

Hyman, A. (1964). *Toledot HaTannaim VeHaAmoraim*. Jerusalem: Kiryah Ne'emanah.

Jackson, B. S. (1975). Liability for mere intention in Jewish law. *Essays in Jewish and Comparative Legal History*, pp. 202–234. Leiden: Brill.

Jacobs, L. (1957). The economic conditions of the Jews in Babylon in Talmudic times compared with Palestine. *Journal of Semitic Studies* 2:349–359.

Jastrow, M. (1975). *A Dictionary*. New York: Judaica.

Kaelber, W. O. (1987). Asceticism. In *The Encyclopedia of Religion*, vol. I, pp. 441–445, ed. Mircea Eliade. New York: Macmillan.

Kampen, J. (1988). *The Hasideans and the Origin of Pharisaism*. Atlanta: Scholars.

Kanevski, R. J. I. (1991). *Etzot VeHadrakhot*, ed. Jacob Greenwald. New York: Torah Graphics.

Kassowski, H. J. (1957). *Otzar Leshon HaMishnah*. Jerusalem: Massadah.

—— (1961). *Otzar Leshon HaTosefta*. Jerusalem: Jewish Theological Seminary.

—— (1966). *Otzar Leshon HaTalmud*. Jerusalem: Ronald.

Kassowski, M. (1991). *Otzar Leshon Talmud Yerushalmi*. Jerusalem: Israel Academy of Sciences and Humanities and Jewish Theological Seminary.

Kieckhefer, R., and Bond, G. D. (1988). *Sainthood: Its Manifestations in World Religions*. Berkeley: University of California Press.

Kirschenbaum, A. (1991). *Equality in Jewish Law: Beyond Equity: Halakhic Aspirationism in Jewish Civil Law*. Hoboken, NJ: Ktav.

Koester, H. (1982). *History and Literature of Early Christianity*, vol. II. Philadelphia: Fortress.

Kohlberg, L. (1968). The child as a moral philosopher. *Psychology Today* (September) 2(4):25–29.

—— (1973). Stages and aging in moral development—some speculations. *The Gerontologist* Winter: 497–502.

Kohler, K. (1964). Essenes. *The Jewish Encyclopedia*, vol. V, pp. 224–232. New York: Ktav.

Kraemer, R. S. (1992). *Her Share of the Blessings: Women's Religions among Pagans, Jews, and Christians in the Greco-Roman World*. New York: Oxford University Press.

Krauss, S. (1898). *Griechisch und lateinische Lehnworter im Talmud, Midrasch und Targum*, vol. II. Berlin; Hildesheim: Georg Olms Verlagsbuchhandlung, 1964 (reprint).

Leslau, W. (1951). *Falasha Anthology*. New Haven, CT: Yale University Press.

Levi, L. (1981). *Sha'arei Talmud Torah*. Jerusalem: Feldheim.

Levine, B. A. (1970). The language of the magical bowls. In *A History of the Jews in Babylonia*, vol. V, app., pp. 343–376, ed. J. Neusner. Leiden: Brill.

Levison, J. (1888). Beyurim BaTalmud. *Otzar HaSafrut*, vol. II, pp. 165–166, ed. S. Gruber: Krakow: Zupnisk and Fisher.

Lewy, H. (1977). Introduction to "Philo." In *Three Jewish Philosophers*. Ed. by Hans Lewy. New York: Atheneum.

Lichtenstein, A. (1989). Does Jewish tradition recognize an ethic independent of Halakah? In *Encounter, Essays on Torah and Modern Life*, pp. 76–100, ed. H. C. Schimmel and A. Carmell. New York: Feldheim.

Liddel, H. G., and Scott, R. (19xx). *A Greek English Lexicon*, vol. I, ed. H. S. Jones. Oxford: Clarendon, 1948.

Lieberman, S.(1931). Tikunei Yerushalmi. *Tarbiz* II:106.

—— (1934a). *HaYerushalmi Kifeshutah*. Jerusalem: Darom.

—— (1934b). Tikunei Hayerushalmi. *Tarbiz* V:100–101.

—— (1937–38). Review of S. Krauss, *Tosafot HeArukh HaShalem. Kiryat Sefer* XIV:224.

—— (1938). Masekhet Soferim. In *Kiryat Sefer*, vol. XV, pp. 56–57, ed. M. Higger.

—— (1950a). *Greek in Jewish Palestine*. New York: Jewish Theological Seminary.

—— (1950b). *Hellenism in Jewish Palestine*. New York: Jewish Theological Seminary.

—— (1973). *Tosefta Kifeshutah*. New York: Jewish Theological Seminary.

—— (1974). On sins and their punishments. In *Texts and Studies*, pp. 29–51. New York: Ktav.

—— (1980). Kach haya veKach yihiyeh—Yehudei Eretz Yisrael

veYahadut haOlam biTekufat haMishnah veHaTalmud. *Cathedra* 17 (October): 3–10.

────── (1984). A tragedy or a comedy. *Journal of the American Oriental Society* 104:2.

Lowy, S. (1958). The Motivation of Fasting in Talmudic Literature. *Journal of Jewish Studies* 9:19–38.

Malter, H. (1930). *The Treatise Ta'anit*. New York: American Academy for Jewish Research.

Margaliot, M. *Hahilukim shebein Anshei Mizrah veAnshei Eretz Yisrael*. Jerusalem: Eretz Yisrael.

Medini, H. (1962). *Sefer S'dei Hemed*. New York: A. Friedman.

Meier, J. P. (1991). *A Marginal Jew*. New York: Doubleday.

Minkowitz, M. (1975). Ishah Perusha, Utzevuim Shedomim LiPerushim. *HaDoar* 54:136.

Montgomery, J. A. (1913). *Aramaic Incantation Texts from Nippur*. Philadelphia: University of Pennsylvania, The Museum Publication of the Babylonian Section.

────── (1932). Ascetic Strains in early Judaism. *Journal of Biblical Literature* 51:184–213.

Moore, G. F. (1966). *Judaism in the First Centuries of the Christian Era*, vol. II, pp. 201–275. Cambridge, MA: Harvard University Press.

Naveh, J. (1983). A recently discovered Palestinian Jewish Aramaic amulet. In *Arameans, Aramaic and the Aramaic Literary Tradition*, pp. 81–88, ed. M. Sokoloff. Ramat Gan: Bar Ilan University Press.

Naveh, J., and Shaked, S. (1987). *Amulets and Magic Bowls*. Jerusalem: Magnes.

Neusner, J. (1965–1970). *A History of the Jews in Babylonia*. Leiden: Brill.

────── (1971). *Aphrahat and Judaism*. Leiden: Brill.

────── (1981). *Judaism: The Evidence of the Mishnah*, pp. 270–283. Chicago: University of Chicago Press.

────── (1983). *The Talmud of the Land of Israel*. Chicago: University of Chicago Press.

*The New Oxford Annotated Bible* (1977). New York: Oxford University Press.

Newman, J. (1986). *Fanatics and Hypocrites*. Buffalo, NY: Prometheus.

Nickelsburg, G. W. E., and Stone, M. E. (1983). *Faith and Piety in Early Judaism*. Philadelphia: Fortress.

Oppenheimer, A. (1977). *The Am Ha-aretz*. Leiden: Brill.

Peters, F. E. (1990). *Judaism, Christianity and Islam*, vol. III. Princeton, NJ: Princeton University Press.

Preuss, J. (1993). *Biblical and Talmudic Medicine,* trans. Fred Rosner. Northvale, NJ: Jason Aronson.

Quasten, J. (1967). Didascalia Apostolorum. *The New Catholic Encyclopedia,* vol. IV. New York: McGraw-Hill.

Quirin, J. (1992). *The Evolution of the Ethiopian Jews.* Philadelphia: University of Pennsylvania.

Rabinovitz, Z. W. (1940). *Sha'are Torat Eretz Yisrael.* Jerusalem: Weiss.

*The Random House Dictionary* (1981). Unabridged ed. New York: Random House.

Rattner, B. (1901). *Sefer Ahavat Tzion ViYerushalayim.* Vilna: S.P. Garber.

Rudin, J. (1969). *Fanaticism: A Psychological Analysis,* trans. E. Reinecke and P. C. Bailey. Notre Dame, IN: University of Notre Dame Press.

Safrai, S. (1965). Teaching of pietists in mishnaic literature. *Journal of Jewish Studies* XVI:15–33.

Sanders, E. P. (1985). *Jesus and Judaism.* Philadelphia: Fortress.

Sarna, N. (1991). *The Jewish Publication Society Torah Commentary.* Philadelphia: Jewish Publication Society.

Schafer, P. (1990). Jewish magic literature in late antiquity and early Middle Ages. *Journal of Jewish Studies* 41:75–91.

Schiffman, L. H. (1975). *The Halakhah at Qumran.* Leiden: Brill.

——— (1985). *Who Was a Jew.* Hoboken, NJ: Ktav.

——— (1991a). *From Text to Tradition.* Hoboken, NJ: Ktav.

——— (1991b). The Law of Vows and Oaths (Num. 30, 3–16) in the *Zadokite Fragments* and the *Temple Scroll. Revue de Qumran,* 57–58, 199–214.

——— (1993). *Halakhah, Halikhah, uMeshihiyut beKat Midbar Yehudah.* Jerusalem: Merkaz Zalman Shazar LeToledot Yisrael.

Schiffman, L. H., and Swartz, M. D. (1992). *Hebrew and Aramaic Incantation Texts from the Cairo Genizah.* Sheffield: Sheffield Academic Press.

Scholem, G. (1972). Three Types of Jewish Piety. *Eranos Lectures* 3. Dallas: Spring.

Schurer, E. (1973). *The History of the Jewish People in the Age of Jesus Christ,* vol. I, ed. G. Vermes and F. Millar. Edinburgh: Clark.

Schwartz, H. E. (1986). *The Human Will in Judaism.* Atlanta: Scholars.

*Sefer Sdei Hemed HaShalem* (1967). New York: Friedman.

Silberg, M. (1961). *Kah Darko Shel Talmud.* Jerusalem: Hebrew University.

Sly, D. (1990). *Philo's Perception of Women.* Brown Judaic Studies 209. Atlanta: Scholars.

Sokoloff, M. (1990). *A Dictionary of Jewish Palestinian Aramaic.* Ramat Gan: Bar Ilan University Press.

Soloveitchik, H. (1994). Rupture and reconstruction: the transformation of contemporary orthodoxy. *Tradition* 28(4):64–130.

Sperber, D. (1991). *Minhagei Yisrael,* vol. II. Jerusalem: Mossad HaRav Kook.

Steinsaltz, A. (1981). *Talmud Bavli.* Jerusalem: HaMakhon HaYisraeli LePirsumim Talmudiyim.

—— (1987). *Talmud Yerushalmi, Peah.* Jerusalem: HaMakhon Ha-Yisraeli LePirsumim Talmudiyim.

Suffrin, A. E. Asceticism (Jewish). *Encyclopedia of Religion and Ethics,* vol. II, pp. 97–99, ed. James Hastings. New York: Scribner's.

Talmage, F. E. (1975). *Disputation and Dialogue: Readings in the Jewish-Christian Encounter.* New York: Ktav and the Anti-Defamation League of B'nai Brith.

Torjesen, K. J. (1992). In praise of noble women: asceticism, patronage and honor. *Semeia* 57, pt. I:41–64.

*The Tosefta* (1981). Trans. Jacob Neusner. New York: Ktav.

Urbach, E. (1960). Iskizim VeYisurim BeTorat Hazal. In *Sefer Yovel LeYitzhak Baer,* ed. S. W. Baron, B. Dinur, S. Ettinger, and I. Halpern, pp. 48–68. Jerusalem: The Historical Society of Israel.

—— (1971). *Hazal.* Jerusalem: The Magnes Press, Hebrew University.

Urman, D. (1985). R. Eliezer haKappar and bar Kappara–Father and Son? *Be'er Sheva* II:7–25.

Voobus, A. (1958). *History of Asceticism in the Syrian Orient,* vol. I. Secretariat Louvain: duCorpussco.

Weinberger, M. (1988). The chumra syndrome—an Halachic inquiry. *Jewish Action* 48:3.

Weinfeld, M. (1986). *The Organizational Pattern and the Penal Code of the Qumram Sect (NTOA).* Universitätsverlag Freiburg Schweiz.

Widengren, G. (1961). The status of the Jews in the Sassanian Empire. *Iranica Antiqua* I:117–162.

Wimbush, V. L., ed. (1990). *Ascetic Behavior in Greco-Roman Antiquity.* Minneapolis: Fortress.

Yadin, Y. (1977). *Megilat HaMikdash.* Jerusalem: HaHevrah LeHakirat Eretz Yisrael veAtikotehah.

# Index

## About the Author

Sara Weinstein received her Ph.D. in Talmud at New York University's Skirball Department of Hebrew and Judaic Studies, and her M.A. in Talmud at Yeshiva University's Bernard Revel Graduate School. She went to Barnard College and majored in history and education, and spent a year studying at Michlalah in Jerusalem. Sara taught Talmud and Halakha at the Yeshivah of Flatbush High School for five years and has been involved in teaching Torah to adults and teenagers for many years. Sara, her husband, and their four children recently moved to Israel. She is presently teaching at a number of institutes for advanced Torah studies in Jerusalem.